Information Systems Management

Revised and Updated 2nd Edition

Series Editor
Jean-Charles Pomerol

Information Systems Management

Governance, Urbanization and Alignment

Daniel Alban
Philippe Eynaud
Jean-Loup Richet
Claudio Vitari

WILEY

First edition published 2019 in Great Britain and the United States by ISTE Ltd and John Wiley & Sons, Inc., © ISTE Ltd 2019.

This edition published 2024 in Great Britain and the United States by ISTE Ltd and John Wiley & Sons, Inc.

ISTE Ltd
27-37 St George's Road
London SW19 4EU
UK

www.iste.co.uk

John Wiley & Sons, Inc.
111 River Street
Hoboken, NJ 07030
USA

www.wiley.com

Library of Congress Control Number: 2023951648

British Library Cataloguing-in-Publication Data
A CIP record for this book is available from the British Library
ISBN 978-1-78630-941-9

Contents

Foreword to the 2nd Edition

More than four centuries ago, Leonardo da Vinci [DAV 87] wrote that "the surface of water belongs neither to air nor to water". An individual wanting to grasp this surface in order to deduce its properties, characterize it or transport it would find nothing in the hollow of his hands! Leonardo da Vinci added: "this surface has a name, but no substance", nor is it an object or material that can be easily analyzed or dissected: it is action, "it forms the contact of these bodies with each other". Emphasizing that the surface of water is influenced by the air (in particular by its motions) and by the water (influenced by atmospheric pressure), Leonardo da Vinci put it into perspective as a link, an interface, or an interaction between air and water.

This brief introduction, taking a historical and perhaps unexpected detour, allows us to turn our thoughts to the artifacts that are information systems (IS). Forming a symbolic lineage with Leonardo da Vinci's suggestions, H.A. Simon [SIM 68] himself proposed to understand IS as the interface between projects and contexts. Simon's invitation was rich and its consequences were significant! In particular, it provided the basis for IS research on a worldwide scale. We have to admit that it is still stimulating: to make the interactions between projects and organizational contexts intelligible. In other words, to seek to understand IS and the organization in all its complexity.

The preceding few lines set out the advantage and credibility of the project of this book, i.e. why it is relevant to undertake "the effort of complexity"! The first arguments in favor of this effort were put forward by J.-L. Le Moigne. As a professor at the Université d'Aix-Marseille III (renamed Aix-Marseille University in 2012), J.-L. Le Moigne founded, among other organizations and institutions, the *Groupe de recherche sur l'adaptation, la systémique et la complexité économique* (GRASCE, a research group on adaptation, systemics and economic complexity), a research center associated with the *Centre national de la recherche scientifique* (CNRS, the French National Centre for Scientific Research). This laboratory came to be one of Europe's leading research centers in management sciences and in the field of complexity. In his first research (published in *La théorie du système général* in 1977), J.-L. Le Moigne [LEM 77] showed that modeling an IS as a complex system primarily means representing it as a system of actions.

More precisely, J.-L. Le Moigne [LEM 99] presents the modeling of complex systems as:

> the action of elaboration and intentional construction, by composition of symbols, of artifact models likely to render intelligible a phenomenon perceived complex and to amplify the reasoning of the actor projecting a deliberate intervention within the phenomenon; reasoning aiming in particular to anticipate the consequences of these projects of possible actions.

The author thus proposes systemic modeling as an alternative to analytical methods, which often reduce the complexity of the social phenomena under consideration to predefined sets of variables or functions to be analyzed or phenomena to be predicted [LUG 09]. In order to study and render intelligible complex systems apprehended in their environment (as is the case with the IS), systems modeling is careful to make explicit the points of view proposed by the observer-designer who implements it and to underline their own project, which is to propose one of the forms of intelligible understanding of the phenomenon without claiming to explain it, as analytical methods seek to do. At the crossroads of cybernetics (as promoted, in particular, by Wiener) and structuralism (as promoted, in particular, by Piaget), systemics can therefore be fully presented as an alternative method that focuses on the interactions and processes of systems without reducing the richness of perceived complexity.

At a time of increasingly massive, even invasive digital presence, from Big Data to generative artificial intelligence, it still seems pertinent to conceive IS engineering as something other than an ideological project seeking to predetermine the "right information", to be provided at the "right time" and to the "right decision-makers". Developed by J.-L. Le Moigne, complex thinking is not about exclusion, but rather about transgressing analytical determinism in situations where it ceases to be operational [MOR 99]. In other words, complex thinking, by the yardstick of which an IS can be represented, is not, contrary to what we might imagine, a competing approach to those that already exist, but a way of going beyond their respective compartmentalizations. On all sides, and in all fields, complexity calls for imagination and innovation: in short, strategy, which is the only way to move forward in the midst of randomness and uncertainty [MOR 70]. It renders closed, inward-looking thinking and science obsolete. As E. Morin suggests:

It is tonic to tear oneself away from the master word that explains everything, from the litany that claims to solve everything. It is tonic, finally, to consider the world, life, man, knowledge and action as open systems [MOR 73].

This book was conceived with this in mind, viewing the IS not as an information technology project, but as an open system. As the reader will appreciate, it draws on concepts that are well known in the field of IS management: *governance*, *urbanization* and *strategic alignment*. In the past, each of these notions has been the subject of numerous scientific or professional publications, and has been widely used in the field by consultants and project managers eager for resolution methods that can be quickly implemented (distorted?) to meet the time and budget constraints imposed on them.

And yet, the Standish Group's various reports over the years have been nothing but reminders of the high failure rate of IS projects. The latest report (from 2022) shows that over 80% of projects still fail (with almost a third of them being stopped midway through). While we cannot, of course, establish a direct link between these results and the management methods used, these figures are enough to suggest that IS projects represent a complexity that invites those involved in the field to rethink the methods in question, and to see how, instead of substituting each other, they benefit from being reconsidered in the light of their potential complementarities.

It is probably in this articulation between *governance*, *urbanization* and *alignment* that the book lays the foundations for a way of thinking that sees the IS as a complex system that requires joint management of the local (of the *actors*, with their changing uses and evolving professions) and the general (of the *territory* within which the IS must operate, and of the *project*, with the strategic objective pursued).

References

[DAV 87] DA VINCI L., *Les Carnets de Léonard de Vinci*, volumes 1 and 2, Gallimard, Paris, 1987.

[LEM 97] LE MOIGNE J.-L., *La théorie du système général. Théorie de la modélisation*, PUF, Paris, 1997.

[LEM 99] LE MOIGNE J.-L., *La modélisation des systèmes complexes*, Dunod, Paris, 1999.

[LUG 09] LUGAN J.-C., *La systémique sociale*, PUF, Paris, 2009.

[MOR 70] MORIN E., *Journal de Californie*, Le Seuil, Paris, 1970.

[MOR 73] MORIN E., *Le paradigme perdu : la nature humaine*, Le Seuil, Paris, 1973.

[MOR 99] MORIN E., LE MOIGNE J.-L., *L'intelligence de la complexité*, L'Harmattan, Paris, 1999.

[SIM 68] SIMON H.A., "The future of information processing technology", *Management Science*, pp. 619–624, 1968.

[SIM 96] SIMON H.A., *The Sciences of the Artificial*, 3rd edition, MIT Press, Cambridge, 1996.

[SIM 04] SIMON H.A., *Sciences de l'artificiel*, Gallimard, Paris, 2004.

Serge AMABILE
University Professor
Aix-Marseille Université, CERGAM, FEG

Régis MEISSONIER
University Professor
IAE de Montpellier, Reliance in Complexity Chair
Université de Montpellier

Foreword to the 1st Edition

We all live and think in boxes, or starting from boxes. It may be those of our practices, our personal lives or our working lives. The same applies to knowledge. Modern science – and therefore techniques – is so specialized that neighbors in a biology laboratory, for example, do not understand each other's work, or only at the cost of lengthy and patient studies. Yet by their own admission, scientists who would like to take an interest in the work of colleagues with slightly different specialisms from their own do not do so, due to lack of time. This observation can easily be made more generalized: we do not take an interest in other people's work due to lack of time, time that flies more and more quickly and nips in the bud our desire to properly understand what is happening in our world and to help ensure that its future is as bright as possible for everyone.

We are all capable of talking about what is going on in the world. Talking about it as non-specialists, talking about it superficially, at the local bar. We can all come up with theories on what *should* be done to make the world a better place, and set the world to rights. When it comes to putting theories into practice, that is a different matter, because changing our practices based on specific problems is a very big ask, and it seems insane – especially, of course, if we would be trying to do this on our own. The effort must be made by a number of people. Changing our practices based on well-expressed theories is a collective or political effort, in the strong sense of the term, encompassing the history and stories of women and men with all their inconsistencies, their chaotic progress and their possible sense. Policy is a position at the point where thought and action meet. In other words, the world progresses towards satisfactory solutions for the dual question of effectiveness and sense without a collective commitment, which consequently must be multidisciplinary and transversal. Until we understand the need to take the time to genuinely share our practices, knowledge and understanding of the world (not just say that we do), we will not be able to genuinely change things to make the world better.

However, there is an urgent need to do this. Developments in science and technology and the subsequent social developments are such that if we do not tackle certain key issues, including the relationship between man and machine, we will soon be overwhelmed not by the machines themselves but by the lack of structured dialog and thought about them. If we do not succeed now in taking control of a minimum of technological development, which is not so much due to the technologies themselves and their manufacturers (on this point, moreover, the issues are more to do with economics and politics rather than science and technology), but rather, it is due to our failure to think about them. We let ourselves be fascinated by technology and the promises of prophets with their visions, such as those of the transhumanists. To put it bluntly, it is all very well to start considering the rights of robots, but that means forgetting the rights of the real live men and women whose numbers are far greater and whose living conditions are morally, socially, economically and politically unacceptable. Developing robust, rigorous and fertile thinking, practice-based and clear on the material conditions of the lives of women and men, in relation to new technologies, is a crucial issue if our humanity and our lives, and those of our children, are to remain meaningful. This is where complex thinking makes a decisive contribution.

This book reflects the authors' preoccupation with the *concrete practice* of the organizational stakeholders on the ground in their day-to-day work. There are stakeholders whose function is indeed, within organizations and businesses, to manage the "information system" *of* the organization, *of* the business, etc. Thus, the authors' starting point was the concrete, everyday life of managers of organizations' information systems. But they do this by integrating the said information system "in its complexity" into the manager function. That is, in its context, taking into account as far as possible all the parameters involved in and via the life of the information system of any kind of organization based on a three-phase approach: via stakeholders, territories and projects. In other words, they step back to get the necessary perspective to relevantly, usefully and meaningfully problematize the issues now being raised by the most routine management of an information system. They thus show, at the most concrete level possible in the daily life of business, how irrevocable relationships are inevitably woven, for the worse if we do not take heed, but for the best if we are careful, between machines and men, between technologies and questions of meaning, and between ownership of the machines by stakeholders and complex, living organizational systems. The usage made to this end of the concepts of governance, urbanization and information system alignment is very enlightening.

This kind of effort towards a concrete understanding of organizational complexity was, of course, embarked on long ago, in particular by Jean-Louis Le Moigne in his *General Systems Theory*, in the context of Morin's complexity thinking. Many subsequent publications have continued the work, and yet, management sciences have still not sufficiently taken ownership of the concepts pertaining to complexity for it to become a central topic in the preoccupations of researchers and teachers on the one hand, and practitioners on the ground on the other hand, ideally in permanent correlation. The task is challenging. It calls for perseverance, the ability to step back, concrete knowledge of businesses and organizations, and tenacity towards the question of the sense of our practices and our knowledge. It is achieved by unfailingly keeping sight of the bigger picture in every concrete situation by leveraging the most productive characteristics of complexity (non-linearity, uncertainty, self-organization, etc.). Through this book, the authors also show how taking stock of stakeholders, territories and projects on the ground requires continuous learning based on trial and error on a daily basis, taking a stance that these days we would call "agile". In other words, a sufficiently flexible stance to lead stakeholders not only to do but also to think about what they are doing. And this, in real life, is not easy for anyone.

Information Systems Management is therefore enlightening. Not only because it takes a fresh look at the concrete, taking as its starting point the tools of complex thinking, which is the essential challenge embarked on by Le Moigne and Morin and to be continued going forward, but because it offers a number of essential elements of the *methodology* of doing this. The best way to thank them is to leverage their work to extend its spirit and its application to all fields that may appear relevant.

Laurent BIBARD
Professor at ESSEC Business School, Department of Management
Holder of the Edgar Morin Chair on Complexity

Introduction

The purpose of this work is to raise awareness among managers in organizations (businesses, administrative bodies, associations and groups of individuals within a collaborative economy) about the issues raised by information systems (ISs). This book does not set out to try to cover all of the questions raised by ISs, or to offer an exhaustive list of ready-made answers. The authors' intention is rather to provide a framework for analysis and the keys to a coherent understanding, in order to help IS stakeholders deal with questions that are rich in diversity and constantly evolving. Information and Communication Technologies (ICTs) are by nature difficult to pin down. They are paradoxical in nature. On the one hand, they are forward-looking, and indispensable in that they pave the way for innovations full of potential (Big Data, artificial intelligence and connected objects). On the other hand, they are vectors of major vulnerabilities (cybersecurity, loss of privacy), and it is still difficult today to gauge their scope and consequences. This is why the study of ISs is both necessary and fascinating.

Beyond the purely operational issues [ALB 09], we can clearly see that IS management deals with ethical questions and the complexity of the world. To the extent that they structure the processes of business departments and increasingly condition the relationships between the stakeholders in a value chain, decisions taken about ISs have a strategic impact. To the extent that they are no longer confined to the world of work, but increasingly offer a continuum to personal spaces, decisions about ISs also have an impact on everyone. This book is pedagogical in nature, aiming to make a contribution towards ensuring that issues relating to ISs are not left exclusively to the experts in this field.

To approach the topic of IS management, we propose to jointly associate and consider three key concepts of IS science: governance, urbanization and alignment.

IS governance entails the implementation of a certain number of resources, bodies and procedures in order to better manage the IS. Governance aims to handle questions such as: how should decision-making for IS stakeholders be structured? How can value creation be measured? How can stakeholders be involved in value creation? How can all information resources be integrated into a single approach? Lastly, how can internal and external challenges be coordinated?

IS urbanization uses visualization methods to help the manager take stock of the different organization levels of an IS and their coherence. Urbanization detects the constraints, opportunities and contradictions that are acting upon the information architecture and can provide the decision-makers with tools to help them envision the continuous development of the IS construction process. Urbanization thus answers the following questions: how can information flows be organized? How can their fluidity be improved? Lastly, how can they be adapted to current and future changes?

IS alignment evaluates the IS's capacity to make a significant contribution to the organization's strategy. In a context of rapid technological change and highly competitive markets, alignment enables responsiveness and aims for proactivity. It is a vector for creativity and promotes the emergence of comparative advantage. As it requires a concrete response and rejects intangible, standardized answers, strategic alignment recognizes the diversity of organizations and issues to be taken into account: how can we make the IS responsive to strategic agility? Also, how can we facilitate the adaptation of tools and humans in the face of changing objectives?

From a pedagogical perspective, the book sets out to make the link between the theory of ISs and the theory of organizations. Thus, we link the three specific IS concepts mentioned above (IS governance, IS urbanization and IS alignment) with three other, more generic, keys: stakeholder, territory and project.

The stakeholder is the crucial element that makes it possible to envision governance, because they are the source of value creation. However, the human stakeholder engages in collective action via socio-technical interfaces and systems. The interweaving in ISs is so strong that it is sometimes difficult to differentiate, within the organized activity, what is human in scope and what stems from computer applications. It is thus possible – as the sociology of innovation proposes [LAT 07] – to think of technical artifacts and ISs in particular as agents.

The territory is the operative field embraced by a self-regulating IS. Territory is a key concept of the urbanization process and is characterized by a multiplicity of levels: geographic, functional, represented, etc. This means that thought must be given to maintaining coherence between the various territorial levels of the IS, in the face of the disruptive influence of the context.

The project is an important element in the IS strategy. Management of the project portfolios allows an implementation of strategic alignment. Once the management direction has been set, the projects will define the path towards the target IS. These projects feed into each step of the IS upgrade: acquisition, processing, storage and distribution of information.

Using these three concepts, we propose to define the IS as: "A set of actors (human and/or non-human) that are interdependent, interacting via socio-material systems on a plurality of territories in the framework of an information management project (acquisition, processing, storage, distribution)."

The great challenge of our three-dimensional proposal (stakeholders, territories and projects) is how this can be turned into a system. To do so, we must, behind this didactic breakdown, open an analysis of the overlaps, intersections and cross-influences. In doing this, the danger is then that the manager will feel overwhelmed by the challenges. Taking these three perspectives into account simultaneously can indeed seem tricky, if not impossible. How should it be addressed? What methodology should be used? Is it reasonable to try to bring these three aspects together in sync? To meet these challenges, we propose the adoption of an operational approach based on complexity thinking [LEM 90; MOR 90].

For the sake of clarity, this book introduces each of the three aspects in turn before seeking to combine them in the final part. The book thus has a four-part construction:

– *Part 1: Governing the Stakeholders.* We offer strategic managers our insights on how their profession has developed by sketching the portrait of the stakeholders involved. Nowadays, these stakeholders are in great demand to drive change in organizational, decision-making and regulatory mechanisms. It is especially important to take stock of these issues in order for them to be given priority status on organizations' strategic agenda. We show that the issue of governance makes reference to assessments in terms of transaction costs, cost-sharing and hidden costs.

– *Part 2: Urbanizing the Territories.* Beyond the urban metaphor, in this part, we consider the modalities of conducting a breakdown of the IS and the vision induced by the IS planner. The issue of the territory is a complex concept. Territory is often referred to in terms of its macroeconomic aspects. Our proposal is to open up a consideration of IS management at the meso level, which seems to be the appropriate observational level of the extended organizational framework.

– *Part 3: Project Alignment.* In this part, we approach the issue of aligning the IS project to the general strategy of the organization. In a competitive environment, there are many changes in strategy and organizations are obliged to adapt to technological developments that quickly render the solutions that have already been implemented obsolete. The management of IT project portfolios enables strategic agility and innovation.

– *Conclusion:* Management of Information Systems in its Complexity. To conclude, we focus on the areas of confluence between the three aspects identified for an analysis of IS management. We show how the coming together of stakeholders and territories raises the need to take into account increased stakeholder mobility in an organizational context, where the organizational boundaries are pushed back significantly, or even broken down. We analyze the coming together of territories and projects and the development of the agility made necessary by new customer expectations. We also look at the assembling of stakeholders and projects around the quest for organizational maturity widely supported by the development of norms and international standards for IS management. At the intersection of the issues of governance, urbanization and IS alignment, there lies complexity management. The use of this term is not an indication of a problem, but rather a solution. In line with the etymological origin of the word (*complexus*: something that is woven together), it entails focusing on the complementarities and continuations between the various points of view.

Finally, this book is a follow-up to a book published in French by Hermès–Lavoisier in 2009: *Le Management opérationnel du système d'information* (operational management of the IS). Its purpose is to address a wide audience: students (business schools and their masters of science in business and masters of business administration) and professionals working in IS management.

The target of the book is to describe and analyze organizational ISs with reference to the problems encountered in businesses and also the problems (always more numerous) that emerge from public, not-for-profit organizations.

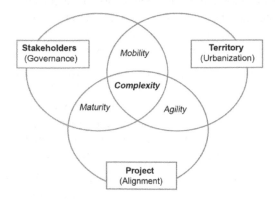

Figure I.1. *IS management in complexity*

PART 1

Governing the Stakeholders

Introduction to Part 1

The first part of this book offers IS stakeholders a reflective contribution to the possible future developments in their roles and responsibilities. In this part, we will illustrate the stakeholders of information systems governance (ISG). We will show how today's stakeholders are driven to seek shared mechanisms for organization, decision-making and audits in order to anticipate successive technological innovations. This sharing is particularly important, to the extent that it is considered a priority in the strategic agenda of organizations. We will show that IS governance encompasses the complexity of the issues arising within organizations (value creation, skills sharing, capitalization of knowledge, etc.).

In Chapter 1, we will address the issue of technological change and describe its impact on the collective organization of IS stakeholders. We will highlight, in particular, the semantic shifts in the job title of this function, which provides evidence of both the growth in opportunities provided by technology and of the acknowledgment of its strategic importance within the organization. Chapter 2 will show the link between global organizational governance and IS governance. We will identify three separate theoretical approaches that enable us to take stock of the issues related to IS management. We will then consider ISs through, in turn, taking stock of transaction costs [WIL 81], the concept of a hybrid coalition organization [AOK 01; AOK 10] and the prospect of the coming together of an organization's stakeholders [FRE 10a; FRE 10b]. Chapter 3 will conclude this first part with a consideration of the practicalities of implementing IS governance. We will describe the organizational forms of governance and good practice benchmarks relating to IS, which are most frequently used as guidelines during implementation and while achieving compliance.

1

IS Stakeholders

THE FUNDAMENTALS.–

1) Technological developments stimulate change to organizational models while at the same time changing production models.

2) The issues raised by an IS involve all human actors within organizations, because they are at the heart of every goods and services production and distribution process.

3) The interface between human actors and technical tools calls for a complex, global approach to IS.

The ubiquitousness of digital tools in both our professional and our personal environments makes the concept of IS stakeholders difficult to grasp. Indeed, a corollary of the widening scope of digital transformation is the increase in the number of stakeholders involved. Thus, when we talk about IS stakeholders, we are referring not only to those responsible for the creation and maintenance of information services but also to all users whose roles and significance have grown steadily along with the development of information and communication technologies (ICTs). By facilitating horizontal operating models, ICT has brought about a profound change in the relationships between the human actors within organizations. ICT has led to a greater decentralization of operations, a peer-to-peer operating model and a decrease (or even disappearance) of middle management who in theory are responsible for supervising those involved in production. We may have talked about the "flattening" of organizations through the generalized use of ICT, with a reduction in the number of reporting levels required. IS users (no matter what their role is within the organization) become key stakeholders in IS governance. In the same way, ICT has helped empower end users by involving them in the production of IS services. The widespread adoption of the so-called "agile" methodologies can be cited as proof of this. But when considering IS stakeholders, we must also take into account the technological tools deployed within organizations. Because they are closely interwoven into the heart of production processes, information reporting and audits, these tools are fundamentally linked to the business activities of today's organizations. As such, these tools have the potential to influence the cognitive capacity of the human actors and to change the way they perceive their environment. It can thus be seen that the concept of stakeholders in ISs, and how to define them, is complex. After describing the development of the technological environment of IS stakeholders, we will seek to show the impact of this development on organizational management. We will then be able to start categorizing IS stakeholders and define the unit of analysis required in order to conduct appropriate IS management.

1.1. The technological environment of IS stakeholders, and its development

Four successive "technological waves" have marked out the history of IS and a fifth is on the way. In the 1970s and 1980s, the IS was centered around what we call "proprietary systems" whose application code was inaccessible to the user. Workstations were slave terminals with no local resources, connected to a central computer (mainframe or "host") on the master–slave model. This earliest period can therefore be described as "host-centric".

The years 1980–1995 were fertile in innovation. The integration of organizational IS led to new, networked patterns of work organization and production. These innovations included, for instance, the emergence of client–server (C/S model) applications. From that point on, the C/S model combined two approaches: client-centric (where resources are managed locally) and server-centric (where resources are centralized). The C/S model assumes implementation of departmental computer systems based on workstations connected to each other by a local network (the invention and rapid adoption of Ethernet technologies). The C/S model was also contemporaneous with the development of relational databases and their associated methodologies (entity–relationship model, SSADM, Prince, Merise methodology) and the advent of the first EDI (Electronic Data Interchange) applications (the birth of Business to Business or B2B e-commerce) using extended networks. The development of EDI was a precursor to the progression of organizational IS into inter-organizational IS, supporting the coordination of logistical flows of increasingly networked businesses [PAC 06].

The years 1995–2010 built upon the previous wave's widespread adoption of ICT. This marked the beginning of the network-centric era. This period was founded on the significant development of networking technologies and the commercial coming of age of the Internet, already firmly established in academic circles. The era was characterized by the birth and growth of intranets (for internal communications and subsequently for all business processes) and extranets dedicated to the opening up of IS to external stakeholders on a massive scale (introduction of business portals). The environment became fully distributed, and the work on the internal integration of the company's IS was effected in the context of wide area networks, in terms of both technology (networks) and economics (networking), boosted by the widespread availability and massive adoption of Internet technologies. This period saw the appearance of entirely new and innovative relationships between the organization and all its stakeholders, in the form of the openness of IS and connectivity with customers (e-commerce with consumers, Business to Consumer – B2C), partners (B2B), partners as stepping stones to clients (Business to Business to Consumers – B2B2C), employees (Business to Employees, B2E), administration (Business to Administration – B2A) and so on, not forgetting shareholders and the general public, through dedicated institutional websites.

From 2010 to 2025, we will continue to see the commercial development of cloud computing. Using a combination of virtualization architectures and distributed operating models, these technologies led to growth of the market for advanced services. Packages on offer were varied and allowed for graduated outsourcing of services. The SaaS (Software as a Service) model is the best known, but other packages were available: Platform as a Service (PaaS) and Infrastructure as a Service (IaaS). The cloud-centric period is oddly reminiscent of the initial host-centric period. There is no need for the user to have significant local resources. The service provider supplies users with all of the resources they need and centralizes them to satisfy the requirement for user integration, with the added conveniences of rolling out the service and providing basic training, which did not exist in the initial period, but which is now made possible by the higher speeds offered by telecommunications.

The next few years could see the arrival of a new type of infrastructure based on a new technological ecosystem linking Web 3.0, the Internet of Things, blockchain and Artificial Intelligence (AI). With these technologies, it is indeed possible to envisage a highly decentralized and user-centric architecture [CHO 22]. The challenge of this change is to give users back control of their private data by freeing them from the control exercised by an oligarchic set of multinational corporations and superpowers. Web 3.0 is defined as the third stage of the World Wide Web. Historically, the first stage gave the Internet user the content of web pages in read-only format. The second gave the user the power to create content (linked to tools like blogs and Wiki pages). This Web 3.0 stage is that of the semantic Web which concerns the interaction between machines and data (IoT, AI), and in which the user is the main agent for value creation and exchange. In this configuration, the user is hybrid and shaped by the complementarity of interventions among human and nonhuman actors. Transactions are secured in peer-to-peer relationships via the blockchain.

This astonishing technological evolution, significant in terms of its vastness, its intensity and its rapidity, has had three major consequences for organizations: a profound redefinition of IS and their impact, an astonishing shift in the uses of computing and a radical change in the computer–user relationship. This is the aspect which we will now consider.

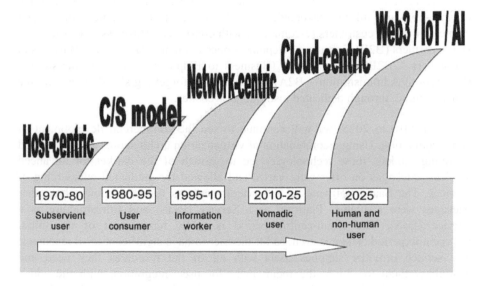

Figure 1.1. *The technological waves*

1.2. Impact of the developing technologies on organizational management

The technological waves discussed above led to IS undergoing a significant evolution in the extent of their impact at the organizational management level. The flexibility and the networking focus of IS for many stakeholders made it possible to manage far-reaching organizational change, stemming from the shifts in policy and strategy adopted by companies from the mid-1980s on: extended business strategy [ALB 09], refocusing on core business activity/activities, a new definition and structuring of the company's business activities, inter-organizational cooperation, outsourcing, offshoring, spatial redeployment of production-related activities, customer focus, seeking a higher return on capital invested and so on.

The evolution of IS is multifaceted, with these facets becoming increasingly complex. The first wave facilitated improved local exploitation and a more extensive integration of tools; the second wave supported the achievement of full internal organizational integration and led to the introduction and subsequent widespread adoption of a new set of management processes, including the appearance of extended IS. The birth and growth of extended IS are directly connected to the new policies of outsourcing and changing the company's value chain, calling for delicate inter-organizational coordination of production in an environment characterized by a fast flow economy (just-in-time, on-demand manufacturing, lean manufacturing, etc.). The setting up of extended networks (network-centric) brought the ability to embrace and sustain more radical developments, such as the redefinition of business networks (B2B, B2C, B2B2C) and the redefining of the company's spheres of operation against a background of global integration (internal and external – the appearance of cooperative IS) [ALB 12]. The most recent wave has consolidated the outsourcing of services and job specialization, developing the concept of the servitization of IS. At the same time, it is weakening local management, insofar as skilled operators are gradually losing control over developments in the environments they use. Cloud computing is another contributory factor in the form of consumerization through growing the market and massifying the range of services on offer. New forms of a collaborative economy are appearing, empowering consumer to consumer (C2C-type) models. Today, in the age of online platforms, new business models (e.g. B2C2C) are being developed and are calling the traditional models [PAR 17] into question. This is for instance the case with printing platforms for 3D engraving and artwork, where the company provides printing services and lets its designer clients liaise with buyer clients.

This evolution in the levels of impact of IS seems remarkable and is important to note, because it both leads on to new forms of value creation and to its analysis. It also brings another consequence, in that it augurs a radical and irreversible change in the area of IS. Henderson and Venkatraman show that the first two levels (local operations and internal integration) can be an incremental evolution, but the subsequent levels bring sudden change, which has implications in terms of managing this change [HEN 91; HEN 93]. However, the greater the degree of transformation, the higher the potential profit which the organization stands to gain (taking the example of Netflix which started out by renting analogue content, evolved into a streaming platform and then became a digital content producer).

In other words, the highly innovative nature of IS goes hand in hand with potentially significant value creation. The notion of breakthroughs being associated with sudden change is based on taking more notice, not of the content of the IS, but of its level of usage and the crucial significance of this level of usage. And this level of usage is linked to the relationship that exists between the user and the IS.

The first level of usage (host-centric) began with the quest for efficiency, with the processing of transactions being automated from the initial computerization of the organization (computer-assisted manufacturing – CAM), and progressed to the second level with the introduction and development of personal and group computing during the client–server era, such as enterprise resource planning (ERP) software packages. The quest for strategic efficiency in the third era leveraged networked computing (network-centric) capable of integrating all approaches so as to simultaneously serve as a powerful operational tool for users, a reporting and decision-making tool for management, and an inter-organizational cooperative tool to support the company's business processes. The growth in IS usage levels and the changes in value creation resulting from this are thus included within the three phases of the computer–user relationship characterized by three operational targets.

In the 1970s and 1980s, the operational objective was the automated processing of the organization's basic operations. The end-user was "subservient" (behaviorist and Pavlovian theories) to the IS, or at least could appear so. Between 1980 and 1995, in parallel with the introduction of client–server architectures, the notion of the subservient end user was gradually replaced by the "stakeholder" concept and made way for an individual who was part of a distributed logic, both personally and as a group, where the user ultimately becomes an IS consumer. Individual consumers of a distributed system interact more and more directly with the IS, and they can be external stakeholders. By the end of 1995, the end user was regarded as being a manager of business activities or processes whose independence was assured by the system which from this point on was dependent on them, making them an "information worker". The customer is an internal and/or external stakeholder. This approach takes into consideration the opening up of the company supported by the "network-centric" phenomenon. In this environment, organizations interact via numerous interfaces. The development of this kind of environment is connected to Internet usage. The end user is an information worker, having a more or less constant relationship with computer tools. This update of the relationship with the user operating the IS, and of the strategic nature of this customer relationship in the process of value creation, has certainly impacted on the development of Chief Information Officers (CIOs). It has strongly influenced IS managers to organize and structure their management in line with the provision of a customer-focused service. From 2010 to 2025, the cloud-centric model will continue to promote freedom of action for the stakeholders and lower the barriers to entry. Small businesses (and even individuals) will be able to access advanced applications and high-level expertise. This will upset the previous equilibrium and restimulate the potential for action at the entrepreneurial as well as the intrapreneurial level.

1.3. Understanding and categorizing the human stakeholders in IS

To categorize a stakeholder, that stakeholder must first be given a title. In the first analysis, it is interesting to note the semantic shift that has occurred during the last 30 years in the job title of the person in charge of the IS. Successively, this person has been called: "Computer Manager", "Data Processing Manager", "IT Manager", "Systems Manager", "Systems Administrator", "Information Development Manager", "Chief Digital Officer" and "Digital Technology Manager". These various job titles – and we could find other variants – cover a rise in the hierarchical positioning of the role within the organizational structure. The evolution of the IT function within organizations has in fact progressed in significant stages. Each stage is characterized by value creation connected with a specific computerization of tasks. We can identify three great strides in the historical process.

1.3.1. *The days of the pioneers*

The first step relates to the 1960–1980s. It begins with the exploratory work of the pioneers (Figure 1.2). Punched card data processing is a set of mechanical techniques which enabled companies to start the industrial processing of information. This process was based on the use of punched cards or tape in purpose-built technical devices. The head of the punched card department (PCD), later known as head of the administrative and punched card department, has staked a place in the annals of history for having automated repetitive tasks, and specifically, for establishing accounting, payroll and invoicing in a role that generally, rather oddly, answered to the Chief Accountant. By the end of this first stage, the Systems Manager had the job title of Computer Manager. On the organizational chart, more often than not, they were placed under the Finance Director. From the point of view of instruments offered by the IS, the Computer Manager implemented applications that everyone readily accepted as complex and advanced.

Value creation was then obtained by optimizing IT resources for each business function taken in isolation (sales, manufacturing, purchasing, etc.), for each level of decision-making (strategic, tactical, operational). The creative and innovative vision of ISs was thus "internal" and limited, but well-suited to the functional structure model implemented by the vast majority of companies. This conceptual approach in silos led to the development of adapted IT tools and also to the implementation of IS that were virtually hermetically sealed (see Chapter 5, Anthony's Pyramid). The era of the pioneers was marked by two phases, leading to the stakeholders in the IT function seeing the importance of their role recognized in hierarchical terms. The appearance of a computer manager liaising directly with the financial management team and the creation of the first team of computer operators to cover data input operations, previously overseen by the Chief Accountant, illustrates this.

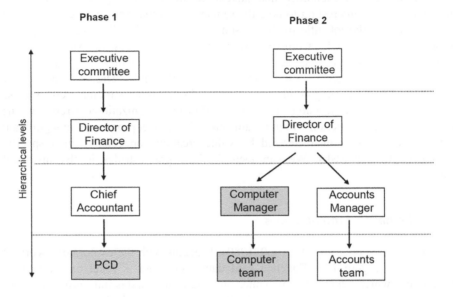

Figure 1.2. *Evolution of hierarchical levels in the days of the pioneers*

1.3.2. *The birth of the IS manager, a change in status*

The second stage happened between 1980 and 1995. This stage saw the advent of the "Systems Manager" or even the "Systems Administrator". This role involved working with operational users towards achieving an IS with application functions that would contribute to making an improvement in working conditions. IS were in demand especially for their capacity to provide a basis for decision-making (advent of decision support systems (DSS), or intelligent decision support systems (IDSS)). Value creation was achieved in this case by improved performance by the organization in its market(s). The "internal" vision of the IS of the 1960s to the 1980s extended to the notion of improving external performance. Massive use of an IT and telecommunications structure is proof of this and resulted in the emergence, followed by rapid and massive roll-out, of ICT in every organizational function within the business and all levels of the hierarchy. The attachment of the IT function to upper management shows the extent to which the role in itself had evolved: the IS manager, promoted to operations director, sits on the Executive Committee on a fairly regular basis.

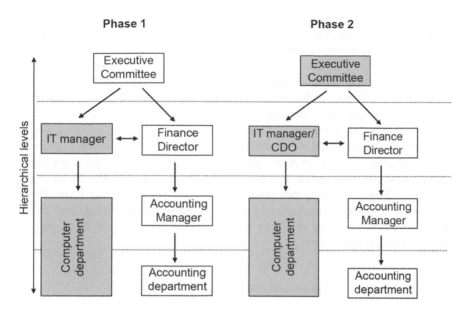

Figure 1.3. *Contemporary evolution of hierarchical levels*

The years 1995–2010 confirmed this shift, and recent years have seemingly intensified it. The emergence of the post of "Systems Manager", "IS Manager" or "Director of IS Governance", and the involvement of the head of the IS function on the company's Executive Committee or Board of Directors, represent significant stages in this change of status of computer managers. Systemic features reinforce this evolution, confirming the strategic position of the computer manager. Regulatory changes that are very restrictive in terms of IS management (Sarbanes-Oxley Act – SOX in the USA, the *"loi de Sécurité financière"* – *LSF* in France, the Basel I–IV Agreements for banks, etc.) and the proliferation of good governance benchmarks for IS (Control Objectives for Information and related Technology – COBIT, Information Technology Infrastructure Library – ITIL, IT Scorecard, ValIT, International Organization for Standardization – ISO 1799, etc.) present many constraints, and it is vital to be aware of and to keep abreast of all of them.

The years 2010–2025 will be remembered for the emergence of a director of computer resources who sits alongside the director of human resources and the director of financial resources. Powered by Cloud tools, this title opens the way to professionalizing the concept of value creation attached to IS and the establishment of boards of directors that include the strategic management aspect of IS, in particular by refocusing on data management and digital sciences (Data Science). The introduction of the Chief Digital Officer (CDO) – in other words, a decision-making stakeholder attached to the board with a cross-disciplinary version – is an indication of this change. Historic recruitments of computer managers or CDOs are the observation criteria of this new trend.

History also highlights a change in the relationship between ISs and value creation. First of all, technological change was responsible for redrawing organizational boundaries and encouraging stakeholders to reconsider value creation. Next, the IS' impact shifted and began to drive new forms of value creation within the organization. More recently, the user relationship is now attracting particular attention for its inherent value potential. With the spectacular progress seen with artificial intelligence, it is clear that AI techniques will have ever greater influence on decision-making processes at the highest organizational level. This in turn leading to general management being increasingly animated and led by nonhuman actors. We must therefore ask what safeguards should be in place to supervise this kind of practice.

1.3.3. *Organizing functions around IS governance*

According to the French school of thought, IS stakeholders can be categorized into two groups: project owners and project managers (see Part 2). The project owner brings together the functions that deal with the organization's core business activity. The project manager brings together the functions that deal with computing. The major managerial problem with this distinction lies in establishing communication between stakeholders who do not speak the same language and do not have the same points of reference. Moreover, project owners and project managers have hierarchical structures, and it is necessary, indeed vital, to establish an appropriate correspondence between the two areas.

Communication between project owners and project managers has for a long time been characterized by different languages and defensive attitudes, a kind of mutual incomprehension institutionalized by preoccupations, culture and skills that are industry-focused for some and IT-focused for others. For as long as IT management consisted of developing tools to facilitate the automation of repetitive tasks and the production of reports, the quality of communication with business managers caused no real issues. Thus, the IT manager could have a relationship characterized by strong interdependence but in which liaison with end users was limited to supervisory functions, and the decision-makers could have no direct involvement in IS.

As the IS became responsible for increasingly complex functions and the services expected of it continued to evolve, it became necessary to clarify the relationship between project owner and project manager. On the project owner's side, an effort to align structurization with client need began to manifest itself. This became firmly established with the creation of a new function: project owner support, the role of which consists partly of bridging the attitude gap and overcoming the language barrier. Project owner support is delivered by a stakeholder who helps the project owner define their needs and draw up a specification for the project manager. In parallel, on the project manager's side, efforts to market IS services have taken shape and grown. This focus on the design of IS services – just as the marketing function designs products aimed at the end user – took the form of the creation of project manager assistant (PMA) positions, of user interfaces and of customer domains, whose role lies in taking the final steps towards reaching an understanding between IS service providers and the clients, the IS users.

These new functions and the new stakeholders made it possible to greatly enrich and improve the relationship between project owner and project manager, creating a complex and effective structure of operational interfaces between all business areas and project leaders in project management. In conclusion, the roll-out of these new resources led to an improvement in the relationship and a closing of the gap between IS director and IS service users, while increasing the number of stakeholders involved in the development of IS. Also, it led at the same time to a redistribution of roles and skills among all these stakeholders.

The introduction of new stakeholders led quite rapidly to a global redistribution of roles and skills in IS organization. A significant factor in building the bridge between project owner and project was the establishment of liaison with an IS administrator, extending functional organization to project ownership, with a specialist from the project management team, in charge of the client domain. This represents a major change. The client has in front of them a stakeholder specialized in understanding the client's business function, not a language, a platform or ICT; and this shows on the systems manager's side a profound shift in the skills required and the application of these skills. The organizational structure has been enriched by this, and the relationships between the systems manager and their environment have been professionalized by the cross-search for operational synergies. De facto, relationships between project owner and project manager have become multiple and personalized.

This kind of organization sets out to identify the business functions and to develop a specific interface for each of them. The systems manager appears in this context as the organizer and the coordinator of a customer focus broken down into major business functions. Redistribution of the roles mentioned above goes hand in hand with the redistribution of skills. These skills can be split into three main levels. At the highest level, the systems manager–project manager has the ability to see the bigger picture covering all of the project owner functions, and provides a global response to the need to align IS performance across the whole of the organization's value chain. At the intermediate level, the systems manager develops an IT architecture and IS that are in line with business function requirements as modeled in their complexity within an occupational or business architecture. Finally, at the third level, the systems manager implements the proposed architecture for IS services, thus integrating the conceptual and physical aspects, in other words, a higher profile in the carrying out of a task, an activity or a process by an end user, a client of the IS service. In this description, we find responses given to demands arising from the model put forward by the Gartner Group in the 1990s. This model basically consists of suggesting an alignment of project owner and project manager at three levels: the global value chain, the company's choice of business organization and operational implementation. Adapting IS management to context has made it possible to develop new functions and new skills inhouse. It has also made it possible to professionalize its services and develop a multi-pronged approach.

The evolutionary stages of the IT governance models (project owner/manager) can be defined as follows:

1) The two worlds are separate with a computer manager carrying out instructions.

2) The two worlds ask each other questions and give each other answers with a service-oriented systems manager.

3) The two worlds mix and interweave, with a systems manager who is a business partner and a service provider.

Governance Institutions

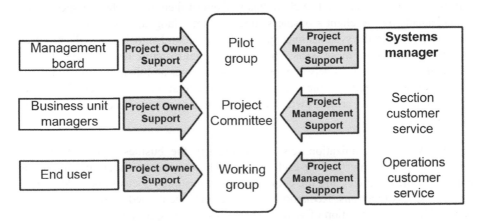

Figure 1.4. *The governance of IS stakeholders*

In summary, IS managers are charged with orchestrating, within the IS governance framework, relationships with key function stakeholders:

– *The board of directors*, which delegates the strategic management of IT to the systems manager, ensures that the systems manager sets up the appropriate governance bodies and contributes to IS management in line with its strategic plan.

– *Operational business directors*, who are clients of the IS management (sales director, marketing director, financial director, etc.). The operational directors own their IS and use it for their own needs. They contribute to managing the ISs in their area of responsibility and also the global ISs.

– *End users*, who can be reached by identifying key users. In this case, consultations take place face to face. Liaison with end users can be routed through project owner support. Project owner support can help users formalize their needs in terms of service level requests (SLRs), as well as tailor the service level agreement (SLA) and take responsibility for SLA. Finally, it can produce the key performance indicators (KPIs) and train users. They can be involved either in the management of one dedicated IS or the management of a number of ISs.

1.3.4. *Extending IS from internal stakeholders to external stakeholders*

From this point on, no business activity can dispense with the utilization of IS resources (workstations, software, architecture, infrastructure, platforms, etc.). For each function, specific processes must be defined and supported between their providers and their own clients. In view of this, and even before considering all of the organizational levels supported by the IS, there is a complex situation to be managed. The systems manager must be able to reach agreements between the executive and the directors, on the one hand, and between the directors of the various functions, on the other. This dual level of complexity requires serious thought in terms of IS stakeholder governance.

The stakeholders in IS governance are numerous, and they have objectives that seldom converge. However, the central, structural nature of IS means that they have to work together and find coherent organizational models. The cooperation to be implemented is tricky because it has to reconcile many levels of action and interaction. An attentive observer looking at an organization's IS will see that the systems manager has to consider first of all the needs of the business in the strict sense, in other words, the needs of the internal clients, i.e. its board and its directors. The directors are tasked with developing the diverse range of skills that make up today's organizations. But the systems manager's job does not end there. A number of other strata of the business environment have to be added in turn to the global management of the system. The same applies in terms of taking responsibility for dealing with the end client and the network of distributor clients, suppliers and subcontractors, who these days are usually structured into different tiers of suppliers, external partners (banks, insurers, logistic providers, service providers and suppliers, etc.), government departments, shareholders, internal auditors and statutory auditors.

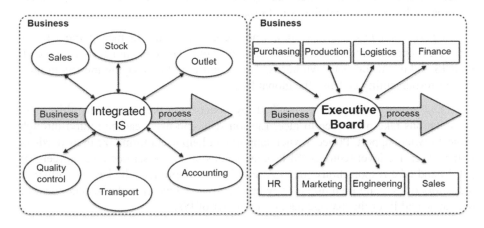

Figure 1.5. *The integrated logic of IS and internal stakeholders*

From a systemic perspective, we can, through Le Moigne's work, see an organization's IS as a subsystem of that organization [LEM 90]. But since the organization itself is a subsystem of a larger system, IS has to be conceived in an expanded, open mode. This means that the boundaries of IS management must be extended to external stakeholders (suppliers, customers, partners) engaged in the same value chain. Moreover, we have to take into account the interactions at play between the various levels. For example, stock management does not stop at local level analysis. IS could provide information on the stock of tier 1 suppliers and, by pursuing the same pattern, of suppliers' suppliers (tier 2), and for the most critical products, the process can move further down the supply channels.

In conclusion, we can see that the issue of IS stakeholders is multi-dimensional. It can be a factor in matters relating to outsourcing, a pooling of resources and shared governance. In every case, the notion of the stakeholder should not be considered only from the human aspect. As regards its analysis objective, IS science is obliged to include a socio-materialistic analysis that takes into account the links interwoven into the materiality of technical objects with the stakeholders who manipulate and sustain them.

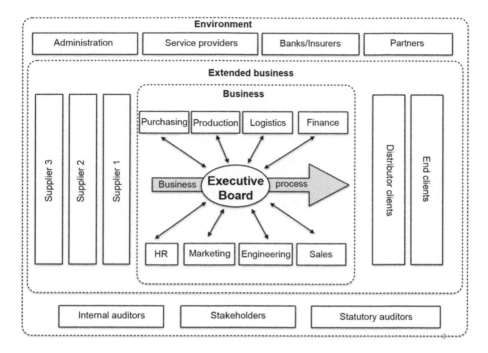

Figure 1.6. *The integrated logic of IS and internal stakeholders*

Figure 3.10: ...

2

From Global Governance
to IS Governance

THE FUNDAMENTALS.–

1) IS governance is related to organizational governance.

2) IS governance has major implications for all the organization's business activities. Therefore, defining their objectives is a prerequisite.

3) The practical implementation of the terms of governance should not be overlooked, since its medium- and long-term impacts have a strategic dimension.

In Chapter 1, we saw that technological change had implications regarding the number of stakeholders involved in IS governance and the roles they play. We also highlighted the need for IS stakeholders to be appropriately positioned in line with the chosen development path in terms of ISs. In Chapter 2, we will put forward an integral vision of the organization as a whole. The purpose of this chapter is to take global organizational governance as our starting point and deduce from that the purpose and nature of IS governance. This will lead us on to a consideration of the coherence of organizational models on these two levels of governance and to questions relating to the dual status of ISs. In fact, ISs provide perceptional tools for both the internal and external environments of an organization (feedback systems) and action models for this same environment (service production systems), all at the same time. This means the quality of global governance may suffer in the case of poor IS governance. After reviewing the challenges of global governance, we will then define IS governance and its objectives. We can then consider IS governance viewed through several possible scenarios: an outsourcing strategy, the potential pooling of resources and a joint-management strategy with third-party stakeholders.

This will enable us to form a conclusion as regards the need to be able to integrate these multiple dimensions within a single approach.

2.1. From organizational governance to IS governance

Consideration of the problems of governance goes back to the 1930s, with the work of Berle and Means [BER 67]. These authors warned of what they felt to be an imbalance of power between shareholders (owners of capital) and directors (business managers) in large, listed US companies. They demonstrated that these two types of stakeholders are in an asymmetric situation in terms of information. Directors have privileged access to the corporate IS and know how it works. Shareholders are excluded. The demand for governance was thus born with the discovery of a requirement for monitoring and counter-power. The natural consequence was the creation of systems to monitor management and the implementation of stock market and accounting regulations (creation of the Securities and Exchange Commission – SEC, in 1934).

In the 1980s, Williamson marked out the boundaries of corporate governance by making the distinction between three institutions: the market, the firm and the network. Williamson's premise was that these three institutions are sufficient to coordinate all economic activities [WIL 75]. Using this approach, he posited the existence of three modes of governance:

– The first is based on externalizing decisions by reference to market mechanisms for which the adjustment parameter is price (where supply meets demand). This model is characterized by an apparent absence of strategy at the organizational level. Stakeholders are guided by the "invisible hand" of Adam Smith (1776). In this scenario, we can adopt Hirschman's view that the firm is a price taker [HIR 70]. An external factor, in this case the pricing system, compels the company to adjust and regulate its production.

– The second governance model is based on a hierarchical and functional organization characterized by the introduction of a corporate management, of some form of strategy (not limited to adapting to a price set by the market) and implementation thereof. The implicit suggestion here is that internal performance is driven by the control of human activities by the hierarchy [CHA 77].

– The third model relates to hybrid or contractual forms that form the link between the market and the internal hierarchy. In this model, unlike the previous two, the manager considers that not all the value creation activities (core or support) are necessarily controlled by the same owners [POR 85] and the owners do not need to control them, and this was the precursor to widespread policies of outsourcing all or part of the value-creation process.

– Thus, we can see that the issue of information (and ISs) is central to the question of governance. Central, because access to information will condition the asymmetries between the shareholders as principals and the directors as agents. The purpose of governance is therefore to provide a framework for the directors' actions to encourage them to manage the company in the shareholders' interests. Therefore, ISs will be used by the controlling parties in hierarchical organizations and by hybrid organizations with the introduction of extended ISs.

– In both cases, the governance institutions, classically represented by shareholders' assemblies and the board of directors, will play a major role in establishing a balance between compliance processes and performance processes.

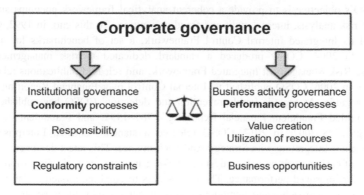

Figure 2.1. *Corporate governance according to COSO (as per IGSI, 2005)*[1]

2.1.1. *COSO standards*

COSO standards (1992, COSO 2 in 2002), established by the Committee of Sponsoring Organizations of the Treadway Commission (USA), provide a benchmark for internal monitoring and a framework to measure the efficiency of an organization. We will see later how IS governance, following the same pattern as corporate governance, can find a balance using COSO's two objectives as its pivotal point. The standard provides for institutional governance, on the one hand, which acts as a process guarantor (conformity, control, accountability, legality), and business governance, on the other hand, which covers the organizational performance processes (value creation, business opportunities). A standard such as this facilitates value creation by leveraging decision-making processes aligned towards the efficient and effective use of resources.

---

1 "The place of IS governance in overall corporate governance, balancing performance and compliance," IGSI, 2005.

The COSO (Committee of Sponsoring Organizations) was set up in 1985 as an offshoot of the National Commission on Fraudulent Financial Reporting, whose work focused on the factors leading to fraudulent behavior in financial reporting. On the basis of these reflections, the Commission developed a comprehensive set of recommendations for businesses, government agencies, auditors and regulators. The commission worked in collaboration with the American Accounting Association (AAA), the American Institute of Certified Public Accountants (AICPA), Financial Executives International (FEI), the Institute of Internal Auditors (IIA) and the National Association of Accountants. This extensive network of actors demonstrates the extent and scope of the regulatory project and the diversity of professions involved in the reflections.

COSO's objective is to provide a coherent analytical framework encompassing the issues of risk analysis, internal audit and fraud prevention. To this end, in 1992, COSO produced its Integrated Internal Control Framework, a set of benchmarks for internal controls. In 2004, COSO produced a standard dedicated to risk management, its Enterprise Risk Management Integrated Framework, and released publications related to this issue. In 2006, COSO published its Internal Control over Financial Reporting in the form of a guide. As regards fraud prevention and detection, COSO has published two reports entitled Fraudulent Financial Reporting: 1987–1997; and Fraudulent Financial Reporting: 1998–2007. In 2017, COSO released a standard entitled Enterprise Risk Management – Integrating with Strategy And Performance. This latest document extends the scope of earlier work on risk analysis by linking it to the strategic dimension and to the drive for improved performance. The idea is thus to combine proactive risk analysis with innovative approaches and continuous improvement around value creation.

Box 2.1. *COSO*

2.1.2. *The Sarbanes–Oxley Act*

The quest for institutional governance is based on the regulatory framework deriving from the Sarbanes–Oxley Act (SOX) and the Dodd–Frank Wall Street Reform and Consumer Protection Act in the USA. SOX was passed by the United States Congress in 2002. Its objective is to prevent fraud by promoting financial transparency in order to protect investors' interests. It addresses accounting for listed companies. The introduction of this law was connected to various high-profile financial scandals, such as Enron and Worldcom. This law seeks to make businesses accountable by promoting integrity in accounting principles: Generally Accepted Accounting Principles (US GAAP).

The law sets out various principles:

– Certified accounts must be signed by the CEO and CFO as a legal requirement.

– The mandatory content of reports is extended to include off-balance sheet items, auditors' report, internal audit report and code of ethics.

– The Securities and Exchange Commission (SEC) is responsible for verifying the proper operation of listed companies.

– An audit committee is established to oversee auditors, and audit rules are defined, as is the obligation to change external auditors regularly.

– The creation of the Public Company Accounting Oversight Board (PCAOB) allows general oversight of audit firms and standards. This body also has the power when necessary to sanction actors (individuals or legal entities) for unacceptable behavior.

– Heavy criminal penalties are prescribed for the falsification of financial statements.

– Internal audits must be adapted to new requirements, and COSO is the common framework adopted to support internal audits' compliance with legal requirements.

SOX has direct and indirect consequences for ISs. Elements of SOX have a direct bearing on obligations within the scope of IS management. Specifically, these include sections 409 Real Time Issuer Disclosure and 404 Management Assessment of Internal Controls. Section 409 deals with the ability of ISs to bring accounts to closure within two days. Section 404 meanwhile deals with IS security, such as the management of user passwords, firewalls, cryptography, antivirus, backup, vulnerability assessments, service continuity, etc.

A similar law on Financial Security (*Loi sur la sécurité financière* – LSF), was passed in France in 2003. The LSF reinforces the legal provisions on corporate governance. In order to respond effectively to these regulatory constraints, organizations engage in the implementation of good practice and the use of international standards to ensure compliance.

2.2. Defining IS governance

IS governance is part of the quest for a balance between institutional governance and business governance. In response to this quest, a schema proposed by the IGSI[2] demonstrates that IS governance consists of the definition and management of a set of processes serving the goals of business governance. In a transposition of the

2 The *Institut de la gouvernance et des systèmes d'information* (IGSI) was founded in 2004 by the *Association française de l'audit et du conseil informatiques* (AFAI) and the *Club informatique des grandes entreprises françaises* (CIGREF).

COSO principles of corporate governance at the IS department level, IS governance thus clearly suggests the alignment of the IS department with organizational strategy. IS governance therefore supports both institutional governance, by controlling regulatory and compliance risks – security, audit, monitoring – and, at the same time, business governance, through the quest for value creation and improved business performance.

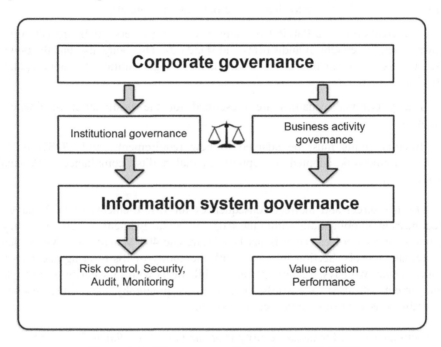

Figure 2.2. *IS governance (taken from IGSI, 2005)*

To achieve these objectives, IS governance proposes good practice guides: Control Objectives for Information and related Technology (COBIT) to define IS governance, control and audit objectives; versus risk control; Global Technology Audit Guide (GTAG) for internal audit arrangements; and International Organization for Standardization/International Electrotechnical Commission – ISO/IEC 38500 for Corporate Governance of Information Technology. For the definition and measurement of value creation, IS governance proposes the use of tools like IT Scorecard and benchmarks that are more open to innovation and investment, such as ValIT, now included in V5 COBIT, Capability Maturity Model Integration (CMMI), Information Technology Infrastructure Library (ITIL), Project Management Body of Knowledge (PMBOK) and International Organization for Standardization (ISO 27000). Matrix approaches are possible between different standards such as COBIT/ITIL or COBIT/PMBOK.

Three levels of maturity exist in organizations. They coincide with the respective weight accorded within the organization to the IS department, to the Executive Council and to the board of directors:

– IS department (ISD) focus: the objective is to ensure transparency (detailed reporting, simplified governance), explain the IS (business benchmarking, personal relationships) and integrate the IS into business governance in order to create an impact on the business.

– Executive Council/board of directors focus: the objective is to reduce IS costs, verify service continuity and functionalities, think more in terms of investment, include IS management and take ownership of the IS decision-making process and the value brought by ISs.

– Liaison strategy between Executive Council/IS department/board of directors: the open perspectives are the transaction (guarantee the performance of the IS and client/server mode), alignment (interpret and translate business strategy into IS strategy) and integration (dialog within the same fora).

Box 2.2. *IS department in value creation (source: Cigref, McKinsey and Company, Dynamics of the relationships around ISs in the management teams of large French companies; white paper [CIG 04]))*

While many companies recognize the benefits of ICTs, only a few have yet taken stock of, and managed, the risks associated with its implementation. For IGSI, IS governance is seen as a way to optimize investment in ICT in order to:

– manage the risks inherent in ISs and implement a security policy;

– enhance the performance of IS processes and their customer focus;

– align ISs with the company's business processes and ensure that they contribute to business performance;

– manage this performance by controlling the financial aspects, i.e. costs and gains related to the IS function;

– predict the development of technological solutions and stakeholder skills based on projections and business development plans;

– globally, support the objectives of value creation, i.e. the capacity of ISs to contribute to optimization of the value chain by its ability to innovate through new competitive edges (see Chapter 8).

2.3. IS governance in an outsourcing strategy

The transactional approach implies a phase of defining the operating forces, their responsibilities and their functions. This phase is associated with a process of financial valorization culminating in the taking of an aligned decision based on the financial cost analysis.

The issue of transaction costs was highlighted by Ronald Coase [COA 37], then taken up in particular by Oliver Williamson amid the 1970s [WIL 75]. The transaction costs theory is based on the concept put forward by Herbert Simon [SIM 76] that economic stakeholders have limited thinking and struggle to foresee all of the costs associated with an activity. These Nobel Prize winning authors[3] show that there are often hidden costs associated with market forces. Thus, they highlight:

– the costs of research and information-gathering upstream of signing a contract (market studies, feasibility studies, prospecting);

– negotiation and decision-making costs (drafting, checking and signing a contract);

– monitoring and enforcement costs (downstream of signing a contract).

The latter factors condition the setting up of ongoing monitoring and quality control of the service provided by the contractor.

These authors take the view that knowing transaction costs thus makes it possible to make an informed choice between keeping the activity in-house or outsourcing. In one case, transaction costs are high and justify the activity being carried out under internal hierarchical control. In the other case, transaction costs are low and it makes sense to leverage the market. Retrospectively, this line of thought can be used to explain companies' presence facing the market.

It is clear that the issue of information management and thus of ISs lies at the heart of the transaction cost approach. Three consequences arise from this:

– Knowledge of transaction costs presupposes that companies are implementing an efficient IS. This must be able to provide traceability on these costs by linking particularly with management control procedures.

---

3 The Nobel Memorial Prize in Economic Sciences was awarded in 1991 to Ronald Coase, in 2009 to Oliver Williamson and in 1978 to Herbert Simon.

– Management control is exercised on the IS department, which must be in a position to estimate its own transaction costs. IS managers are thus themselves led to consider outsourcing the IS.

– ISs are internal and external vectors for new forms of collaborative working. The development of open architectures and the Internet has had the effect of focusing on reducing transaction costs. The emergence of an open-source software economy, then a collaborative economy, has shown that it is possible to set up networks without a formal hierarchy. Between hierarchy (the firm) and the market, ISs have supported the development of hybrid networking structures that the transaction cost theory had anticipated. Marcia Aoki [AOK 86] introduced the concept of J-Form (a Japanese firm form, the founding model being Toyota) or J-Firm Group, a horizontal structure for the circulation of information as opposed to the A-form, an American multidivisional firm, based on a vertical structure for the circulation of information.

Thus, IS governance built around the transaction cost issue leads to:

– frequent recourse to outsourcing, to the point of becoming systemic;

– the establishment of a dual strategy, one to manage internal services and the other to manage outsourced services;

– a quest for cost savings that involves managing a plurality of service providers.

2.3.1. The scope of outsourcing and the stakeholders involved

Making use of facilities management for ISs is a common practice within organizations. However, application parameters are variable insofar as the objectives and forms of outsourcing vary from one organization to another and develop along with technological changes and degrees of connectivity. In terms of features and services, the most common are the outsourcing of customer relationship management, human resources and accounting ISs. In terms of type, facilities management is most frequent for hardware outsourcing (computer hardware, servers, network connections, etc.) and third-party maintenance. However, many other forms of facilities management are emerging on an ongoing basis: business process outsourcing (BPO) (outsourcing a section of business activities, such as HR). The most common outsourcing tool is cloud computing, whether private, public or hybrid, joint venture or technology partnership (see Chapter 6). These new forms of outsourcing have an ongoing impact on the IS department's territory and thus on the definition of the role of its stakeholders and also their governance. Strongly rooted and orchestrated by a financial-type transactional approach, the massive spread of outsourcing significantly redefines the role of IS department actors.

2.3.2. *A dual strategy*

The management of governance in a transactional prism leads to a dual perspective, in that it must overarch the management of outsourced and in-house services. The challenge for an IS department operating in this operating mode therefore lies in managing this duality. Often, agreements on functional cover, shared responsibility and also maintenance management differ from one provider to another. Moreover, the scope of services developed and maintained in-house can sometimes be blurred or poorly documented. Finally, the functional split resulting from an outsourcing approach based on a financial model is not always appropriate in operational terms. This dual strategy involves a special effort in managing the sharing of responsibilities. Essentially, the challenge is how to assure a stable and satisfactory level of services for users while achieving scalability of the IS as a whole and service continuity.

Subcontracting, formerly restricted to the hardware and network connectivity aspects, now extends to functional and application areas that are as vast as they are shifting. A lot of organizations have taken the decision to outsource many of their applications, including email and shared calendar management, and also the management of shared documents. These are classed as services and hence the term Software as a Service (SaaS). The concept of outsourced (and very often paid-for) application services is no longer limited to communication and storage services, as well as extends into the heart of business organizations. This is particularly the case for publishers in terms of enterprise resource planning (ERP) software packages that provide contractual solutions with their customers across increasingly broad functional parameters, along with the potential for extended interfacing with other software packages covering services that are not integrated (or not supported) within the ERP.

For the target organization, or client, the development of these multiple contracts covering services and deliverables brings significant disruption for stakeholders both internal and external to the IS department. The race to contract-out is seen by the IS directors and other directors as a solution to the quest for agility in ISs. This is in fact the advantage of shifting the responsibility for applications outside the IS department's territory. Thus, tasks such as maintenance, security and application updates are taken care of by external providers, skilled in their sphere of activities and able to provide appropriate state-of-the-art solutions.

As part of the process of negotiating service level agreements (SLAs), the internal stakeholders in the IS department define the sharing of responsibilities with all service providers in their network. In such contracts, providers agree on a set of measurable factors, key performance indicators (KPIs), such as the robustness, maintenance and development of leased solutions. This then results in an ultra-specialization of the organization's external stakeholders, acting in the interests of the organization giving the orders. Internally, this means that the IS department's role is evolving towards multi-project management.

2.3.3. Transactional governance

The race for subcontracting must be informed by the need to differentiate application-heavy processes, such as the in-house deployment of an integrated management software package like ERP on premise (treated as capital expenditure – Capex) and paid-monthly services such as public cloud email clients (treated as operational expenditure – Opex). These types of software are often combined within organizations. The development of Software as a Service (SaaS) tends to make it easier to arbitrate.

Often, the purchase cost is less than the cost of leasing a service. However, when we include the indirect or consequential expenses related to using the purchased software, and hardware support (space taken up, electricity, air conditioning, equipment management, managing its renewal, managing its maintenance, service updates), the bottom line can change. In a crisis economy, companies tend to move towards operating expenditure (Opex), because access to investment finance is difficult. In a booming economy, companies are more likely to opt for Capex. This general trend naturally impacts the IS department's budget and its expenditure policy. Facility outsourcing has the advantage of making it possible to adjust the fixed costs and provides a clear answer to the question of the cost of providing services. Transactional governance is centered on the steering committee that deals with facility management contracts and their cost management. In the case of an organization that sees itself as operating a transactional strategy, the approach to value creation through cost optimization is thus central. This vision of IS stakeholder governance will determine the parameters of outsourcing and define where the organization draws the line between internal (what it does) and external (what it has done). The structure of stakeholder governance will thus be oriented and institutionalized around this pivotal point.

The main problem with this type of governance is being able to monitor and steer the facility management contracts. Fora will therefore tend to exclude, de facto, outsourced project management. Governance fora should thus subscribe to a technological and operational watch in order to be able to respond to the necessary technical developments. The emphasis will in this case be placed on governance fora in their ability to monitor at the local level:

– service level requests (SLRs) to define requirements and service levels;

– service level agreements (SLAs) to establish a link between service levels and IS client expectations;

– service level management (SLM) to manage IS service levels;

– key performance indicators (KPIs) to monitor the performance of the services cataloged in outsourcing contracts.

2.4. IS governance in a resource pooling strategy

In a resource pooling strategy, the IS department organizes the provision of services to its customers via partners and subcontractors providing level-one services and who are themselves in control of level-two service providers. The clearly stated strategy of the IS department is thus archetypal of leader firm governance, the strategy of a vertically structured (V-form) business as described by Aoki (see Chapter 1) that seeks to be in control and not to be subjected to flux with its service providers. As an extension to the transaction cost theory, Aoki's work is of interest in this context insofar as it opens the door to hybrid forms between hierarchy and market [AOK 01].

The Aokian firm is conceived as a coalition deriving from an inter-organizational partnership approach. The company is seen as an association of directors and stakeholders (shareholders, employees, lenders, customers and suppliers). Governance is viewed as a set of constraints and rules, creating a framework for decision-making by the directors. According to Aoki, the objective is to understand how your own value can be created and shared. Governance is envisioned as the facilitator of this role, as an innovation system [AOK 10].

One of the singular points of the Aokian model lifts one limit to the transactional approach. Alongside the quest for monetary benefits driven by transactional analysis, Aoki introduced the concept of the value or quasi-value of the relationship, the fruits of a long cooperative relationship between stakeholders.

2.4.1. *Hybrid forms between hierarchy and market*

Aoki has studied network organizations in the J-form group, whether of the V-form or the H-form type. If we follow Aoki's thinking, IS stakeholders are regarded as a collection of interests to be pooled. This means that their governance should not seek to separate them, but on the contrary to unite them so that they can act in harmony. This is characterized by governances formed from alliances, partnerships, unions and collaborations.

These studies show the pertinence of a horizontal operation of the firm, where all stakeholders form an alliance and organize themselves into a shared governance structure. The flexibility and agility of the partner network are promoted. The focus is thus put on internal partnerships with a strong return on investment. Partnerships are formed and dissolved in line with the services required by business activities. Each stakeholder is sovereign within their sphere of action, but they all work in unison towards the fulfillment of a joint, concerted, productive project. Partnerships are vectors of social cohesion and organizational coherence.

Pooling here makes reference to win–win strategies. These nonzero games are aimed at reducing the uncertainty resulting from this kind of cooperation. Pooling can limit the information asymmetry between stakeholders and promotes savings of time, means and resources. The issue of empowerment as a profitable investment positions the IS as a catalyst. It is considered an instrument whose governance is at the service of the stakeholders who use it in a positive interaction leading to organizational learning and increased capacity for action.

American form – A-form

This form is about resource insourcing, vertical integration (administrated transactions) and the alternative model of coordinating productive activities alongside market transactions. The A-form is based on a hierarchical coordination of resources within an organization. It combines two types of structure: U-form and M-form.

Unified form – U-form

This is a centralized structure with functional departments. Theorized by Williamson, it represents the traditional American company described by Chandler. It is unified because it is based on centralized management. In most cases, the business owner relies on a strong hierarchy (company directors, business activity directors, divisional managers, heads of department, etc.) to ensure coordination. The classic functional structure relies on splitting it down into the major organizational functions: production and processing, sales and marketing, administration, accounting, finance and security.

Two key points regarding U-form must be highlighted:

– It is a clear structure that is well suited to companies that fulfill "one economic function, one product category, in one geographic area". By loosening the constraints of the model proposed by Chandler, this appears as a structure well suited to small businesses, still regularly adopted by European SMEs (which would tend to indicate that it has evolved to adapt itself to today's context).

– It is a limited structure characterized by the rigidity of the organization (partitioning, creation of silos), centralization of information in the company (top-down for decision-making, bottom-up for reporting; horizontal communication is poor), one vision per specialization (fragmented view taken by highly specialized stakeholders and ranked by hierarchical level). The functional structure reflects the earliest organizational theories prioritizing authority, specialization and hierarchical control over resources.

Multidivisional form – M-form

This is a multidivisional structure. It corresponds to the archetype of corporate enterprise of the early 20th century America. It is essentially about having a structure that can work in different places, perform different economic functions and produce various categories of goods and services.

Japanese form – J-form

This is a corporate network structure (networked firms), or an extended enterprise which is an alternative organizational form, in that it challenges the traditional hierarchical model. Originally, the J-form was implemented within the Japanese company Toyota in the 1950s. A J-form firm is characterized by the horizontal coordination of resources in a network of organizations. In Europe, it is known as an "outsourcing structure". It is a structure based on vertical disintegration and interfirm cooperation (agreements, contracts, treaties). It is explained by two theoretical frameworks: transactional (with its general pattern of interfirm strategic and operational relationships, i.e. between economic actors) and conventional (with its relationship strategy adapted to the new economic environment). The J-form can be achieved via two different organizational configurations: a centric network (vertical form – V-form) or a noncentric network (horizontal form – H-form).

Vertical form – V-form

This is a structure organized around a leader firm in a centric-type network. The network firm is organized on a vertical model of production operations. Toyota, for example, is divided into upstream (multilevel suppliers and subcontractors), downstream (structuration of a customer-facing network of distributors and retailers) and internal (assembling functional elements purchased at 80% from the upstream network). Suppliers, subcontractors, distributors and retailers are either subsidiaries, or affiliate companies with an equity share, or independent businesses. Among V-form firms can be found Benetton, which manufactures products using approximately 500 independent businesses upstream and distributes downstream via 6,000 or 7,000 independent distributors. Carrefour, McDonald's, Nestlé, Danone, Ikea, Dell, France Telecom, PSA, Renault and Air France can be considered V-firms.

Horizontal form – H-form

A network of firms organized on a horizontal pattern of production operations and cooperatively as a partner association. It is a type of noncentric network whose form is close to an economic interest grouping (EIG). This is a commonly used form for structuring SME networks, networks that share common challenges and complementary, customer-oriented networks. However, some large groups do use them. Sky Team, for example, is an H-form company consisting of major airline businesses (including Air France), each of which is V-form.

Box 2.3. *Organizational forms*

2.4.2. Self-organized forms

The pooling of ISs can be fulfilled by fluid, flexible processes that maximize the horizontal organization. This then fully exploits the potential of ICT systems. In a self-organizing strategy, the organization acts like a community of stakeholders adopting the rhizome paradigm [DEL 80]. Collaboration between stakeholders is based on adaptable, flexible models. Agile approaches using few resources are preferred.

The organizational issue in this case is to distribute the knowledge that has been created to a wide variety of stakeholders. Thus, IS plays a key role [SCH 14a]. The use of tools that help keep physical meetings to a minimum is favored. Collaboration supports action. Governance processes are not defined in absolute terms, but in terms of contingent need. Organizational principles are founded on ad hoc approaches and on modular and open tools. The stated objective is to maintain the lightest possible operating model to focus on innovation with the emphasis on economy of resources. Stakeholders form a coalition if necessary to make the organizational structure sustainable.

However, such a structural arrangement is also envisioned as a learning organization [ARG 78; SEN 90; ZAR 00], and the focus is on knowledge capitalization and continuous improvement strategies. Carried through to its conclusion in technological environments, such as software development, this pooling and sharing strategy has showed astonishing organizational capabilities, as evidenced by the success of open-source software (see also Chapter 6).

By definition, open-source software is first and foremost software that respects the freedom of its users. Specifically, the Free Software Foundation defines free software according to the following four freedoms:

– the freedom to execute the program, for any purpose;

– the freedom to inspect the programming and adapt it according to the need;

– the freedom to distribute copies of the program;

– the freedom to improve the program and distribute improvements.

These four freedoms are essential and complementary. They change computing in how users relate to it. For example, the first freedom allows the program to be used on all computers, with no limit on numbers. Thus, a volunteer or employee whose job is to deal with IT issues does not waste time managing licenses. The second and fourth freedoms provide the opportunity to improve and adapt the software or have this done by a third party with the necessary knowledge. These freedoms are an illustration of knowledge-sharing and are in line with a logical strategy of not having to continually reinvent tools that already exist. We take advantage of existing software, and in return, we can help the community benefit from further improvements, simply by sharing them. Finally, the third freedom allows copies of the software to be shared. For example, a person attending a training session on free software can go away with the tool on which they have been working. A volunteer can use the same free software, at home or at their charity, without having to worry about the licensing fee.

Advantages generally attributed to free software:

– the ethics of knowledge-sharing;

– reducing the cost of access to IT;

– legal copying of software, which is a natural and obvious solution to counterfeiting (often improperly referred to as "hacking");

– adapting software to the need, totally independently;

– reliability;

– interoperability and compliance with standards;

– immunity to viruses;

– sustainability and development of an IS;

– new versions with new features;

– second life for old computer hardware;

– protection of personal privacy;

– control over what computers do.

Box 2.4. *Free software (source: "Guide Libre Association – April", June 1, 2012. To find out more about the free software movement: Richard Stallman and the Free Software Revolution (Boston, MA: Free Software Foundation) or online at the Framasoft website [STA 13])*

"Linux is subversive. Who would have thought even five years ago (1991) that a world-class operating system could coalesce as if by magic out of part-time hacking by several thousand developers scattered all over the planet, connected only by the tenuous strands of the Internet? Certainly not I. By the time Linux swam onto my radar screen in early 1993, I had already been involved in Unix and open-source development for ten years. I was one of the first gnu contributors in the mid-1980s. I had released a good deal of open-source software onto the net, developing or co-developing several programs (nethack, Emacs's vc and gud modes, xlife, and others) that are still in wide use today. I thought I knew how it was done.

Linux overturned much of what I thought I knew. I had been preaching the Unix gospel of small tools, rapid prototyping and evolutionary programming for years. But I also believed there was a certain critical complexity above which a more centralized, a priori approach was required. I believed that the most important software (operating systems and really large tools like the Emacs programming editor) needed to be built like cathedrals, carefully crafted by individual wizards or small bands of mages working in splendid isolation, with no beta to be released before its time. Linus Torvalds's style of development – release early and often, delegate everything you can, be open to the point of promiscuity – came as a surprise. No quiet, reverent cathedral-building here – rather, the Linux community seemed to resemble a great babbling bazaar of differing agendas and approaches (aptly symbolized by the Linux archive sites, who'd take submissions from anyone) out of which a coherent and stable system could seemingly emerge only by a succession of miracles. The fact that this bazaar style seemed to work, and work well, came as a distinct shock. As I learned my way around, I worked hard not just at individual projects, but also at trying to understand why the Linux world not only didn't fly apart in confusion but seemed to go from strength to strength at a speed barely imaginable to cathedral-builders. By mid-1996 I thought I was beginning to understand".

Box 2.5. *Excerpt from an essay by Eric Raymond entitled*
The Cathedral and the Bazaar, published in 1994

2.5. IS governance in a co-management strategy with stakeholders

When we regard IS stakeholders as being of strategic importance, IS governance takes on a partnership aspect. The prism of transaction costs or pooling operations is not eliminated as such, but it is no longer a decisive factor in decision-making. The idea is to not reduce the complexity of interests at stake by marginalizing certain peripheral actors. The partnership approach to IS stakeholders is influenced by the seeking out of hidden costs and the desire to make them transparent. The issue of governance thus unfolds across a wider and more open playing field. In a context such as this, the first issue to be considered is the stakeholders who have been forgotten or sidelined, and also to listen to the plurality of this group. In highly competitive universes, this special attention can be a powerful lever to drive operational innovation. This, of course, happens through stakeholder governance based on the mobilization of actors and through a strong recognition of their contributions. It also happens through taking into account the interdependence of the stakeholders in IS governance and implementing mechanisms of co-construction and

---

4 Full text is available online at: http://www.catb.org/esr/writings/cathedral-bazaar [RAY 99].

co-decision. This level of openness may lead to a closer relationship between IS governance and human resources.

2.5.1. *The forgotten stakeholders*

IS governance is not immune to the mistakes repeatedly made by management. In focusing on efficiency, or simply responding to the pressing injunctions of senior management, some stakeholders may be neglected. This can happen to an IS customer, an important figure in the marketing strategy as well as an often-ignored figure in internal strategic decisions. Significant progress has been made in IS management through the widespread adoption of Information Technology Infrastructure Library (ITIL) certification and good practice. Identifying an internal customer, defining a deliverable, agreeing a service contract, supporting change and providing a Service and Support Center are all processes that have been standardized to improve the professionalization and industrialization of IS departments.

All this naturally entails significant costs, but the cost of not taking account of client needs can still be higher, as has been shown by the total cost of ownership (TCO) approach of the Gartner Group. When customers are neglected, they will try to find their own solutions, to get around the problem. This results in significant costs, which can remain totally unknown in the absence of a partnership governance of IS stakeholders. Another stakeholder too often ignored by governance is the end user. To put it bluntly, their existence is sometimes ignored until it is time to distribute and implement a new computer application. At this point, they will be accused of resisting a sudden and sometimes brutal change. The IS department will then make it their mission to force the end user to give in and adopt the solutions imposed on them.

The responses do not all come via training programs and support teams in the event of major infrastructure migrations. It is necessary to design a governance that allows users and beneficiaries to become involved and mobilized at the earliest possible stage. We can note some developments in this direction with the widespread dissemination of agile methodologies such as Scrum and XP, in which the end customer is involved throughout the process. To summarize, adopting a partnership governance also means refusing to make IS stakeholders actors take sides against each other, refusing to marginalize IS beneficiaries in the face of shareholder demands and refusing to sideline the user against the decision-makers.

This is a method of approaching IT costs introduced by the Gartner Group in 1986, directly inspired by the evaluation methods used in industry at that time. The idea is to look for an actual investment cost that goes beyond the simple purchase price to determine cost of ownership. Thus, we must put a value on indirect costs, reflect the life cycle of the product and estimate the hidden costs. In fact, in the 1990s, TCO was a precursor to the institution of a dialog between the financial controller and the IS department. In the 2000s, IS departments went further and internalized this tool, putting themselves in a position where they had financial information on their business activity and could gain in internal credibility.

Direct costs (provisionally estimated at approximately 40% of TCO) are as follows:

– hardware;

– software;

– operation;

– network;

– office management;

– service management.

Indirect costs (60% of TCO):

– training;

– application development;

– data management;

– lost time;

– staff troubleshooting;

– assisting colleagues.

Direct costs typically represent no more than 40% of TCO. Of these, it is estimated that the purchase costs of hardware and software account for approximately 15% of total cost. Most of the cost is thus related to indirect costs that reflect difficulties faced by users and their lack of experience.

Box 2.6. *Total cost of ownership (TCO)*

2.5.2. *Recognizing stakeholder contributions*

Once set up, governance forums do not only have an operational role. Being authorized to sit on this or that committee, and being able to participate in decision-making at this or that stage in the development of an IS project, is a way of achieving recognition of our abilities from others. Governing IS stakeholders thus means, for the CIO, being able to bring them together around the table and create an environment conducive to reflective discussion. This involves setting out to make a critical and attentive reading of the IS on the basis of an initial diagnosis. Questions can then be asked: how do we take into account the business needs of stakeholders from different environments and with different levels of responsibility? Are all users represented in the fora? If yes, at what level? For what purpose? What account is taken of external partners resulting from extended enterprise strategies? So many questions, so many findings. Finally, an analysis of the functioning of the governance fora of stakeholders on the strategic level can be an instrument for the implementation of a proactive organizational model.

The better developed, formalized, communicated and understood governance is, the more it allows stakeholders to appreciate the importance and the advantages of their interdependence. This appreciation can limit the instrumentation of fora for the purposes of internal politics and power grabs by a minority. When governance is dealing with a truly collective project, it can equate to joint identification of the challenges, joint financial decision-making and joint action in the field [BAL 10]. To bring us back to the title of this paragraph, it is necessary to bring about a situation where stakeholders see themselves reflected in their mutual interdependence in order to improve their interactions in the context of value creation for the organization.

2.5.3. *A multifaceted approach with a strong HR emphasis*

If IS governance can act in the interests of the stakeholders by recognizing their contribution and including them in the decision-making process, it can also pave the way to a closer relationship between the IS department and HR. This may begin with the strategic development of an HRIS [CER 12], which, in turn, can influence IS governance in its entirety. Between individualization and collective management, HRIS management opens up new avenues for the governance. Its strength lies in its ability to reconcile the transversal nature of the project while bringing together the actors involved [MID 12]. In this model, governance fora will be defined by a comprehensive vocational matrix. All kinds of projects can benefit from this type of organization. They will be driven and serviced by the plurality of perspectives and skills. Of the three models mentioned, it is this last model that probably goes furthest in taking into account the importance of stakeholder interaction in value creation. This stakeholder governance model seems to offer the potential to unite the three approaches put forward, retaining the good practices, or nomadic practices, conveyed by the other two [STE 87].

It is defined by establishing liaison between individuals, in a peer-to-peer relationship. It requires new organizational forms, made possible by the appearance of digital platforms allowing horizontal functioning. The collaborative economy is based on the pooling of resources and knowledge. It takes many different forms, such as collaborative consumption (e.g. car-sharing), collaborative finance (e.g. alternative currencies, crowdfunding), collaborative work (e.g. coworking) and collaborative production (e.g. fablabs, makers).

The collaborative economy is a controversial concept. Some see it as an alternative to capitalism and others as an evolution of capitalism. It is true that many capitalist enterprises adopt collaborative functions in order to break into new markets. In this regard, we talk about "uberization" of the economy, after the international success of Uber, a company that has established itself in many countries as an alternative to traditional taxis. This collaborative economy has upset the previous balance and brought social security systems into question. In effect, the company is a digital platform, and the self-employed worker is a user of services offered by the platform. They are therefore not a salaried employee of the company. If there is exploitation, it therefore takes the form of self-exploitation (see also Chapter 6).

Other stakeholders in the collaborative economy want to distance themselves from capitalism. Thus, platform cooperativism is a movement whose objective is to arrange a meeting between active Internet stakeholders and actors in the social economy who share their interests [SCH 16]. Unlike capitalist operators in the collaborative economy, they call for transparency in organizational models and governance of digital platforms. In this, they are inspired by the cooperative model, which was spawned by the social economy. Platform cooperativism thus claims a defense of shared rights by leveraging open design, open source (soft and hard) and shared 3D printing. Ten principles have been set out to guide stakeholders calling for this approach:

1) the rejection of exclusive ownership in favor of shared access to resources;

2) a living wage and a secure income for workers;

3) transparency on what data is managed by the platform and how this data is managed;

4) the forms of recognition for work carried out;

5) joint determination of labor;

6) legal protection, tailored to the platform in order to differentiate it from commercial operators;

7) appropriate social protection for the contributors;

8) protection within the organization against any potentially arbitrary decisions;

9) rejection of any kind of unfair control over work done;

10) the opportunity to claim the right to unsubscribe.

From this, we can see that technology gives rise to policy issues with regard to its management. The challenge for these cooperative platforms is to be able to compete with capitalist stakeholders who are already well established and running their businesses on an almost monopolistic model.

Box 2.7. *The collaborative economy*

2.6. Open innovation-type software

If the dual strategy of transaction costs helped develop partnership strategies of pooling within organizations, the expansion of the IS issue to a larger number of actors paves the way for a radical transformation of our societies.

This transformation is not limited to digital issues. As the growth of the free or open-source software movement and the collaborative economy has shown us, ICT promotes the path towards redrawing the shape of collective action and redistributing operational roles.

Innovation steps outside organizations and moves ahead outside of them or between them. In this respect, we use the term "open innovation" when talking about procedures where businesses interact with private individuals within communities of practices. The world is changing, along with the classic face of the economy, which used to separate the producer figure from the consumer figure. Between markets and governments, between personal property and public property, a space is opening up for shared property and its governance.

Living labs are experimental areas organized outside organizations' R&D departments. The idea is to experiment in open living areas where innovators, users and interested third parties can associate and interact freely. Open innovation brings organizations and individuals together within one collective. Links are forged between the actors in the collective based on a spirit of sharing and a community of practice. Living labs share a capacity for action and a collective innovation that render organizational boundaries permeable and permit transversal individual trajectories in a field that is not purely competitive, but which is open to competition.

Box 2.8. *Living labs*

2.7. Exercise: PingPongApp

In a northern European country, the practice of table tennis – which has long been very popular – is no longer so. The National Table Tennis Federation wants to act in order to maintain its good results at the international level by locally restoring vigor to the sport. Facilities exist but are beginning to be underutilized. In addition, the development of disabled sports raises the question of their specific facilities and the need to invest. The Federation aims to restore greatness to this sport by generating enthusiasm among players and the general public. To do so, it has created a digital platform accessible on Android, IOS and also on the Web. The main objective of this platform is to become the key social network for table tennis at the national level and to connect all stakeholders interested in practicing the sport. In fact, some of the problems frequently reported by table tennis enthusiasts include the lack of information on sports facilities, the difficult in finding partners of the same level interested in training together, the lack of information on coach availability, lack of private training to improve skills, etc.

PingPongApp is a multi-stakeholder platform bringing together all the partners involved in practicing table tennis. It is based on a two-sided market[5] with two interfaces:

– For the players, the mobile application provides a wide range of choices. Players are thus put in contact with other players taking into account geographical proximity, level of play, age and availability. In this way, players can form groups and set up discussion forums. They are informed about the location of sports facilities near their homes. They can pool the use of tennis tables between them.

– For institutional partners, sports associations and commercial companies, the online platform offers a certain number of targeted services. Table tennis associations and clubs can distribute their information about their services and competition tournaments. Coaches can advertize their services and organize training sessions.

Those that manage sports facilities can open an account on the platform to be put in touch with players and coaches. Municipalities can report tables that are available in open public spaces. Equipment sellers can advertise online via the platform. The National Table Tennis Federation can also validate coaches' qualification levels.

The platform's business model is based on a commission paid by institutional partners and on advertising revenue paid by sellers of sports equipment. For players, the service is free. On the technical side, the company has chosen open source software to build its platform. As a result, it does not have to pay license costs. The platform is available on virtual servers in the cloud. The cloud service provider is a market-leading global company. This choice was made at the very beginning of the project to make the first official presentations and demonstrations. It is the head of infrastructure, production and support for PingPongApp users who monitors changes

---

5 A particular type of market requiring the existence of two different groups of customers whose particularity is to be interdependent.

in offer and adapts the subscription as the platform's needs grow. The infrastructure manager also monitors competing offers. For the moment, he declares that he has not found anything better and that the service is reliable, inexpensive and good quality. Despite everything, he recognizes that the initial choice was quick and little thought out from an economic point of view. In his opinion, the choice was a winner, because it led to the rapid rise in the application's power. However, criticism has been made by member associations of the Federation who complain that they were not involved in decision-making, and who question who truly owns the application's data managed on the cloud.

Practice your skills

1) How is the platform innovative in technological and economic terms and enables meeting the objectives that prevailed when it was created?

2) Do you think that the choice made by the PingPongApp's development team to work with open source software is justified? Why?

3) How can cloud computing help the PingPongApp grow?

4) What do you think of the criticisms expressed by the associations about the signing of the contract with a large international cloud operator and the controversies relating to data ownership?

5) What governance model would you suggest adopting so that the PingPongApp can maintain a multi-stakeholder dimension in its decision-making processes?

IS Governance in Practice

THE FUNDAMENTALS.–

1) The organizational model of IS governance is strategically critical.

2) Knowledge of best practice benchmarks helps strengthen IS governance.

3) Successful implementation of a benchmark is conditional on defining the objectives of the IS.

The phenomenon of globalization of the economy has seen a rise in the power of multinationals, with a sphere of activity covering every continent. The strategic and managerial steering of these global players was made possible via the territorial coverage provided by extended ISs. Given the operational significance of these tools and the expansion of their fields of action, a strong need for standardization and norms emerged. This led IS management to multiply its own objectives: a better evaluation of operational performance and of the value added by the IS, more effective management of resources and skills, improved service value, greater visibility, optimization of sales activity, a better fit between the IS and the business strategy, compliance with the laws and regulations in each country, management of IS risk and security, etc. To achieve all this, there was a need to document best practices and define standard requirements.

Two working perspectives are necessary for this. The first stems from the internal reflection, which leads organizations to look for the IS governance organizational model best suited to their own needs. The second involves the adoption of external benchmarks that will determine the organization's capacity to engage in a process of international compliance. After addressing these two aspects, we will conclude this chapter with a reflection on how they link together.

3.1. IS governance organizational models

IS governance is strongly correlated to the governance model implemented by the company directors in relation to their strategic business units, regional offices and subsidiaries. Therefore, one question takes on full significance: who steers and monitors the IS between the group and the subsidiaries? There are several possible answers to this question.

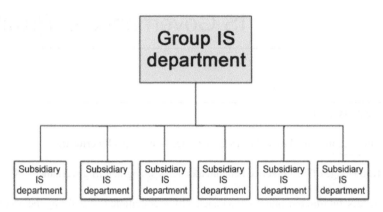

Figure 3.1. *IS department/subsidiary*
IS department

3.1.1. *Centralized governance*

In large, centralized organizations, the IS department plays a key role. Attached to the executive, the group IS department is usually seen as a bloated governance structure responsible for IS strategy, steering and monitoring. Governance is decided upon and monitored by the group IS department, which manages the majority of computer resources centrally: development teams, production teams, the technical infrastructure (servers, networks, workstations, etc.), the application's portfolio used by all subsidiaries, norms and standards, budget, projects, HR, security, urbanization, and also external service provider relationships. The subsidiaries' IS departments manage the local technical infrastructure (workstations, servers, LANs, printers), a few applications such as VAT management, accounting and reporting to administration. The subsidiaries' IS departments implement head office strategy and steering on a devolved basis.

The IS department has set up a centralized organization, with designated contact persons for business departments and regional branch offices (shared service centers vs. localized IT teams) for greater proximity with users.

During project implementation, the project manager/project owner responsibilities are shared out by activity, adjusted according to project size. When projects are relatively small, a simplified roadmap is proposed.

For certain major projects, all of the teams are brought together at a single site (organized along the lines of a project team). This allows for greater responsiveness, particularly at critical phases of a project such as defining needs, feasibility studies, revenue and monitoring.

Special attention is paid to defining the requirements and commitments shared between business departments and the IS department and to reducing the complexity of the solutions.

Box 3.1. *Example of centralized governance in a major automotive group*

3.1.2. *Decentralized governance*

In large, decentralized organizations, the role played by the IS department is just as critical as in the previous case, but in a completely different form. Responsibility for the strategy and steering of the IS belongs to the subsidiaries. The group IS department's governance is weak at the operational level, because it manages only a very small proportion of IT resources. At its own level, it is responsible for controlling applications required to consolidate the accounts and produce statistics for the dashboard. Its external activity is focused on recommending shared norms and standards.

Meanwhile, the subsidiaries' IS departments locally manage most of the computing resources they need, in compliance with the norms and standards determined by head office. Specifically, this concerns the application portfolio, development teams, production teams, technical infrastructure (servers, networks, workstations, etc.), budget, HR, security and urbanization. Strategy and steering of local ISs fall within the area of responsibility of the directors of the subsidiaries.

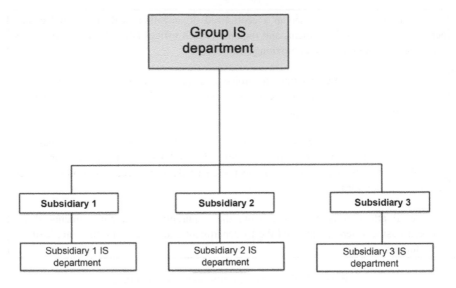

Figure 3.2. *Decentralized governance*

The IS department takes care of:

– coordination of the business departments' IS departments;

– supplying transversal services for branches;

– anticipating strategic developments of ISs to meet business needs.

Within each business unit, an IS department is responsible for its alignment to the business department concerned.

Box 3.2. *Example of governance in a large oil group decentralized into business units (refining, marketing, exploration, production and chemistry with a corresponding number of IS departments)*

3.1.3. *Federal governance*

A third type of major organization refuses to choose between centralization and decentralization. In these organizations, there is an explicit wish to use a matrix organizational structure. In this configuration, the responsibility for IS strategy and steering is shared between the IS department of the group and those of the subsidiaries. The group IS department centrally manages the shared part of IT, hardware and human resources. In particular, this covers norms, standards, technical infrastructure components (servers, networks, workstations, Internet access), the architecture and benchmarks for business, and other resources and skills (strategic IS management, business IS expertise, project management). Pooling can thus be as much an operational as a strategic objective. The subsidiaries' IS departments locally manage the unshared IT resources that they need, the application portfolio, development teams, production teams and the technical infrastructure: servers, networks, workstations, etc.

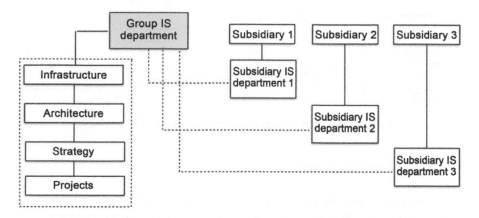

Figure 3.3. *Federal governance*

3.1.4. *Internal software and computing service-type governance*

A variant of federal governance may consist of taking care of the IS strategy, choice of business architecture and management of transversal projects for the group IS department. It centrally manages the bulk of the IT infrastructure resources: development teams, production teams, technical infrastructures, application portfolio used by all subsidiaries, and also the norms and standards.

The subsidiaries' IS departments manage the local technical infrastructures and applications. The primary objective of the group IS department is to contractually meet internal customer requirements, through identifying customer needs and interests. The group IS department positions itself as a profit center and a service contract provider. The group IS department has a duty to be proactive and competitive towards the subsidiaries' IS department to compete with external software and computing service companies.

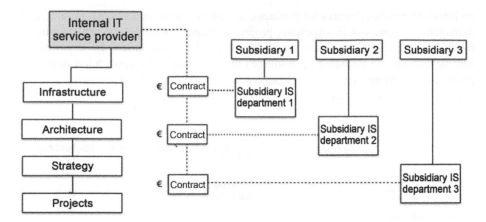

Figure 3.4. *Internal software and computing service provision*

3.2. IS governance benchmarks

The need for standards, norms, certifications and other benchmarks is strong in the field of ISs and their governance. There are two main reasons for this. On the one hand, ICTs are vectors of major policy issues. Furthermore, dialog between business stakeholders (initiators of needs) and programmers (providers of application solutions) is difficult. In fact, business stakeholders may have problems in defining their overall needs in a technical specification. Programmers, on their side, have to provide application solutions in business departments where they often know very little about the practical issues. Since project owners and project managers do not speak the same language, the need for norms is all the stronger. Benchmarks and good practice guides thus appear as unifying tools that can establish a common language. In this sense, they are much needed.

Raising the issue of IS governance standards also raises the issue of audits. In fact, when norms are adopted, this also authorizes a certain degree of deviation from the norm. This is not a simple matter, in that the IS audit considered as a governance tool again refers back to a multitude of stakeholders and national and international organizations: the Institute of Internal Auditors (IIAs), the Information Systems Audit and Control Association (ISACA), the Public Company Accounting Oversight Board (PCAOB), the Institut français de l'audit et du contrôle internes (IFACI), the Association française de l'audit et du conseil informatiques (AFAI) and the Haut conseil du commissariat aux comptes (H3C).

These various actors sometimes have different interpretations of the audit concept and in each case are referring to different standards: Global Technology Audit Guides (GTAGs), Control Objectives for Information and related Technology (COBIT) and Auditing Standard 2 (AS2). To contextualize this work on analysis and its associated missions, audits have been based on professional standards and best practice for a long time. As with most management activities, the various stages of the IS audit can involve the use of computer-assisted audit techniques (CAATs).

However, the proposed standards are to a large extent concurrent, in part complementary and sometimes redundant. Therefore, the auditor has to be capable of seeing the bigger picture, and this will help them to use the proposed standards wisely. They also have to be able to apply them to meet the legal and organizational requirements for IS governance.

In this section, we will look at the difference between:

– generalist benchmarks, aimed at covering all of the issues related to IS management;

– more specific benchmarks, focused on one particular issue.

3.2.1. *Control objectives for information and related technology (COBIT)*

COBIT sets the objectives for auditing information and associated technologies through the creation of a common language. It was developed in 1994 by a group of American experts specialized in IS audits, as part of the ISACA. The benchmark is based on a process-type approach. It seeks to position itself as the benchmark for IS governance and audit. It also seeks to provide key indicators for the success of the alignment of the IS strategy to that of the company by the optimal use of resources. Its objective is to meet the needs of stakeholders, cover the business end to end, apply a single frame of reference, separate governance and management, and promote a global approach.

COBIT Version 5 defines 37 processes, split into five areas:

– *Evaluate, direct and monitor:* ensure governance framework setting and maintenance, benefit delivery, risk optimization, optimization of resources, stakeholder transparency, and the definition and maintenance of a governance framework.

– *Align, plan and organize:* manage the IT management framework, strategy, enterprise architecture, innovation, portfolio, budget and costs, human resources, manage relationships, service agreements, suppliers, quality, risk, security.

– Build, acquire and implement: manage programs and projects, requirement definition, solution identification and building, availability and capacity, organizational change enablement, changes, change acceptance and transitioning, knowledge, assets, configuration, programs and projects, and organizational change.

– Deliver, service and support: manage operations, service requests and incidents, problems, continuity, security services, business process controls, and operations.

– Monitor, evaluate and assess: monitor, evaluate and assess performance and conformance, the system of internal control, and compliance with external requirements.

COBIT Version 5 incorporates the benchmarks ValIT and RiskIT presented in sections 3.2.2 and 3.2.3.

3.2.2. *Enterprise value, governance of IT investments (ValIT)*

ValIT was developed by the ISACA and the IT Governance Institute (ITGI) to complement COBIT with regards analyzing the quality of the processes of decision-making and governance of investments linked to IS projects. ValIT provides a frame of reference for value creation and management that identifies three areas (or axes) of governance of IS investment projects and 40 good practices.

The first area relates to *value governance*. This looks at how the decision-making process is organized for IS projects, at the definition of criteria that facilitate arbitration between projects, and at confirmation that the objectives have been achieved. Eleven good practices are used to support and organize this area, with the objectives of ensuring informed and committed leadership, defining and implementing processes, defining roles and responsibilities, ensuring an appropriate and agreed final responsibility, defining information requirements, identifying reporting requirements, creating organizational structures, setting strategic direction, defining investment categories, determining the composition of the target portfolio and defining the assessment criteria by category.

The second area covers *portfolio management*. This focuses on understanding the dependencies between projects, resource management, the definition of common criteria for arbitration and monitoring of portfolio performance. Portfolio management is based on 14 practices: keeping an inventory of human resources, identifying resource requirements, conducting a gap analysis, drawing up a resource plan, monitoring resource requirements and utilization, setting an investment threshold, evaluating the profitability analysis of the initial program concept, evaluating and scoring the program profitability analysis, creating a general view of the portfolio, making and communicating the investment decision, progressing the selected programs through the stages and funding them, optimizing portfolio performance, reorganizing portfolio priorities, and monitoring and reporting on portfolio performance.

Finally, the third area is concerned with *investment management*. This addresses the identification of business requirements, knowledge of investment programs and analysis of alternatives, profitability analysis and program management throughout its economic life cycle. This area falls into 15 key processes: establishing a general definition of the investment opportunity; developing a profitability analysis of the initial program concept; promoting a clear understanding of program projects; analyzing alternatives; developing a program; developing a benefit achievement plan; identifying full life cycle costs and benefits; developing a detailed profitability analysis of the program; clearly assigning final responsibility and ownership; initiating, scheduling and launching the program; managing the program; managing and monitoring benefits; updating the profitability analysis; auditing and reporting on the execution of the program, and closing the program.

All in all, ValIT claims to answer five big questions that arise regularly with respect to current IS governance: (the strategic question) Are we doing the right thing? (the architecture question) Are we doing it properly? (the implementation question) Are we having it done properly? (the value question) Will we obtain benefits?

3.2.3. *IT framework for management of IT-related business risks (RiskIT)*

RiskIT was developed by the ISACA to complement COBIT and ValIT. While COBIT identifies good practice regarding ways to control risks, RiskIT is concerned with the governance of IT risk management. Based on a process approach similar to COBIT and ValIT, RiskIT covers three areas, nine processes and 47 monitoring activities. The first area is risk governance, and the aim is to establish and maintain a common view of risks, integrate IS risks into the risk strategy at the corporate level, and make business decisions that take the risks into account. The second area addresses risk assessment and consists of collecting data, analyzing risk and maintaining a risk profile. The third and final area is risk response, which covers handling the situation as regards risks, managing IS risks and reacting to events.

3.2.4. *Global technology audit guide (GTAG)*

The GTAG is a practical guide to ICT auditing and is issued by the IIAs. Since the early 2000s, the IIA has produced 22 GTAGs – practical ICT audit guides that describe best practice covering internal IS audits. The various GTAGs focus on IS auditing, patch and change management auditing, continuous auditing and its implications for insurance, risk control and assessment, managing IS audits, managing and auditing risk of privacy violations, managing and auditing ICT vulnerabilities, facilities management, auditing application controls, identity and access management, managing business continuity, developing an audit plan, auditing IT projects, fraud management, auditing applications, security governance, data analysis technologies and ICT governance.

3.2.5. *Information technology infrastructure library (ITIL)*

The ITIL focuses on satisfaction with delivered IS services. This benchmark, which originated in Great Britain, provides in its Version 4 (published in 2019–2020), a set of good practices on IS organization at the operational level, on improving its efficiency, risk reduction and improving the quality of services delivered, by being attentive to the service life cycle. The adoption of ITIL by an organization authorizes it to implement a quality-driven approach to the IS department's internal and external customers.

This focus on the service life cycle enables the management of IS services to be structured around the five stages in their life. Service design leads to the creation of the expected architectures and processes. Service transition schedules the move from planned services to exploitation. Exploitation of the services puts the operational plans into implementation. Continual service improvement makes it possible to analyze the functioning of the solutions put in place and improve them. ITIL is based on the creation of a service center and a process approach built upon two central ideas: service support as close as possible to the users, on a day-to-day basis, and the quest for a service provision as close as possible to business needs, over time. An application guide for ITIL in small- and medium-sized enterprises completes this benchmark.

Implementation of ITIL processes calls for the creation of a new operational unit, the Service Center, which ensures the interface with service support processes for the services at the heart of IT production on a daily basis. It is also the single point of contact for users of delivered services.

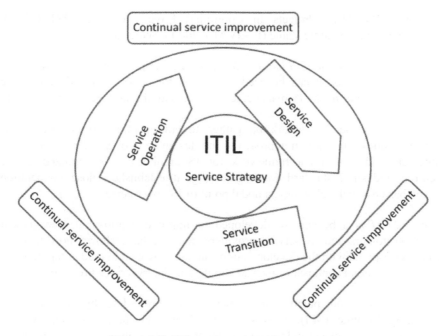

Figure 3.5. *ITIL and continual improvement*

3.2.6. *International electro-technical commission (ISO/IEC)*

ISO 27000 (International Organization for Standardization/International Electrotechnical Commission) is a series of norms that deals with information security governance. ISO 27000 introduces the concept of the information security management system (ISMS). The field covered by this suite extends from physical intervention on a website to software attacks, and from managing one simple process to complex processes calling for specific equipment and resources. ISO 27001 is the most important standard in this series, because it relates to security requirements. ISO 27002 provides a good practice guide. ISO 27005 enables the carrying out of a risk analysis.

3.2.7. *Specific benchmarks*

Here, we will discuss the existence of particular benchmarks for the management of good IS practice on specific themes: a classification of IS job profiles, The Open Group Architecture Framework (TOGAF), e-Sourcing Capability Model (e-SCM), Capability Maturity Model Integration (CMMI), Project Management Body of

Knowledge (PMBOK), Projects In Controlled Environments 2 (PRINCE 2), Intellectual Capital dynamic Value (IC-dVAL), and IT Scorecard.

Cigref's classification of IS job profiles gives a description of the roles that exist within IS departments. It can be used as a basis for an IS skill audit and more generally for structuring the IS management in line with the strategies implemented.

TOGAF is an open benchmark that gathers together good practices with regards to urbanization. It provides an approach to the design and governance of enterprise architecture and proposes a framework for IS architecture. Recognized as the concurrent industrial standard for engineering, it establishes close cooperation between business and technology, a nodal point of IS governance.

The *e-SCM* is a benchmark developed to improve relationship management between customers and IS service providers, and we have shown how this has become widespread with the development of outsourcing e and cloud computing. Its objective is a mutual appraisal of the stakeholders in the IS service provision.

CMMI is a good practice benchmark, kept up-to-date by the Software Engineering Institute (SEI). It sets out to define, evaluate and improve the management of IT projects and the development processes; in other words, to assess capacity to manage an IS project and bring it to a proper conclusion. What is different about this benchmark is that it proposes a scale of maturity in approach by defining five levels:

– Level 1, the *initial* level, indicates that development processes and projects are not stable.

– Level 2 looks at the *reproducibility* of the processes and builds on learning.

– Level 3 presupposes standardization, making it possible to precisely *define* all processes such that improvements will be seen in all projects.

– Level 4 validates the *controlled* processes for which the measures taken and the associated forecasting make it possible to adapt certain projects without interfering with the rollout of others.

– Level 5 is attained when the capacity to adapt reaches the point where processes are *optimized* and improvement has become incremental, anticipated and managed. We are now in a perspective of continuous improvement.

PMBOK and PRINCE 2 are project management benchmarks. They are built on a process-based approach to project management and are complementary with approaches to process improvement, such as CMMI.

IC-dVAL is a benchmark that sets a framework for the steering and valorization of intangible capital generated by the IS.

IT Scorecard is a tool that can be used to organize benchmark management and gives concise feedback on indicators of maturity relating to governance. IT Scorecard proposes the building of a dashboard composed of five perspectives: business contribution, financial profitability, user-friendliness, operational performance and future proofing. This benchmark contributes to a foundation upon which the IT director and manager can together build a balanced positioning of the IT function.

Reading this presentation of specific benchmarks reinforces the idea of overlap, not to say entanglement, between the range of standards. This raises the issue of the quest for an adaptive framework that would enable the understanding and implementation of benchmark coherence and their development through regular updates.

3.3. Implement a best practice benchmark

Faced with the multitude of standards, good practices and benchmarks, IS professionals have to make difficult choices. Implementing a benchmark is long and costly. Since the benchmarks on the market differentiate themselves from each other in their profile and emphasis, it is not unusual for a large company to use a number of benchmarks. This being the case, the implementation of benchmarks can be linked to a support contract with service providers (consultancies, IT service provider, etc.) and the rollout of a training and certification program.

In addition, any adoption of a framework paves the way for a reorganization of (often complex) processes and of changes in actors' working methods and IS governance modes.

With these impacts in mind, the IS department must consider the issue of productivity versus counter-productivity of benchmarks. The implementation of standards must be thought through and planned. However, all benchmarks can be seen as following their own particular logic, linked to their history: governance, production, development, security, urbanization, skills, project management and even in other words, quality. It is these unique features that give strategic, organizational and operational value to the benchmarks.

Six Sigma is a structured management method aimed at improved quality and efficiency of processes, which can be applied to the management of an IS department. The methodology is based on:

– measurable customer expectations;

– reliable measures to measure the performance of the business departments relative to these expectations;

– statistical tools to analyze the root causes that affect performance;

– solutions to address these root causes;

– tools to monitor whether the solutions are in fact having the expected impact on performance.

The method is thus based on five steps that can be shortened to the acronym "DMAIC": Define, Measure, Analyze, Improve, Control.

Each stage has different tools that are grouped together in a coherent approach. Typically, the range of tools used in each phase is (this list is not exhaustive):

– Define: the project, the process to be improved, identify operational and financial gains, understand customer expectations, also called "Yi", map the process and identify factors that have an impact on the process, known as "Xi".

– Measure: monitor the process to simultaneously measure Yi and Xi, having verified the quality of the measurement process.

– Analyze: carry out data analysis to identify the Xi factors that have the most influence on Yi, and conduct a detailed process mapping.

– Improve: identify improvement actions in relation to the most influential Xi factors.

– Control: put tools in place to steer the process.

Box 3.3. *Six Sigma*

For instance, ITIL can be seen as the ideal method for managing operational control of an IS and the management of delivered IS services; COBIT can be seen as the ultimate audit and external consultancy tool, thus covering the vast field of governance, steering, control, risks, investments and audit in its strict sense; the GTAG is the international benchmark for external audit; CMMI is the appropriate vector for gaining maturity in process approaches, etc. However, at the same time, the best-known and most popular benchmarks at the international level are seeking to expand their spheres of competence – top-down for COBIT and bottom-up for ITIL – and to position themselves as essential tools.

Against a background of strong pressures in terms of standards and best practice, the implementation of a benchmark must be able to ensure the IS's institutional and regulatory compliance, ensure a high standard of security, allow added value to be unlocked, and foster an audit and continuous improvement approach.

3.4. Exercise: GreenNRJ

GreenNRJ is a group specializing in renewable energies at the global level. Its mission is defined around principles such as the answer to energy needs, optimization and security of supply and the fight against global warming. Its sphere of activity is organized around a number of energy sources: hydropower, solar, wind and geothermal. The group invests heavily in research and development (R&D) to maintain a competitive advantage over its competitors. The group is structured into branches: GreenNRJ Europe, GreenNRJ International (outside Europe), GreenNRJ Infrastructure and GreenNRJ Cross Disciplinary. Within each branch, the activity is organized around business units (BUs). For example, the GreenNRJ Europe branch has four BUs. In the GreenNRJ Cross Disciplinary branch, one BU is exclusively geared towards R&D and works for other branches' BUs. The Infrastructure branch includes an IS department and the unit in charge of audits.

The distinctive feature of the group is that it must coordinate traditional energy production units (hydraulic and geothermal) with far more modern energy production units (solar and wind). This differentiation poses problems in terms of optimization and steering of the overall energy production and distribution network. In practice, the dedicated ISs of each sector are not of the same generation, which makes interoperability and reporting difficult. It was therefore decided at the executive level to launch a massive restructuring program via a general digitization program within the group. The aim was to harmonize all IT within the organization. This program had two goals: to improve the performance of the energy production network and to drive the company's digital transformation, with its key being innovations, with the potential of offering new services to customers.

The IS department took the project over. In dialog initiated on its own initiative with the Infrastructure branch, the IS department defined a strategy based on four tasks to be conducted as projects in the following chronological order:

– Task 1: standardization project. A broad process of industrialization was initiated within Infrastructure to promote outsourcing of application maintenance to a single service provider.

– Task 2: intelligent network project. This was to develop a smart energy production and distribution network, to make it easier to better predict, or control, energy consumption with the rollout of smart meters, in order to better regulate flow, leveling out peak consumption and decreasing production capacity at off-peak times.

– Task 3: virtual office project. This was to promote flexibility and remote working with workstations. Virtualization would permit unification and globalization of access offered to business departments, improved security and network optimization.

– Task 4: data warehouse project. The objective of this project was to improve GreenNRJ's data hosting capacity by rationalizing and also reducing the number of data warehouses. This task focused on the setting up of a private cloud and providing the BUs with a shared architecture on the Infrastructure as a Service and Software as a Service model. This would be an opportunity to reduce fixed costs and simplify the exploitation processes.

In the Cross Disciplinary branch, the internal audit and quality business unit produced a report on IS bugs which it passed to the BU's IS department. This report showed up many existing problems in the architecture. In particular, it underlined the heterogeneity of applications and infrastructure, and showed that it acted as a brake on establishing dialog between various energy production units. The report highlighted the cost of this failure: the group was in effect driven to buy energy from its competitors when it was unable to manage the balance between production and customer demand. The report concluded by recommending a Six Sigma approach combined with a lean management strategy: a Lean Six Sigma. The recommendation defined five stages with the acronym "DMAIC": *Define, Measure, Analyze, Improve, Control*. It sets out to answer the following questions:

– Define: What is the objective? How do we understand the problem?

– Measure: What is the nature and scale of the problem?

– Analyze: What are the underlying causes of this problem?

– Improve: What must be done to resolve the problem?

– Control: How can we ensure sustainable performance?

The digital strategy proposal was put to the Executive. The Executive approved it, but did, however, change the order of priorities: the Data Warehouse project was now put in the second place (instead of fourth), after the Standardization project. The Virtual Office project therefore moved to the last place in terms of priority. The Executive then asked for these tasks to be turned into a blueprint with a target IS and levels of achievement. The Executive also ordered a specific governance provision to be implemented to supervise this major digitization program. It proposed that:

– The Steering Committee should be composed of one board member and one representative from each branch.

– The technical monitoring committee should be chaired by the Infrastructure branch with members of the IS department, the internal audit and quality business unit, and representatives of the subcontractors involved in the project.

– The Leading Change committee should be steered by the IS department, in partnership with the internal audit and quality business unit, and should bring in a young firm of consultants keen to form an ongoing relationship with the IS department and work for the company.

Test your skills

1) How can GreenNRJ's digital transformation project potentially create sustainable value for the group?

2) Why did the Executive change the order of priority of the tasks set by the branches? What might have motivated its decision? Do you feel it was justified? Will this have an impact on the target IS? If yes, in what way?

3) The governance structure proposed by the Executive has not yet been approved. How could it be improved to better meet expectations for this major project for the group?

PART 2

Urbanizing the Territories

Introduction to Part 2

The second part of this book aims to inspire the strategic managers of the IS to reflect on the development of the territory of their organization and their IS. We will start with a presentation of the organizational territory and its counterpart, the IS territory. Note especially the territorial representations because they describe and also determine our understanding of the organization of an IS. Finally, beyond this description, they have an influence on organizational reality.

The urbanization of an IS, similarly to the urbanization of a city, is a way of controlling the territory and its changes. Urbanization thus aims to understand the current IS, define IS targets and the associated trajectory, and provide tools to steer its development. We will demonstrate that the issue of IS urbanization does not stop at the organizational boundary. IS urbanization can cross boundaries via the development of an IS that extends to other organizations or via the cooperative IS.

In Chapter 4, we will address the conceptual framework of organizational territory and IS territory, and envision different ways to represent the organization and the IS: according to hierarchy, functions, processes, software, hardware and information content. Chapter 5 will focus on the issue of IS urbanization. We will introduce the principles of operational IS urbanism and the advantages brought by urbanization: upgradeability, sustainability and an IS that is independent from any external organization. Chapter 6 concludes this second part by touching on the approach to IS urbanization in the inter-organizational domain and the specific issues this raises: shared protocols, free software, standardization and collaboration on standards.

4

The IS Territory

> THE FUNDAMENTALS.–
>
> 1) The organizational territory and the IS territory develop in parallel with economic, societal and technological transformation.
>
> 2) Territory can be charted in many different ways: according to hierarchy, functions, processes, software applications, technical hardware, information content and so on.
>
> 3) Each representation of the territory influences the territory being charted in one way or another.

4.1. The territory

The concept of territory is important, because the history of IS is linked to the issue of representation. In this section, we present different visions of the concept of the organizational territory and IS territory.

The word "territory" is polysemous, thus its meaning differs depending on the angle of approach, the disciplines studying it and the era. In the social sciences, territory can be defined as "an arrangement of material and symbolic resources capable of structuring the physical conditions of existence of an individual or a social group and in return making this individual or group aware of their own identity" [LEV 13]. This definition highlights the presence of material resources and cultural or symbolic resources. Material resources cover the physical world: earth, air, water, buildings, etc. Cultural resources include economic, social and cultural components, such as the value of pure water, relationships between neighbors and the historical significance of a monument. Thus, territory is not only the physical space represented by a physical map, but also a symbolic value to the individuals and groups who built it. Hence, the varied, and sometimes stubborn, resistance when buildings symbolizing a certain history are demolished: unused churches, places of anti-fascist memory. In fact, in social terms, the appropriation of territory mostly happens cognitively and symbolically; such as handing over the keys to an apartment or laying the first stone of a building. This appropriation of territory is often done through the transformation of space by human labor, thus opening up space for organizations to use in a dynamic process of transformation. The burning or felling of a forest and its cultivation are still very widespread activities in terms of appropriating a territory.

The appropriation of a territory entails the existence of borders that are regularly subject to revision due to changes in the territory itself and the neighboring territories. The growing use of cars within a territory leads to roads being widened which then encroach on the surrounding land that communities appropriate for construction needs. Finally, the spatiality of territory is conceived in general as an interlocking of a multitude of scales. In France, for example, land is attached to a municipality, a municipality to a department, and a department to a region.

Figure 4.1. *A territory consisting of physical resources such as water, plastic signs and people. In addition, symbolic resources such as the relationships between people, the meaning of the information on the plastic signs and the cultural aspect of ritual bathing in these waters. The fence identifies the territory's border. Author: Kannanshanmugam, shanmugamstudio; attribution: 2.0 Generic (CC BY 3.0)*

4.2. Organizational and microeconomic territory

In every organization, there are also territories, with their material and symbolic resources, their borders and their transformation dynamics. A manufacturing company may have a significant demarcation between the manufacturing floor and the administrative offices. Different rules aim to guarantee safety on the manufacturing site and different clothing, in particular with workers in overalls, marks the different affiliations. However, the introduction of automation, robotization, computer-aided production or subcontracting can upset these boundaries, with, for example, workers who control their machines remotely from a desk.

However, achieving a degree of materialization and stabilization of the territories and their boundaries is a key managerial imperative in order to ensure that the organization's common objective is pursued. This is how certain functions within an organization grow in terms of personnel, and others see their staff reduced without necessarily changing the floor area available for each function, neither with each recruitment or departure. This imperative runs up against the issue related to the question of power over the territories [BID 06]. The growing function, perhaps, will eventually lead to new organizational influence, to annex part of the territory's shrinking function.

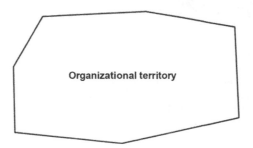

Figure 4.2. *Representation of an organization's territory with its boundary (perimeters)*

We will see how an organization's territory is structured according to the perspective fed by the microeconomy, in other words on the small scale of an organization seen as independent and delimited by its organizational boundary. This territory has been established in a hierarchical–functional way and according to business processes.

4.2.1. *The hierarchical–functional territory*

The hierarchical–functional territory characterizes organizations where the executive establishes a hierarchy within the organization and imposes subordination on the workers through structuring the organization in a pyramid form, with a handful of business-critical decision-makers at the top and a mass of action-takers at the bottom.

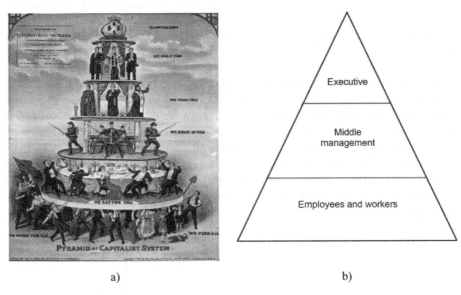

a)   b)

Figure 4.3. *The hierarchical pyramid. a) Allegory of a pyramid belonging to a capitalist society, published by the journal Industrial Worker of the World (IWW) in 1911, with some decision-makers at the top and a multitude of workers at the bottom and b) pyramid of an organization*

The hierarchical perspective outlines that different types of activities are performed at different levels of the organization by members with specific responsibilities. From the hierarchical point of view, three levels can be clearly defined.

The operational level deals principally with ongoing business activities, impacting directly on the business in the short term. These activities are extensively structured, by procedures that leave the workforce little room for leeway or interpretation. The vital goal is efficient in the execution of the various operational tasks. The operational level tends to encompass the majority of the workforce who mainly have office-based and shop-floor qualifications.

The management level of an organization is principally concerned with decisions on medium-term impact for each business function. Activities performed by these managers tend to be partially structured, with a certain amount of uncertainty, potential to interpret events and significant leeway for freedom of action. These managers tend to seek to meet management expectations in terms of results achieved by the department for which they are responsible, as per the strategic objectives defined by management.

The organization's Board tends to be involved in strategic decisions, impacting the organization as a whole in the long term. These decisions are often loosely structured, with very heterogeneous data equally drawn from internal and external sources, and partial information. In general, the Board must evaluate current trends in order to identify the best upcoming opportunities.

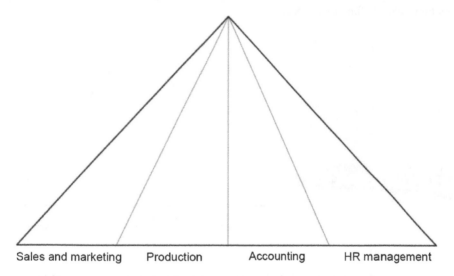

Activities	Timescale	Hierarchical level	Activity structure type
Strategic	Long term	Board (Executive Officers and Directors)	Loosely structured
Tactical	Mid term	Middle management	Moderately structured
Operational	Short term	Administrative and shop floor staff	Highly structured

Table 4.1. *The different activities of an organization according to timescale, hierarchical level and activity structure type, adapted from Anthony [ANT 65]*

Complementary to this, the organizational territory is envisioned as a set of business activities split into core functions, corresponding to the principal business activities of any firm, irrespective of size and complexity: sales and marketing, production, accounting and HR management [FAY 99]. Each different function operates with its own business logic, which leads intrinsically to the formation of functional silos that are relatively independent of each other. As agricultural grain silos are fed from the top and the product comes out from below and the grains are not mixed between silos, the functional silos receive orders from management and products and services are rendered by the workers and employees at the bottom of the pyramid, without there being any exchanges between one function to the next. In this model, the firm's optimum is reckoned to be achieved by maximizing the performance of each of the functions seen as autonomous. The combination of the hierarchical pyramid and functional silos has led to the formalization of the territory in a hierarchical–functional form.

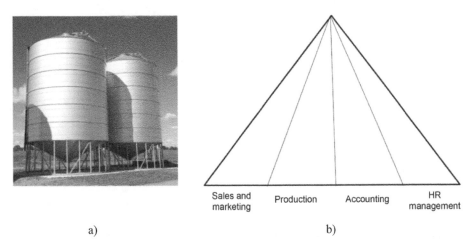

a)   b)

Figure 4.4. *Functional silos a) The organization's territory according to its hierarchical–functional silos; b) analogies of agricultural grain silos*

In this scenario, the organizational chart is the firm's preferred method of territorial mapping to depict all the functional territories within which the relationships between stakeholders, their responsibilities, their legitimacies and their skills are set out. Through the organizational chart, we can understand the posts, responsibilities, functions and respective skills of the stakeholders [BID 06].

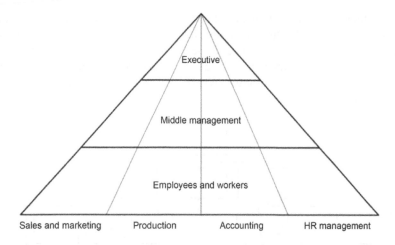

Figure 4.5. *The hierarchical–functional territory, as a combination of the hierarchical pyramid and functional silos*

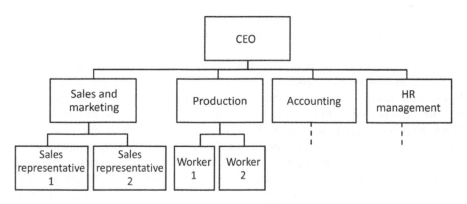

Figure 4.6. *The organizational chart outlines the hierarchical levels and functional silos of an organization*

At the top of the organizational chart, we find management, in the middle is middle management, separating into different functions, and the bottom are employees and workers.

The increase in the size of organizations and the diversification of activities has given rise to new organizational structures. This first view has been described as the unitary form (U-form). Organizations that have broken with this unitary form have structured themselves into divisions. Each division is responsible for a strategic business unit (SBU). Within each division, all functions of the company are represented, such as marketing and sales, production, accounting and HR management. In a complementary way, all divisions report to general management. This structure takes the name of multidivisional form (M-form), where each division is organized within a U-form.

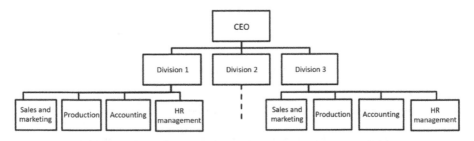

Figure 4.7. *Organizational chart of an organizational structure in multidivisional form (M-form)*

4.2.2. The territory of business processes

Another perspective of an organization's territory makes it possible to highlight the importance of business processes and the inclusion of the different functions and hierarchical levels in these organizational processes. The logic of representing organizations according to their processes means separations between functions and hierarchical levels are pushed to the background. This is because everyone finds a role in an organization's business processes. Thus, a manufacturing company would see the functions of marketing and sales, production, accounting and HR management, all invested in a business process that would lead to the sale of a product, in turn leading to it being manufactured to order. Then, the sale of the production would be recorded and cashed by the accounting department and HR management would finally pay the commission to the salesperson responsible for this sale.

Functional silos are thus interspersed with processes. The process mentioned thus involves marketing and sales, production, accounting and HR management functions. Cross-functional collaboration is promoted and information is supposed to flow faster between the different functions. Hierarchical levels are also entangled in processes. In the manufacturing and sales process discussed, perhaps the commission paid to the salesperson, input by an employee from HR management, must be validated by the line manager, but this validation will be considered as an additional step within the same process, involving all hierarchical levels.

Figure 4.8. *An organization's business process*

Thus, different representations of the organization's actual territory have emerged in attempts to create a representation of organizational territory that is as close as possible to reality, while also simplifying it. The same territory can also be represented in different ways, to highlight certain elements more than others.

However, none of these representations is objective and impartial; furthermore, they, in return, influence the territories they represent. For example, in our societies, campaigns for the recognition and nondiscrimination of transgender people lead to their integration into our territorial representations. Canada began to count transgender people following the 2021 census. In a complementary way, public spaces are evolving, with, for example, the introduction of transgender toilets and their specific signs.

To this complexity of reciprocal influences between the actual territory and the territory as represented, we must add the territorial dynamics. Territories develop over time, in parallel with economic, societal and technological transformation.

A company that sells more and more products in a foreign country could open a subsidiary in this country and recruit staff. Thus, it is necessary to take this new territory of the organization into account when considering the company's representations. New recruits may well ask who their points of contact and superiors are at the parent company: does the subsidiary report directly to general management or to the managers from marketing and sales, because the subsidiary does not (yet?) manufacture on site?

Nevertheless, representations of a developing territory must follow the development of the actual territory to seek alignment between representation and reality.

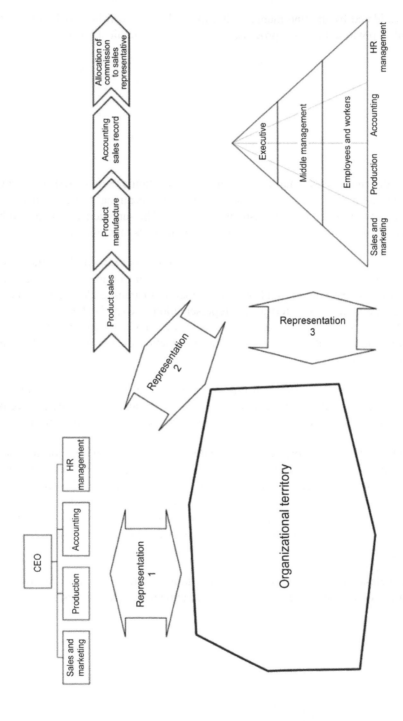

Figure 4.9. *The territory of the organization and its representations with double arrows between territory and its representations, because there is a reciprocal influence between the territory and its representation*

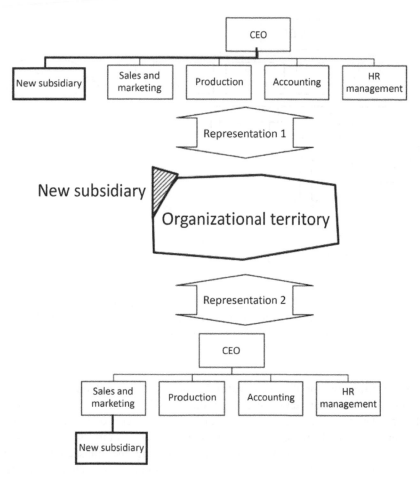

Figure 4.10. *The new real territory must be integrated into the territorial representations but decision-making is neither automatic nor unequivocal, as in this case the addition of a new subsidiary in the organizational chart and two possible options for its representation*

4.3. Organizational territory and mesoeconomics

As a reminder, while microeconomics focuses on observing and analyzing small-scale interactions, macroeconomics studies the economy at the national and international levels. Mesoeconomics retains a level of analysis that favors the intermediate branch or sector between the microeconomy and macroeconomy. Mesoeconomics expands the view of an organization by including the environment external to the organization with the aim of analyzing reality through economic sub-sets midway between macro- and microeconomics.

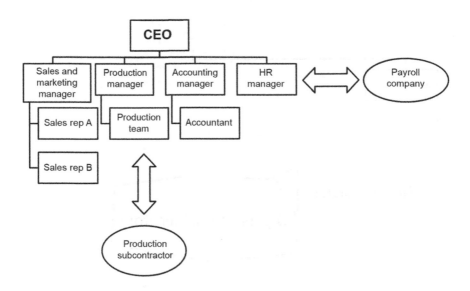

Figure 4.11. *According to mesoeconomics, organizational form is linked to transaction costs for the firm in relation to its environment. In the illustrated scenario, the company has outsourced payroll to one company and subcontracted part of its manufacture to a second company*

The justification for the organization's form will depend on quasi-automatic controls, linked to transaction costs for the firm in relation to its environment [WIL 75]. The transaction cost refers to all costs of an economic exchange, which go beyond the simple price of the exchanged product: commissions, prospecting costs, time or effort spent negotiating and verifying the transaction. The firm compares these transaction costs with its organizational costs, such as coordination or HR management costs. If organizational costs are lower than transaction costs, then the firm keeps activities in-house because it is more efficient than the market. If transaction costs are lower than organizational costs, then the firm outsources, because the market is more efficient.

To do this, the firm builds strategic market relationships with its environment using a rational approach that can be the result of an economic calculation. An organization's mesoeconomic environment completes its internal territory. The mesoeconomic environment is thus recognized as a source of specific assets and the arrangement of material and cultural resources capable of structuring the conditions for the organization's existence and informing the organization about its own identity, in addition to the organization's only internal territory. Finally, an organization's territory expands, integrating the mesoeconomic environment into the organization's internal territory.

Dynamically, the mesoeconomic environment puts each organization in a position of ongoing development in line with the changes in its specific assets, transaction costs and skills. The temporal dynamic becomes an essential element, with the constant need to decide between short-term effectiveness and long-term efficiency.

This enlarged territory can play a strategic role in the organization thanks to learning processes and can promote the development of specialized and specific skills [JOF 99]. The latter are crucial, because an organization's workforce is less mobile than other resources available within the territory. Therefore, learning and skills development require special attention in order to find a balance between building for the long term and use in the short term. This is how competitiveness clusters take on their full meaning. By combining in a given geographical space, several companies, training centers and research units develop synergies around joint projects of an innovative nature.

Conversely, the organization can also have a major impact on the enlarged territory. A company, via its business activities, becomes (voluntarily or involuntarily) part of a process of territorialization [AME 88; GAF 90]. This process shapes this enlarged territory, builds and destroys resources, and plays a part in defining the territorial trajectories. The successive choices of a firm involve an element of commitment, which can make them irreversible for this enlarged territory. Every choice made by a business impacts on its enlarged territory, and these choices are cumulative. The history of coal-mining regions, in France for instance, which have seen an economic boom, followed by difficult attempts at socio-economic reconversion during mine closures, clearly shows how companies have an impact on the trajectories of large territories.

In the same way as there are technological trajectories, [DOS 84], there are also territorial trajectories. From the management point of view, it becomes important to understand the risks of an organization becoming entrapped within a given territory. This entrapment would weaken the company because its destiny would be inextricably linked to its territory. The end of coal mining in France meant the end of Charbonnages de France, while still having coal-fired power plants throughout the country. Conversely, the end of uranium mining in France did not put an end to the activity of the Cogema-Areva-Orano company. Preserving a certain openness and flexibility towards other territories would make it possible to avoid these pitfalls and keep the balance in the firm–territory relationship [VEL 93].

4.4. The IS territory

The IS also has its territory and is rich in information content, functions, software applications and technical equipment.

The informational content refers to the elementary descriptions of the realities recorded, in the broad sense, by the organization and available to it. Information about the organization's workforce (e.g. first names, surnames, employee hire dates), orders placed by customers (order number, customer name, order date, etc.), list of suppliers, production volumes, accounts transactions, etc., all of these things, whether recorded on computer or on paper, are part of the IS territory and particularly its informational content.

Example of an IS's informational content:

– sales: order number 0028, product name Delta, quantity 10, price €1,000, sales rep Paul Dupont, etc.;

– production: production date *May 21, 2023*, Batch 34, product name Delta, etc.;

– accounting record: date of sale *May 10, 2023*, customer Pierre Roux, VAT charged €200, merchandise sales €800, etc.;

– sales commission: name of rep Paul Dupont, amount of commission €10, payment month *June 2023*, etc.

In a complementary way, the IS territory is rich in functions. The word "function" refers to activities possible via the IS and the word "function" refers to functions of the organization (sales and marketing, production, etc.). Thus, all the activities of an IS are divided into different functional areas. These functional areas can be more detailed, and the distribution of the IS's functions becomes increasingly fine-grained. In terms of dilution, we speak of an IS's functional area, functional division and functional block. This distribution creates structures where each function of the IS belongs to a single block and each area to a single functional area of the IS.

An example of a structure of IS functions with areas, divisions and blocks:

– "sales and marketing":

  - "marketing" division,

  - "market research" block,

  - *target definition function*,

  - *data collection function*,

- data analysis function,

- etc.,

- "marketing campaign management" block,

- etc.,

- "sales" area,

- etc.;

– "production" *area*;

– etc.

Software applications are all computer programs accessible to employees. A company should thus have the Salesforce customer management application used by salespeople to enter customer details and their orders and know, in return, the amount of turnover made by the company with each customer, for example, to better target discounts to larger customers. The same company might have SPSS statistics software that would be used by marketers to process data from research to estimate sales forecasts by type of customer for their new product coming to market.

Examples of software applications:

– *salesforce customer relationship management application*;

– *SPSS statistics application*;

– *computer-aided manufacturing (CAM) software: Odoo*;

– *accounting software: Grisbi.*

Finally, the IS territory includes technical equipment. It combines the hardware components supporting the software applications. We also speak of the technological base and the infrastructure. These hardware components include computers, tablets, smartphones, servers, printers, cables, as well as wireless networks and network access devices such as routers.

Examples of an IS's technical equipment:

– *laptop for sales reps*;

– *desktop for production management team*;

– *desktop for accountants*;

– *desktop for HR management*;

– *server to host the CRM software with remote access for sales reps*;

– intranet;

– etc.

The technical equipment represents the IS territory in its physical materiality. In 3300 BCE, when writing was invented, clay tablets were used to record and track the trading of food. Today, tablets, now electronic, are used to do the same thing: record and track trade in food products. Through the millennia, tablets have been made with different materials. Modern-day tablets have a glass surface on one side, and aluminum or steel alloys for the frame. But, under the surface, there are various materials: a lithium battery, resin motherboard, electrical and electronic circuits made of copper, silver or gold and a silicon microprocessor. In total, up to 50 different metals are found in a tablet. There is no great difference between one form of computer hardware to the next.

All of these materials constituting the technological base and the infrastructure of an IS are essentially of nonrenewable mineral origin, and require multiple polluting transformations, such as extraction and refining, and require a lot of energy, chemical and fresh water, before they can be used in an IS. The French public energy agency, ADEME, introduced the metaphor of an ecological "backpack". This ecological backpack takes into account all of the natural resources mobilized from the extraction of raw materials to the manufacture of the finished product. For manufacturing a laptop, ADEME has deemed it necessary to mobilize 800 kg of resources (fossil fuels and minerals), to which must be added several thousand liters of fresh water.

When using the IS, electricity is an essential input and the electricity consumption of the IS increases from one year to the next. Even if the computer equipment is designed to consume less energy than the previous version, the multiplication of uses and computer equipment generates new electricity consumptions that exceeds progress in energy efficiency. This rebound in consumption was first observed by Jevons 150 years ago for coal in opposition to improvements in the performance of steam engines. Since then, it has been repeatedly observed for technological improvements in different sectors.

Finally, the life span of an IS's hardware component is a few years. These components quickly become waste from electrical and electronic equipment (WEEE). Only a small amount is collected for recycling. The rest is buried, incinerated often illegally in countries lacking effective means of control. Another dose of soil, water and air pollution adds to the grim picture of the IS's ecological impacts.

This presentation shows how what it touted as immaterial or dematerialized in not immaterial at all. The materials have changed, but above all they have not disappeared, on the contrary they have multiplied. Hence, the importance of considering a partial "decomputerization" of the computerized IS to overcome today's environmental challenges [VID 19].

Box 4.1. *The materiality of an IS*

4.5. The IS territory and the organization's territory

In the same way that the representation of the organizational territory in return influences the organization's actual territory, the territory of the organization's IS is also influenced by this, insofar as IS territory is a subset of the actual organizational territory.

The studies on the form of the company have greatly influenced the classic vision of an IS, which associated the functional approach with the hierarchical approach [MIR 00]. The management information system (MIS) is the IS model of classical microeconomics. The MIS establishes the link between the organizational functions the hierarchical levels. We then speak of the MIS as a coupling system of a hierarchical functional territory. This coupling means that each function and each hierarchical level is dependent on a specific IS. The building block of the IS is the business application that has been programmed to satisfy its target. Thus, tendentially, each profession has its particular application, architecturally independent of other applications. In a complementary way, the organization's IS will tendentially be structured also on the hierarchical levels of the organization's territory, with informational content, functions, applications and material components specific to each hierarchical level. Deferred unidirectional flows enable the dissemination of interfunctional and interlevel information and in particular ensures that information from the base of the pyramid reaches management and that decisions come down for execution. The benchmark document for describing the IS is an application map.

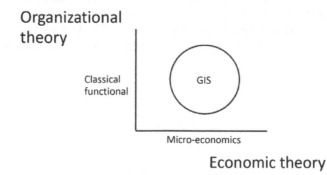

Figure 4.12. *The MIS at the crossroads of "classical functional" organizational theory and "microeconomic" economic theory*

4.5.1. *The IS territory and the hierarchical pyramid*

The hierarchical perspective recognizes that different types of business activities are performed at different levels of the organization by members with specific responsibilities. From the hierarchical point of view, three levels can be clearly identified and each level has its specific IS [ANT 65].

The IS at the operational level ensures the organization's day-to-day management. It integrates processing procedures, like order preparation, and records transactions carried out, like a sale, by the workforce. The system is called a transaction processing system and insists that transactions are automated and standardized.

The IS supporting the management level is known as the decision support system and provides core information to functional managers so that they are able to control management activities and take mid-term policy decisions. For example, the decision support system makes it possible to monitor the nonconformity rate of products and decide, if the rate increases, on staff training programs, a change in production processes or even renewal of work tools.

The IS supporting the Executive is known as the Executive Information System. It enables strategic planning and frequently provides highly synthesized information on the company's macro-activities, but with the potential to explore specific elements more deeply using aggregated data. For example, the change in a company's customers makes it possible to decide on the opening and closing of branches according to customer location. If new customers come from the north, it may be appropriate to open new branches in the north. The MIS makes it possible to monitor these demographic changes in order to feed strategic decisions, such as the opening of a branch.

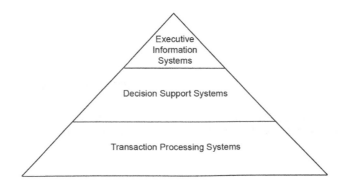

Figure 4.13. *The IS supporting each level of the hierarchical pyramid*

4.5.2. *IS territory and functional silos*

The functional approach proposes an MIS delivered to the functional manager, by instituting the idea that firms are organized by function, primarily around sales, marketing, production, HR management and accounting. This will lead to the development of IS in silos, by function, and more often "hermetically sealed". From the functional point of view, the four main functions thus each have their own IS.

The sales and marketing IS collects data for the marketing managers from the markets in which the business operates. First of all, this IS collects transactional data linked to product sales to customers, according to the various distribution channels. This data can then help the various sales and marketing managers to understand the revenue and margins for each product, each customer and each distribution channel. The same data can also measure the sales reps' performance in terms of revenue generated and sales activities of each rep. On a more "as-and-when" basis, this same data enables the company to evaluate the impact of specific one-off events, such as a marketing campaign or a product price increase. Market studies, meanwhile, aim to understand the reaction of potential customers to changes in the company's offer in terms of marketing mix. Finally, competitive intelligence systematically analyzes the economic, social, demographic, legal and technological context to identify weak signals that give advance warning of possible risks and opportunities in the medium and long term for marketing and sales.

The production IS supports the manufacture of goods and services, the focus of the company's core activity, through acquisition of raw materials and intermediate goods, setting production targets, production planning, organization of production workers and production plant maintenance. An essential element of this production IS is stock control of the components required for each finished product. This is known as material requirement planning (MRP). Extensions of MRP systems integrate the management of other corporate resources, not only components, such as machine production capacity and manpower availability. This means production can be steered more efficiently from sales forecasts. These systems become Manufacturing Resources Planning systems (MRP2 or MRP II).

The accounting IS tracks monetary transactions in order to produce accounting and financial statements for the various stakeholders, such as directors, shareholders, banks and tax authorities. Thus, its focus is on the automation of accounting records and the automatic translation of these records into the various output reports. The production of these documents is an essential feature of this IS, with reports being customized for each type of stakeholder. While configuration work is needed at the outset to define the various reports required, the accounting IS is supposed to automatically produce these reports as per the defined needs (once set up). One-off statements can be produced, but development work is generally necessary. This IS is designed for use in connection with audit, governance, risk management and compliance.

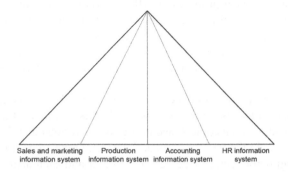

Sales and marketing   Production   Accounting   HR information
information system   information system information system   system

Figure 4.14. *ISs supporting each functional silo*

As we saw in some detail in Chapter 2, IS governance can be put at the service of stakeholders in acknowledging their contribution and involving them in decision-making. Among the stakeholders of the company, a special role is played by the employees, who can be considered both as subordinates and partners. A more "staff-oriented" IS governance may promote a strategic development of the IS for HR management and in turn influence IS governance in its entirety.

In a classic approach, IS governance of IS for HR management seeks to satisfy the need for integration to handle the essential services, in accordance with law and at the lowest cost. This is how payroll management and the related IS have been largely outsourced by companies in the face of processing costs for each report of around 10 euros requested by these external service providers. At the same time, company employees find their HR management services too distant and not very relevant to their concerns their inadequate IS.

However, in a more advanced version of IS governance for HR management, it will be necessary to design personalized employee reports. For example, teleworking should be chosen and accompanied by an offer of an adequate and personalized IS. Thus, a certain equilibrium between individual management and team management may emerge. In a complementary way, the new HR management IS integrates the hierarchical vision and the horizontal vision within the same decision-making equation, via, for example, business social networking tools.

Box 4.2. *The HR management IS as a device for IS governance*

The IS for HR management manages an organization's employees. This system records each employee's personal data, their post, professional activities and their performance evaluations. The main short-term objective is to facilitate the payment of wage. The function for processing pay slips automates the process of collecting data on the presence and absence of staff and calculates the various taxes and contributions in order to determine the sums due to each employee under their employment contract. In the medium and long terms, this IS helps to manage human capital according to the organization's strategic decisions. The functions available in this IS for HR management include recruitment, planning and training.

4.6. The IS territory and process systems engineering

A process systemic vision of the organization allows us to break away from the hierarchical–functional approach and think of the IS as a whole, noting in particular the necessary and beneficial interactions between all stakeholders and all functions. The IS is in this case defined as an organizational information system (OIS) [LEM 86]. The OIS meets the needs of a system to unite space and timescale. From a spatial point of view, in an OIS, the three hierarchical levels are interconnected by interactional loops via a single operational-decision support IS. In an OIS, corporate timescales are also interrelated. Finally, the OIS can be seen as the IS of a business system integrating a range of processes.

Translating this systemic vision of the organization into an IS often takes the form of an integrated management system (IMS) package, enterprise information system (EIS) or enterprise resource planning (ERP).

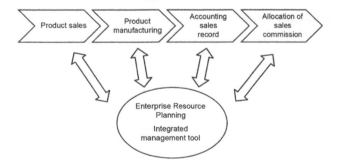

Figure 4.15. *The OIS as the combination of a range of processes*

Historically, ERPs came into being as a gradual extension of the functionalities of MRPs, but nowadays these solutions go beyond the functional boundaries of production and build the OIS around the processes that cover the various organizational functions. In practical terms, an ERP is a modular, integrated software application that crosses organizational functions and hierarchical levels, relying on a single unique database. The modularity allows the organization to choose from the various modules available. Thus, all the company has to do is to activate them and use them to meet its needs. Then, integration enables the automatic release of software developments that overlap the various modules and thus various functions and levels. Unidirectional flows in real time and also when automated enable dissemination of information between units. All data stay recorded in the ERP database. For example, the placing of an order by a client automatically triggers the issuing of an invoice, a finished product inventory, start of production, a raw material order from the suppliers, assignment of commission to the sales rep responsible for that customer, etc. To conclude, the final key characteristic of an ERP, beyond modularity and integration, is its flexibility in configuration. ERPs have customizable settings so that the basic ERP can be adapted to suit each company.

The benchmark document is the authorization map. These authorizations concern the rights of access to the functionalities and the data and the duties of execution of the operations of consultation, modification, printing, recording, destruction, distribution and validation of data. These authorizations therefore decide which employees have access to which modules and with which rights to the data.

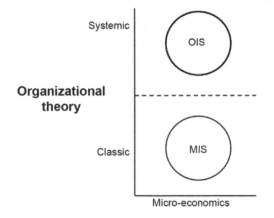

Figure 4.16. *The MIS at the juncture of the theory of "classic functional" organizations and microeconomics and the OIS at the juncture of "systemic" organization theory and microeconomics*

Although the systemic vision is often translated into an ERP, complementary initiatives flourish, with a vision of the business as a community of networked stakeholders: enterprise 2.0 [MCA 09]. This new organizational framework makes borders more permeable, and social networks, online communities, Wikis and other collaborative tools are recognized as collaborative spaces vital to the company's success. This concept should promote greater cooperation between business functions, the stimulation of collective intelligence, freer access to information, greater responsiveness and flexibility from the part of the business, more open communication, a more innovative culture and a less authoritarian and more collaborative leadership style.

Source system	Organization		IS	
Territory	Of the firm		Of the IS	
Economic theory	Microeconomics			
Theory of organizational structure	Classic functional	Systemic procedural-driven	Classic functional	Systemic procedural-driven
Typology	Functional	Systemic	MIS	OIS
Elementary block	Function	Process	Business application	Module
Architecture	Functional by silo	Transversal by process	Independent applications	Modular
Benchmark document	Functional mapping	Business process mapping	Application mapping	Access mapping
Formalization	Procedure	Process	Program	Configuration
Interunitary distribution mechanisms	Hierarchy	Process manager	Deferred one-way flow interdependence	Real-time one-way flow automation

Table 4.2. *Putting organizational and information system territories into perspective (inspired by [BID 06])*

Like existing influences between the organization's real territory and the representations of the organizational territory, the IS territory is influenced by its representations and by the representations of the organization's territory.

We find here the same kind of complexity of reciprocal influences between actual territories and charted territories, identified in relation to organizational territories, and their development in line with economic, societal and technological transformation. Extending the IS territory, by adopting a new application, for example, requires updating the IS's representations. As part of an MIS, the mapping of business applications would thus be enriched with a new application.

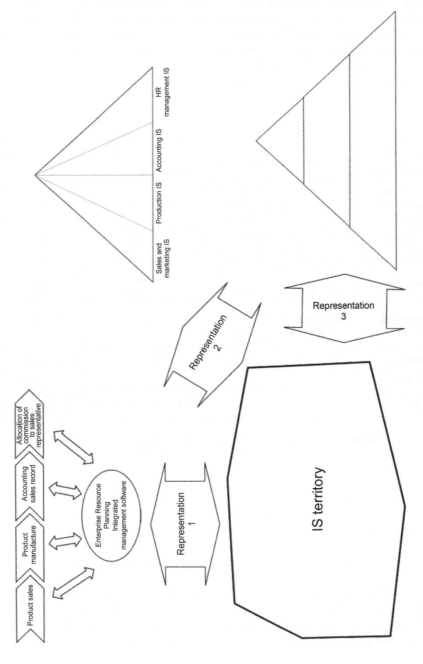

Figure 4.17. *The IS territory and its representations*

4.7. Alignment between the firm's territory and the IS territory

However, the potential benefits of IS for the organization can only become a reality for the organization if there is an alignment between the territory of the firm and the territory of the IS. This alignment means that any IS can be at the service of any part of the organization and that each part of the organization has an IS to support their business activities. Representations of the territories, both of the organization and the IS, are an important step to facilitate their alignment. For example, alignment can be formalized by the superposition of job mapping, according to the organizational chart, and application mapping. As a first approximation, if each position in the organizational chart has an application and each application serves at least one position in the organizational chart, then an alignment exists. On the contrary, if certain parties in the organizational chart do not have an application or vice versa, certain applications are not used for any position then misalignment exists. This superposition allows potential areas of conflict to be flagged up. The company can then focus on making these coherent and on ways of resolving potential boundary conflicts [BID 06].

If stakeholders in the business defend a territory of the firm that is not aligned with the territory of the IS, or vice versa, risks emerge in the form of inefficiencies, conflicts and blockages in processes. If an organization, for example, is structured into functional departments (HR management, marketing and sales, production, accounting), the implementation of an ERP can generate a misalignment between the firm's territory and the IS territory. The logic, by process, recorded in the ERP is not compatible with the organization's functional silos, and thus conflicts may emerge at the boundaries between one function and another. This being the case, when a new IS is introduced, it is normally accompanied by a project to align the territory of the firm with the new territory of the IS through business process re-engineering (BPR) [SRI 11].

However, some stakeholders in the organization may resist change for fear of losing power, autonomy and freedom due to centralization and integration. In the logic that information is a source of power, for example, the centralization of information in a single database shared across the entire company deprives the initial holder of this now centralized information power. A stakeholder can hold a certain power within an organization by way of behavior, a false pretense or unpredictability. The fact of not being able to predict a stakeholder's behavior leaves those around them in a position of relative weakness. The automation of manual operation, at the origin of stakeholder's power, can be seen as a personal attack in their eyes.

In other cases, the users see their IS as an instrument of their oppression [MAR 58; HAN 09]. Indeed, efforts to improve IS performance can hard some users. For example, some technical "improvements" could make human exploitation more likely, insofar as the IS user must produce more information in the same period of time. But these so-called improvements could at the same time generate social exclusion. By making it possible to produce the same quantity of output information as the previous version of the IS, but with fewer resources required (users included), the new IS could justify layoffs.

Finally, the division of labor is another classic lever for improving performance. It also regularly applies to IS users. IS users whose work has been divided up may develop a sense of alienation, because they no longer call upon their intellectual skills or dexterity, which generate pleasure and well-being, relating to the body and the mind [MAR 58].

We are far from the intentions outlined by the UN in its declaration on an information society:

> We, the representatives of the peoples of the world, assembled in Geneva from 10–12 December 2003 for the first phase of the World Summit on the Information Society, declare our common desire and commitment to build a people-centered, inclusive and development-oriented Information Society, where everyone can create, access, utilize and share information and knowledge, enabling individuals, communities and peoples to achieve their full potential in promoting their sustainable development and improving their quality of life, premised on the purposes and principles of the *Charter of the United Nations* and respecting fully and upholding the *Universal Declaration of Human Rights*. Our challenge is to harness the potential of information and communication technology to promote the development goals of the Millennium Declaration [ITU 04, p. 20].

Due to the diversity and resistance of stakeholders, the complexity of the processes and dynamics of the territories, even if the organizations aim for alignment, this alignment of the territories is infrequent [BID 06].

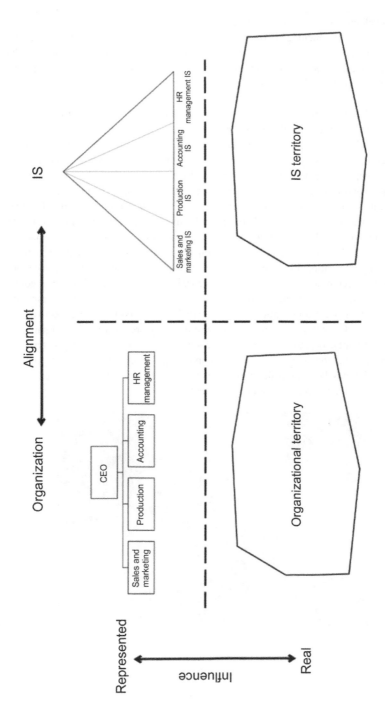

Figure 4.18. *Alignment and influence between real and represented territories of the organization and IS of the organization*

The development of information and communication technologies has been a powerful driver in the opening up of the corporate territory. The sphere of opportunities for gathering, processing, storing, sharing and communicating information has become greatly enhanced and nowadays offers a set of methods and tools supporting hyper-mobility, hyper-localization and augmented reality.

Hyper-mobility refers to IS users who move around frequently and for whom the organization thus provides an IS that is accessible from anywhere in the world via any device (ATAWAD – anytime, anywhere, any device). On the one hand, these users may be employees of a company, for instance sales reps who travel the world promoting and selling the company's products and services and can stay connected to the corporate information network while they are with clients. On the other hand, users may be customers who wish to be able to access the company's online store at any time from any place via their various IT tools. This hyper-mobility means the company must ensure that its IS is compatible with the widest possible range of systems and devices. Unable to deploy its private IS across the globe, the company must make it compatible with the various existing international telecommunication standards. This allows it to be accessible via third-party telecommunication networks, over which it has no control. Lack of control is a source of insecurity and uncertainty. A source of insecurity, because the company is borrowing third-party communication networks which are shared with other borrowers of these same networks, with no means of being sure that they are all trusted third parties. A source of uncertainty, because third-party telecommunication networks may offer lower quality services and lower capacity. For example, high-speed Internet connection via mobile networks may be seen as the norm in major French cities, but high-speed mobile connections are still an exception on the global scale.

Figure 4.19. *Hypermobility can be at the service of botanical data collection in the wetlands. Author: Alesia Gritsuk; attribution: 2.0 Generic (CC BY 4.0)*

Hyper-localization refers to the pairing of mobile devices including GPS-type localization technologies and software that can tailor the user experience to their geographical position. Hyper-localization enables interaction between the user of the device and their environment. Thus, the IS knows the exact location of the mobile device user and can provide information specific to their location. Interactions can take a variety of forms. For example:

– A retailer's IS can send notifications of promotional offers to customers coming geographically close to their store.

– An urban transport service provider's mobile application can instruct a potential traveler, step-by-step, how to get to the nearest stop.

– A camera can automatically include in the photo the name of the street on which the photo was taken and the names of the buildings photographed.

Figure 4.20. *An example of a mobile app that geolocates the phone and offers proximity searches. Author: David Berkowitz; attribution: 2.0 Generic (CC BY 2.0)*

Augmented reality is the superposition on reality of physical elements produced by the IS in real time. Thus, it is no longer physical stakeholders connecting to virtual space, but virtual space connecting to physical space. Augmented reality is often associated with enhanced visual perception through the integration of images, drawings and texts onto physical reality. However, augmented reality also includes the improvement of other senses, such as hearing aids, by accentuating some sounds and diminishing others. Augmented reality thus makes it possible to virtually insert objects such as buildings that only exist on a computer, into real environments, to assess how they integrate into what already exists. Augmented reality can moreover simulate changes in existing objects, for example, to remodel a room in a house or a production line. Product catalogs include augmented reality elements to enrich the information provided to the prospective purchaser (the discussion of new technologies continues in Chapter 8).

Figure 4.21. *An example of augmented reality with a representation of furniture in an empty room. Author: Oyundari Zorigtbaatar; attribution: 2.0 Generic (CC BYSA 4.0)*

Box 4.3. *The increasingly close interrelationships between territories and IS*

4.8. Representing the IS territory

Representing an IS territory ultimately means mapping it. Mapping aims to represent a structured set of all the elements that contribute to information management. In order for this mapping to remain useful across space, for other interested parties such as project owners and project managers, and time, it is essential to map it in accordance with very specific modeling rules. Modeling allows us to analyze, understand and break down an often complex system in order to confine it to a set of finished objects that are measurable and controllable by all the stakeholders in the organization. The model must be a simplified representation of a real system in a precise perspective and a defined objective. As we mentioned earlier, the IS territory can be represented by a mapping of software applications, in a classic functional perspective, or by a mapping of authorization, in a systemic procedural perspective. A multitude of other representations exist and a number of models are possible for the same reality, depending on the perspective and the objective. Modeling and mapping is therefore an element of common language for communication about the IS.

Modeling of an IS territory can be focused on a description of the business processes, in which case it is called process mapping. The term "business process" relates to the sequencing of actions and operations performed by the organization's stakeholders in carrying out their business activities. However, these actions and operations are rich in used and produced information and require IS. Mapping business processes makes it easier to identify the events that trigger them, their progression and IS used.

The modeling of business processes makes it possible to open a productive dialogue between the project owner and the project manager. Indeed, the modeling of business processes proves to be a very effective tool for developing mutual understanding between the different areas of the company and IS specialists. Thus, this process modeling is often the link with other IS modeling. Modeling can be focused on a description of the IS functions, in which case it is a functional mapping of the IS. As discussed previously, the word "function" refers to activities that are possible via the SI. Mapping the functions formalizes business functions in areas or blocks. The functions interact with each other through functional flows by helping to identify the information needs to accomplish each activity.

Modeling can be focused on the description of the IS structure – focused on IT. This is an architectural mapping of the IS. The term "architecture" refers to the hardware and software components, their construction and their behavior within the IS and above all their interaction for the operation of the IS as a whole.

Software components relate to the applications accessible by employees and/or installed on the technical infrastructure. This modeling requires identification of the IS software applications and the information flow into and out of each application. The IS territory is then represented as being composed of software applications which receive information as input, process it and produce other information as output.

When the IS, from a software point of view, is reduced to a single application which takes the form of an integrated management system package (IMS), then the mapping of software applications is often replaced by a mapping of authorizations. These authorizations relate to the rights of access to the functionalities and to the data and duties of executing the following operations: consultation, modification, printing, recording, destruction, diffusion and validation of data.

Hardware components relate to the technical infrastructure that supports the software applications. This mapping makes it possible to view the IS's hardware heritage, age, level of obsolescence, renewal needs and potential for improvement.

Modeling can be focused on a description of the informational content, in which case it is called data mapping. The data in an informational system are basic descriptions of a reality. Data mapping makes it possible to identify what data exist in the IS, where they are and how they are handled.

Some models seek to integrate multiple forms of mapping in a complementary fashion to achieve greater coherence in the representation of the IS and to facilitate communications between the various parties involved.

Finally, approaches invite us to question the capacity of the analytical models mentioned above to solve complex systems. Systemic modeling is an alternative method that focuses on the interactions and processes of these complex systems without reducing the richness of their complexity. Systemic modeling is defined as:

> The action of development and intentional construction, by composition of symbols, of artifact models likely to make a complex perceived phenomenon intelligible and amplify the actor's reasoning, projecting a deliberate intervention within the phenomenon; reasoning aimed in particular at anticipating the consequences of these possible actions plans [LEM 99].

Intelligibility is here an understanding of the complex system, rather than its explanation and its resolution which are confined to simple or complicated systems.

4.9. Unified modeling language (UML)

Several model propositions exist. Some are focused on process modeling (e.g. business process modeling notation), others on functional modeling (e.g. functional flow block diagram), others again on architectural modeling (e.g. Acme) and finally, some focus on data modeling (e.g. entity–relationship model). More and more propositions are seeking to include multiple forms of IS modeling using integrative approaches (e.g. unified modeling language).

Of the few existing models, unified modeling language, from Object Modeling Group[1], is one of the most widely used models, with its objective being to cover all IS modeling requirements. This language offers 14 different maps. Among these, the activity diagram makes it possible to model the processes, the class diagram makes it possible to model the functions and informational content, the component diagram makes it possible to model the software applications and the deployment diagram can model technical equipment.

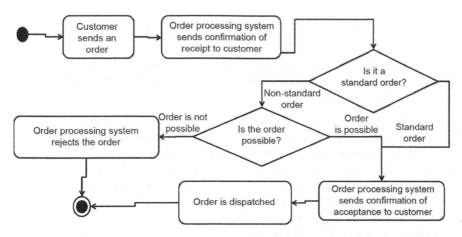

Figure 4.22. *Activity diagram of an order management system*

4.9.1. *Process modeling*

The activity diagram represents, in the form of a flowchart or activity sequencing chart, the behavior of a process, a system or its components. It can meet the needs of business process modeling. An activity diagram includes the following components:

– a rounded rectangle representing an action;

– a diamond representing a decision;

– a bar representing a beginning (separation) or an end (conjunction) of concurrent activities;

– a black dot representing the beginning of a process;

– an outlined black dot representing the end of a process;

– an arrow representing the direction of the link between components.

1 UML website: www.omg.org/spec/UML/.

4.9.2. *Function modeling*

The class diagram represents the classes, the interfaces and the relationships between them. A class is a semantic collection of functions and attributes. In object-oriented programming, a+ class describes a set of objects called "instances of class". In other words, classes are instantiated to create objects that contain their own values for each attribute of the class.

A class diagram can meet the requirements of modeling the IS functions. A class diagram includes the following components:

– A rectangle represents a class. It is divided into three parts comprising respectively: the name of the class, the attributes of the class, the methods of the class (functions of the IS).

– An arc represents a relationship between two classes. Relationships can be through inheritance or through association. Inheritance is represented by a line linking the two classes, and their origin (parent class) is marked at the other end (subclass) by a triangle. Inheritance is a principle of division by generalization and specialization. Association is represented by a dash linking the two classes, plain in the case of a bidirectional association, with an arrow in the case of a monodirectional association, with a blank diamond in the case of an association of aggregation, with an infilled diamond in the case of an association of composition and with a dotted arrow in the case of an association of dependence. An association is a semantic connection between two classes.

4.9.3. *Modeling information content*

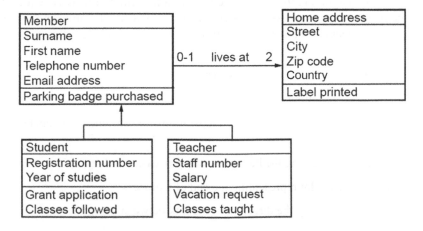

Figure 4.23. *Class diagram of members of a school*

The class diagram can also be used to represent the informational content of an IS. Because a class is a set of functions and data, the class diagram can simultaneously be used to describe the functions and the informational content of an IS. When classes are instantiated to create objects, the objects created contain their own values for each attribute of the class to which they belong. Relationships between data are displayed with links of association.

4.9.4. *Modeling software applications*

The component diagram represents the organization of the IS from the point of view of software applications. The software elements are called "modules", whether they are packages, source files, libraries, executables, data in files (or databases) or configuration elements (parameters, scripts or batch files). All of these elements are interconnected by interface links explaining who uses what.

A component diagram includes the following components:

– A rectangle (possibly with a small rectangle in the top right corner with two smaller rectangles extending out on the left) represents a component. A component is an independent unit and must provide a specific service. Its internal behavior is completely hidden in the component diagram and only its interfaces are visible.

– A circle, linked to a component rectangle, represents an implemented interface.

– A semi-circle, linked to a component rectangle, represents a required interface.

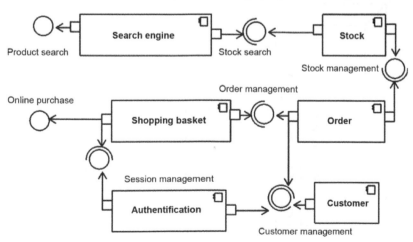

Figure 4.24. *Component diagram of an online store*

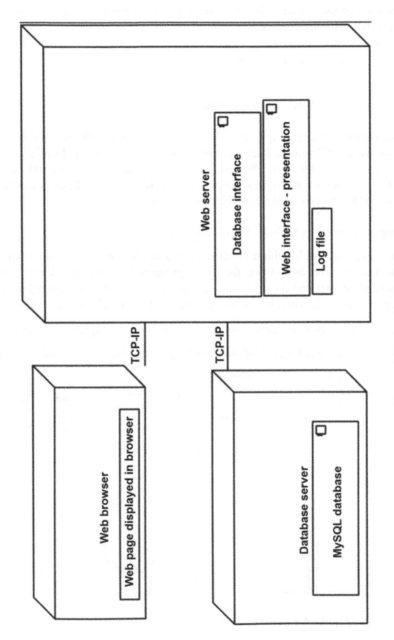

Figure 4.25. *Deployment diagram*

4.9.5. *Modeling the hardware*

The deployment diagram represents the use of the physical infrastructure for the components of the IS and the relationships between different resources. This deployment diagram is often used to model the technical structure of an IS. A deployment diagram includes the following elements:

– A cube is a node, i.e. part of the physical infrastructure equipment such as a router or a computer.

– A rectangular box with two rectangles extending out of the left side is a component.

– A plain line is a connection of association between elements.

– A rectangle is an artifact, which corresponds to a concrete element existing in the real world: a document, executable, file, database table and script.

4.10. Exercise: Linky and Enedis' IS territory

Linky is the name of the new meter developed by the French electricity distribution network administrator, Enedis. The rollout plan anticipated installation in all French households by 2021. This meter is considered to be a communicating or "smart" meter due to its ability to be interrogated and operated remotely. The communication is ensured by Power-Line Communication (PLC) technology, which makes it possible to build a telecommunication network on the power grid. This allows Enedis to replace manual meter readings, taken every six months, by automatic remote interrogation via PLC. Smart meters can also be remotely operated, which means activating a new subscription, changing the power rating and also cutting off the electricity supply remotely and automatically.

There is a heated debate about Linky for various reasons [FLÜ 17] and there is much resistance. This is how Enedis changed its plans and displayed, more modestly than expected, on its website, in February 2023, that "more than 8 out of 10 French people have a Linky meter". Several controversies and forms of resistance revolve around the territory of Enedis' IS and the extension of this territory via the installation of Linky. Its installation has shaken up the boundaries between Enedis and French households because Linky is able to transmit simple energy consumption, as well as more. In fact, this meter also transmits information on maximum apparent power output and input, and potentially also the load curve. In practical terms, this information gives information on the household's usage of electrical appliances [SCH 14b]. The following is how members of Pièces et Main d'Oeuvre, a "workshop for the construction of critical thinking in Grenoble" [PIÈ 00], responded to notification of an upcoming Linky meter installation:

For the attention of the Linky customer service manager:

Dear Sir,

We recently received an advertisement from EDF for the new Linky meter, together with your letter announcing the forthcoming installation of this meter at our premises by your local sub-contractor.

EDF's customer liaison department sets out the "benefits" of this meter for our electricity contract: remote readings "without a visit from the technician from the supplier Enedis"; a "fairer billing system" based on the reading and not on an estimate, advice from EDF to help save energy thanks to "*e.quilibre*, EDF's digital solution to help you better understand and reduce your electricity consumption" – "if you have registered for this". Thanks, but no thanks. None of these selling points is an advantage in our view. We prefer to deal with our fellow creatures rather than with machines. We believe that a world with contact is better to live in, more interesting, reassuring, human in a word, than the "remote" world you are trying to impose on us. We have a brain, equipped with functions to sort out the practical details of life without electronic assistance. We have not registered for EDF's "digital solution", because we know how to reduce our electricity consumption. This is in any case low, and is reducing thanks to measures that we ourselves have decided on, without your so-called "smart" meter. We do not want your service providers to poke their electronic nose into our private space. You do not need to know if we are in, and when, if there are more people here than usual, or any other changes in our habits. We do not want data relating to our private lives to be collected, by you, or anyone else.

Here, we have a territorial conflict. With the rollout of these meters, Enedis is equipping itself with an SI that meters not only our monthly electricity consumption, but also provides knowledge about electrical appliance use and consequently behavior in homes. It is as if the Enedis IS territory now reaches every switch and every socket in every home. Individuals see their personal, private territory eroded by Enedis' potential surveillance of their behavior at home. This tension is exacerbated by Enedis' potential to share information gathered to other companies.

This extension of Enedis' IS territory took shape in the fall of 2022. The decree of September 22, 2022, published in the *Journal officiel* of September 27, 2002, "relating to meter devices regarding electricity distribution" gives Enedis even more power, within home, via its Linky meters. Enedis has thus received authorization to temporarily deactivate the power supply to water heaters in approximately 5 million households for the purposes of energy savings.

This kind of territorial conflict can, for example, be found on social networks, where the boundary between the staff, the public and the salesperson is very often challenged and is very contentious.

Test your skills

1) What is the historical boundary of Enedis' territory towards its clients?

2) What changes is Linky bringing in terms of Enedis' IS territory?

3) What alignment is Enedis pursuing between the firm's territory and the IS territory?

5

Territorial Urbanization

THE FUNDAMENTALS.–

1) Urbanization of an IS translates the principles of urban planning of a city into the context of an organization's IS.

2) Urbanization of an IS facilitates the upgradeability, sustainability and autonomy of the organization's IS.

3) Urbanization of an IS sets out to understand the existing IS, define the target IS and the associated trajectory, and provide the tools to steer its development.

5.1. Urbanization

Urbanization is a historical movement portraying the increase in the numbers of city dwellers in relation to the general population [VER 07].

In the face of this historical movement, a new field, urbanism, emerged over time, covering the study of the urban phenomenon, the urbanization process and the organization of cities and their territories.

This includes the implementation of urban policies in terms of developing public and private spaces, organizing the built environment, socio-economic services and networks in order to achieve a certain harmony between uses, and for the sustainable well-being of users.

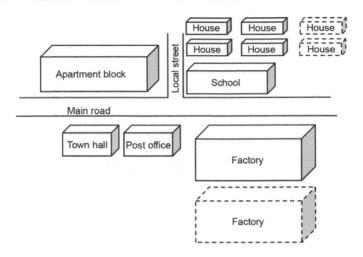

Figure 5.1. *Mapping of the urbanization of a town with the roads, public services, economic activities, residential areas and the location of future facilities in dotted lines*

Organization, processes and regulations
Organization of public authorities, residents' mandates, organization of the police, fire and ambulance services, regulations relating to building, etc.
Usage and services organized into areas/districts/blocks
Making a home, traveling, working, studying, developing social bonds, shopping, debating, personal care, etc.
Built environment and facilities
Housing, schools, workshops, miscellaneous buildings, sports facilities, etc.
Networks and utilities infrastructure
Electricity, gas, water, transport, telecommunication, etc.

Table 5.1. *Level of analysis in the urban planning of a town. Adapted from the French state IS urbanization policy: "Cadre commun d'urbanisation du SI de l'État français – version 1.0 – Direction interministérielle des systèmes d'information et de la communication", November 2012*

The urban planners' goal is thus to represent the city and its territory. In addition to describing, urban planning projects plan for the future of the city. Thus, these representations should be consistent across the territories, in relation to neighboring territories and in relation to larger-scale territories. It may be tempting for a city to place facilities that generate difficulties, such as polluting companies, on the outskirts of its territory. This decision could be unfavorable to neighboring cities and therefore create inconsistencies between adjacent territories. On higher scales, if the territory is within the perimeter of a national park, the polluting factory may not be able to establish itself at all. More specifically, town planning can cover the regulatory and operational aspects. On the one hand, the regulatory aspects restrict or, conversely, encourage certain actions. Thus, for instance, we have town plans. On the other hand, in relation to the operational aspects, urban planning covers particular actions on the ground, such as building a new road.

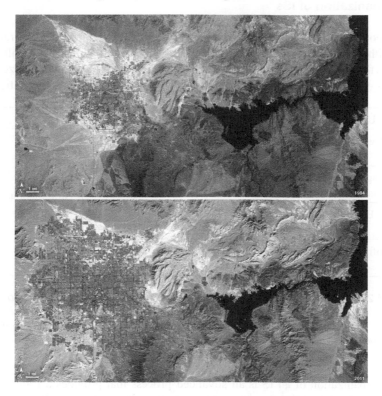

Figure 5.2. *Example of urbanization in Las Vegas (1984–2011). Author: NASA Goddard Space Flight Center, attribution: CC BY 2.0*

Formally, the urbanization of a city concerns four different levels of analysis. A first level lists the organization of the public authorities, the mandates of the inhabitants, the organization of the police, fire and rescue services and regulations in terms of construction. If the city is part of a national park, the regulations dictate what the governance of the national park decides and what remains of the city's autonomy in terms of for example, the location of polluting factories. At another level, town planning is interested in uses and services organized in areas, districts and blocks. There are many uses: housing, getting around, working, studying, building social ties, shopping, public debate, receiving treatment, etc. At another level, town planning looks at the buildings and facilities individually: location of housing, schools, sports facilities. Finally, the last level of analysis focuses on infrastructure networks and facilities for electricity, gas, water, transport, telephony, etc.

5.2. Urbanization of ISs

Corporate management draws on the principles of urban planning and translates them within its business for its IS [LON 09]. Like a city that expands in parallel with the growth of its population, an IS expands in parallel with the growth in size of the business, the data to be processed and the computerization of business activities.

Urbanization of a city	Urbanization of an IS	
Organization, processes and regulations	Processes	Informational content
Usages and services arranged in areas/districts/blocks	Functions	
Built environment and amenities	Software applications	
Infrastructure networks and utilities	Hardware	

Table 5.2. *Parallel in levels of analysis of the urbanization of a city and an IS. Adapted from: "Cadre commun d'urbanisation du SI de l'État français – version 1.0 – Direction interministérielle des systèmes d'information et de la communication" November 2012*

The urbanization of an IS is an advanced process that provides a framework of analysis in the interests of rationalizing, transforming and improving the IS. As such, it is the creator of value. Just like town planners, whose terminology they adopt, the IS planners call for engineering focused on the organization of the territory and understanding how it has developed over time. Thus, the urbanization of the IS looks at the IS's history and dynamics. It seeks to analyze the current IS in terms of the inherited IS, while planning the target IS. Urbanization of the IS does not wipe out the past and start afresh, but it takes into account the existing system and the technological opportunities to develop the IS.

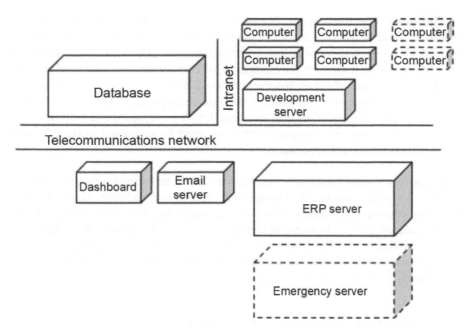

Figure 5.3. *Mapping of the urbanization of an IS with its networks, servers, databases, computers and the location of future facilities in dotted lines*

Behind the often complex technical aspects, the process of urbanization is in particular an aid to strategic decision-making. Urban planning means, first of all, seeking, in an organized framework, the optimal allocation of financial, human, application-driven and infrastructure resources. In this, urbanization is essential for a professional approach in terms of IS management. Urbanization of the IS is a prerequisite to enhancing the upgradability, sustainability and autonomy of the organization's IS, through strengthening the organizational capacity for integrating heterogeneous solutions. This approach targets an IS capable of supporting the business strategy through a series of coherent IS development projects.

IS urbanization entails the mastery of specific techniques and methods, and compliance with precise rules. The two main rules are: weak links [ORT 90] and strong ties. The rule about weak links helps ensure that each object of the IS is relatively independent of other objects at the same level of analysis. Taking into account the level of software applications, each application should be independent of other applications. The number of exchanges between objects such as applications should then be reduced and flows between applications should be simple.

The strong ties rule ensures that each IS object contains only sub-parts that directly respond to the expectations of the main object. Taking again as an example the block level of analysis of software applications, the HR management system is coherent insofar as it includes the registration of employees, the printing of payslips and the management of leave; however, it would become inconsistent if it enables registering the company's customers in addition to employees. This last individual registration operation must be split into two. Employees must be registered in the HR management system; however, customers must be registered in the customer relationship management application.

The association of these two rules, weak coupling and strong cohesion, makes it possible to add, remove or change one application without disrupting the other applications with which it communicates, according to a modular logic. In the urbanization of a city, changing an application would be comparable to knocking down a building, and it should be possible to do this without disrupting the lives of the entire neighborhood. This means the IS planner is able to give analysis elements on the modularity and development potential of the IS.

5.3. Urbanization: approaches and objectives

There are two approaches to urbanization: top-down or bottom-up. The top-down approach is based on a technical process and typically consists of two steps. In the first step, the IS planner works for the Executive and their proposal is purely informative. Thus, the urbanization process has no impact on the actual development of the IS. In the second step, the Executive will make use of what the planners have produced to set strategic orientation plans for the business departments.

The bottom-up approach is based on pooling and sharing, and involves dialog with the stakeholders. The planners' work will thus be useful in supplying the elements of understanding necessary to develop reasoned, well-argued debate between all stakeholders involved in IS governance.

Irrespective of the approach taken, IS urbanization sets out three main objectives: to understand the existing IS, to define the target IS and the associated trajectory, and to provide the tools to steer its development.

5.3.1. *Understanding the existing IS*

This entails identifying the functions covered by the "as is IS", how they are translated within applications, how they are implemented in the technical infrastructure, and what data is processed in the IS.

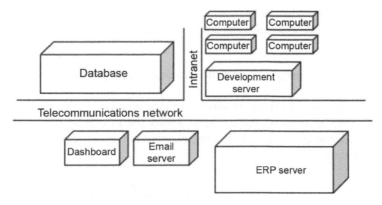

Figure 5.4. *Mapping of the existing
IS in the IS urbanization process*

The deliverables are of two kinds. On the one hand, they are a repository that will centralize all the information about the IS. On the other hand, they are a mapping process that will give a visual representation of the IS. Mapping plays an essential role in the urbanization process. The IS is thus described as a composition of maps whose parameters must be controlled.

Among the different representational models of an IS (see Chapter 4) in the context of IS urbanization, the map is often called an IS "land use plan" (LUP) and primarily adopts a functional point of view. As discussed in the previous chapter, the term function refers to the activities possible via the IS, echoing the organization's functions (sales and marketing, manufacturing, etc.).

Thus, depending on the desired granularity and the least granularity, we speak of the IS's functional area, its functional district and its functional block (or functional islands), and finally of the IS's function. A grouping of concurrent functions with the same capacity as the IS takes the name "functional blocks". The functional block is then identified by the functions it brings together, the objects of the IS that it handles and the services the block provides to other blocks of the IS, via its interfaces. Coarsening the granulometry still further, a set of function blocks groups itself into an area. At this higher level, the same logic applies. The functional area is characterized by the blocks it groups together, the IS objects that it manages within it, and the services that the district offers to the others IS districts, via its interfaces. At the most synthetic level, a set of districts is grouped into areas and the area is characterized by the districts it groups together, the IS objects that it manages within it, and the services that the area offers to other areas of the IS, via its interfaces. This distribution creates branches where each function of the IS belongs to a single block, each block to a single district and each district to a single functional area of the IS. We find, thus applied, weak coupling and strong cohesion.

5.3.2. Defining the target IS and the associated trajectory

Defining the target IS firstly means being in a position to identify the business strategy in order to envision the extent to which the IS can be of use to it. This process should extend to a study of the organization in context in order to establish a broad vision of the IS "to be".

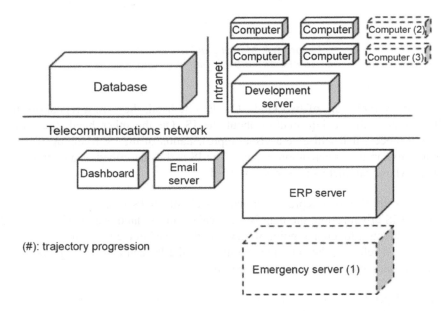

Figure 5.5. *Mapping of the target IS with the new installations in dotted lines and the development trajectory in terms of priorities, numbered, in the progression of urbanization*

Any approach to IS urbanization thus entails a description of the business goals, before being able to identify the objectives of the IS to be urbanized and consequently ensuring strategic alignment of the IS with business strategy, or in other words, to establish a connection between these two kinds of goals. This clarification process happens through a quest for rationalization and simplification of the IS structure by eliminating duplicates and establishing cross-functional checks. The main deliverable of this phase of the process is the roadmap. This concretely describes the target IS and how it will be deployed to meet the objectives set and provide the expected services. Concretely, we find: the decisions made on the target, the staging and programming of the projects, the selection of the means and resources necessary and sufficient for the objectives targeted, and therefore an overall budgeting. The roadmap is supplemented by maps, the main one remaining the mapping of target IS functions.

5.3.3. *Providing the tools to steer development*

Steering the development of the current IS towards the target IS while respecting the associated trajectory requires mastering the given urbanization framework, while allowing it to develop. This control means concretely updating the maps and other documents connected to the urbanization process. Furthermore, managing the development of the IS requires good IS governance and good communication around the urbanization process.

The deliverables from this phase are project framework documents to ensure compatibility with the rules associated with IS urbanization. These project framework documents set out the main features of the IS urbanization process and the various functional and technical choices to be made, together with a work schedule. Beyond these documents, IS planners participate in the selection and support of IS projects, in order to ensure the coherence of projects during their realization in relation to the target IS defined in the IS urbanization process.

5.3.4. *The IS urbanization approach proposed by CIGREF and IFACI*

CIGREF (*Club informatique des grandes entreprises françaises*) and IFACI (*Institut français des auditeurs et contrôleurs internes*) have adopted the principles contained in ISO 9001 to set a framework for a quality approach to business systems urbanization [CIG 11]. The advantage of the approach is that it applies equally at the global corporate level, IS management level, level of IS urbanization and at the level of IS project management. It suggests three types of processes: steering processes, support processes and operational processes.

The steering processes can be split into two:

– steering and measuring the effectiveness of the IS urbanization policy;

– participation in strategy and project selection committees, in order to contribute to decision-making on IS projects.

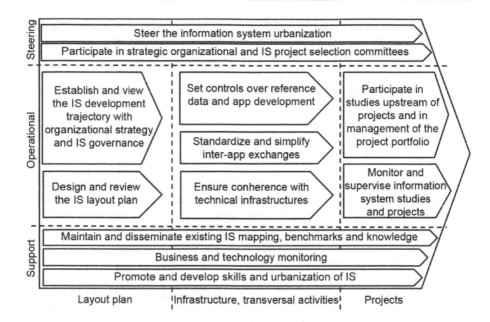

Figure 5.6. *The information urbanization process, adapted from [CIG 11]*

The operational processes include two processes directly related to planning, three processes linked to transversal and infrastructure activities, and two processes linked to project management processes. In the two operational processes that have a direct bearing on the IS layout plan, we have, on the one hand, the activities of defining and revising the IS's development trajectory in order to align it to developments in business activities; and, on the other hand, the processes of drawing up and reviewing the urbanization's reference classifications. The three processes linked to transversal and infrastructure activities cover the management of reference data and development of applications, the standardization and simplification of information flows and the maintenance of the consistency of hardware and technical infrastructures available.

Finally, the three main support processes cover:

– tooling activities, maintenance and dissemination of knowledge on the company's IS, such as maps and repositories;

– monitoring of developments in professions and technologies;

– activities to promote and develop skills in IS urbanization.

5.3.5. *The urbanization process, software packages and ERP*

Software packages, in general, and integrated management software packages (IMSs), in particular, are increasingly finding their place in organizations. Their arrival in companies questions the urbanization process: is it possible to implement an IS strategy from software packages?

In practical terms, this means considering whether it is wise to construct your IS urbanization via a structure created from software packages, like a Lego set. This option has been chosen by many businesses, not always consciously. In fact, many studies show that numerous major organizations made the decision to implement an ERP-type IS and then incorporated or added on other software packages to complement its range of functionalities. This means that the IS's functionality provision is shared in an area consisting of interoperable software [ULL 16].

In practice, this raises interoperability problems connected to the compatibility of data standards between one software package and another, as well as precise management of the versions in place for each solution, in protecting the consistency of the overall software mapping.

The nested software can only be managed seamlessly if the IS urbanization has established, in advance, a policy of choosing software solutions aligned to recognized and widely adopted norms and standards.

Another choice made by companies is to opt for an IS that structures the organization, through the adoption of ERP (Enterprise Resource Planning) that covers, on its own, all functional needs. Therefore, with ERP, the company does not nest or articulate other software packages that complete ERP's functional offer. The previously mentioned Lego game for combining software packages no longer exists. IS urbanization, inspired by the metaphor of developing a city, loses meaning. ERP structures the organization, and it is no longer up to the organization to give structure to the IS. More than a city under construction, adopting single ERP for the organization is like embarking the entire organization onto a big ocean liner. There will be almost everything, but there will be no possibility of extending over the sea, as it could have done on dry land. It is up to the organization to properly configure the ERP parameters and possibly pay for some customization.

The support processes for business and technological monitoring remain important in order to recognize the arrival of other ERPs, or other technological solutions that would be more in line with changes in the company's businesses. If such a case occurs one day, then the urbanization process will have to contribute to the changer of liner-ERP or to the disembarkation, by abandoning ERP and by founding a new city-IS to be urbanized.

5.4. The planner's job

The planner must have solid experience in IS, know precisely the professions concerned and have a significant capacity for conceptualization, a synthetic mind and great qualities in terms of communication and being a negotiator. However, the planner is not the strategist, any more than the town planning office votes in the place of elected local officials. The planner's job is to ensure that the complete IS develops consistently in line with corporate goals, the functional domain, external and internal constraints, while fully exploiting technical opportunities. The planner's achievements will thus be judged in the light of the IS's agility and responsiveness to any given change.

The planner's tasks cover three different areas [CAI 22]. They work on the design of the IS, ensure the IS's coherence and disseminate information about the IS.

With regards to the design process of the IS, the planner manages IS mapping, ensures its integrity in terms of the IS blueprint and approves the IS urbanization standards and benchmarks, and puts forward proposals to develop and simplify the IS. Alert to the issues and also well informed about technological solutions, the planner anticipates and is attentive to past, present and future technologies to achieve an efficient and effective IS within the shortest possible timescale. However, the planner is not an architect and should not view their work as being focused on project implementation or on technology at the heart of their work. In this regard, the planner is responsible for delivering IS mapping, plans and proposals for development of the IS and opportunity studies.

In relation to assuring IS coherence, the planner evaluates the relevance of IS projects to the target IS and to the "as is" IS. The planner resists the introduction of local dialects (technical or functional). The planner is also responsible for identifying overlaps, contradictions, shareable market propositions and divergent developments.

Finally, as regards communication, the planner promotes IS mapping to the company's Executive through consultation and develops the relationship between departmental managers on the one hand, and IS managers on the other hand. Their role also includes obtaining the joint consensus of the project owner and project manager, with the support of the decision-makers. The planner must be able to see the full picture, which gives them the opportunity to overcome the divisions between functional departments of the company, and to analyze both the potential short-term impact and the medium-term achievable targets. It is a nodal position at the crossroads of strategic, technical and managerial concerns.

Domain	Skills	Level
Plan	IS and strategic business alignment	4 out of 5: wide scope of responsibilities, has a great ability to integrate into complex environments. Full responsibility for the strategic development of staff working in unpredictable and unusual situations.
	Architecture design	
	Technology watch	
	Innovation	
Enable	Needs identification	5 out of 5: general obligation and responsibility, recognized inside and outside the organization for applying innovative solutions and for designing the future through exceptional and innovative knowledge and spirit.

Table 5.3. *The planner's main skills. Skills at levels 1 to 3 are not displayed, because the skills required at the first levels (1–3) are not sufficient to assume the responsibility incumbent on the planner [CAI 22]*

5.5. The limits

The limitations of this approach are human, methodological and also financial. In terms of human limitations, any classic approach to urbanization will run into the issue of the complex relationships between the project owner and the project manager. Thus, the qualities needed to exercise the profession of planner are relatively difficult to find. In terms of tasks, it is necessary to have the ability to model and prioritize processes.

Figure 5.7. *Overview of urbanization*

In terms of methodological limitations, IS modeling is often perceived as a purely descriptive exercise. This approach is of limited value. Producing pretty charts is of no use if they do not result in progress at the technical level. Conversely, modeling and mapping are at risk of being fruitless when faced with severely limited realities.

Finally, in terms of the financial limitations, urbanization involves the use of expertise that is difficult to find and also expensive. It is thus a high consumer of resources, and organizations in practice rarely pursue the process to the end.

5.6. IS urbanization and the ecological transition

Classic urbanism is increasingly taking into account the ecological aspects. In France, all local urban development plans include a sustainable development project, and the 2007 Grenelle Environment Forum (France's environmental pact) urged the creation of eco-districts. The 2001 Climate and Resilience law aims to achieve zero net land take by 2050.

This attention to green issues has also gained a footing in urbanization. On the one hand, some ISs promote ecological sustainability [HIL 05, WAT 10], through what we commonly refer to as "green IT". Applications optimize parcel distribution routes by making trucks travel fewer kilometers and therefore leading to less fuel consumption and polluting emissions. Software anticipates the variations in temperature and sunshine expected for the day to minimize the electrical consumption of lighting and heating.

On the other hand, several initiatives aim to reduce an IS's ecological impact. One of the scourges of ICT is electricity consumption, which is rising very sharply year on year due to the increasingly widespread use of ICT. For example, Google alone consumes more than 2 GW of electricity each year, the equivalent of two nuclear reactors, to directly and indirectly power the various Internet services it provides. The relatively good news in this particular case is that Google, from 2017, has bought 100% of the electricity it consumes from renewable energy producers, including wind power generation [HÖL 16]. A lot of other companies have followed the same path; nevertheless, the use of renewable sources is still in the minority.

Another strategic choice to reduce electricity consumption is green coding. This consists of writing computer code that improves the energy consumption of software applications. This objective can be pursued in different ways. For example, data center managers have software to direct customer requests to data centers that are better exposed to intermittent renewable energy sources (solar, wind). Another way to reduce the IS's ecological footprint includes frugal (or low tech) approaches, i.e. an IS capable of satisfying the needs of users by requiring fewer resources during their development and use [BIH 14; BEL 18]. Frugality is a principle that applies both to the IS in place, to reduce its obsolescence, and to the emerging IS, to minimize its impact, in order to globally reduce all uses of the IS.

Obsolescence is a major problem of ICT due to the pollution caused during the production of IT equipment. In addition, this obsolescence is often planned or in-built [SLA 07]. However, companies are going against this obsolescence. For instance, the company Fairphone offers a modular phone that is robust and easy to repair to extend its life span. Note that the average life span of a mobile phone is four years, as consumers change their phone on average once every 20 months [COD 08]. This means that the phone, when changed, is still functional, even though certain capabilities have been superseded by other features. In this context, modularity will make it possible to replace the superseded feature without changing the complete phone.

In order to gain a better means to accomplish this IS ecological transition, the life cycle approach can also play an important role. In particular, it allows us to stop focusing our attention on the use of the IS and its economic effects, as has been the case for most dominant models. While, in the IS field, the life cycle concept is present for project management; what we propose is the extension of the approach by using an ecological analysis of the IS's life cycle. The first initiatives date from the 1970s, standardization from the 1990s, and since then the practice has spread to many sectors. It is a key instrument in the circular economy. However, the IS is, and remains, a little analyzed object in terms of its life cycle.

> If shanty towns are the future of urban planning, end-user computing (EUC) and bring your own device (BYOD) are the future of IS urbanization.
>
> Today, 40% of urban expansion worldwide takes place in shanty towns in a rapid and uncontrolled manner. One-third of the urban population is already crowding into slums and this proportion is set to reach 40% in 2030, according to the Global Risks Report 2015 [WOR 15].
>
> According to Valérie Clerc, a researcher at the French Research Institute for Development:
>
>> These informal settlements are not inferior to the official town. They are 'fringe' towns, like festivals held on the fringes of the main schedule: places that grow up spontaneously with input only from the inhabitants, without urban planners or architects, whose only aim is to manage to live as well as possible as a community. [...] The hygiene is not acceptable, but their layout copies the sustainable city model: compact, dense, pedestrianized, with narrow, shady streets, skillfully blending business and residential use in a public space shared by all, thus strengthening social bonding[1].

---

1 Available at: https://www.lesechos.fr/idees-debats/sciences-prospective/021588746784-le-bidonville-est-il-lavenir-de-lurbanisme-1189430.php.

In terms of ISs and IS urbanization, similar trends can be observed. BYOD is the practice of using personal computing equipment in the business context [HAY 13]. The *boundary between the tools (or technology solutions) called "personal" or "business" is becoming extremely permeable.* This practice is becoming increasingly widespread within companies, with wide differences according to employees and regions of the world. This reflects major disruption in access and security management for application resources in particular.

EUC covers all computer applications installed by end-users themselves to automate and improve their workstation [DWI 12]. With increasingly intuitive graphic programming languages that are close to natural language, employees find it easier to develop applications by themselves, using Excel spreadsheet-type programs as a basis. Again, "artificial intelligence", such as ChatGPT, is able to understand human natural language and develop computer programs on user demand. Computer development applications also exist which enable the creation of programming code to be completely hidden from users (no-code development platform) or which greatly reduce it (low-code development platform).

BYOD and EUC do not create a problem for the IS urbanization process, if they are steered by the IS department who made arrangements to "invite" staff to bring their own computer tools and develop their applications in a defined framework. The problem for IS planners is that employees use their equipment and develop their applications without permission or in spite of an explicit ban by their employer. The term "shadow IT" covers all parts of the IS made and implemented within an organization without the approval of IS management.

Major security risks are emerging in the end IS, in the processing of data via a user-developed application and also in the company's confidential data being accessed via personal devices which might contain any kind of malware. However, just as shanty towns have their advantages, so do BYOD and/or EUC. Hence, the information departments of a growing number of organizations have agreed to supervise these phenomena. In some cases, the outcomes are astonishing: increased productivity, increased employee satisfaction and a reduction in IT costs.

Box 5.1. *The ISs of shanty towns*

5.7. Exercise: urbanization of France's government IS

States (like businesses) take a close interest in information systems urbanization. As part of its general review of public policies (RGPP – *Révision générale des politiques publiques*) launched in 2007 and the modernization of public action (MAP – *Modernisation de l'action publique*) in 2012, the French government has focused on the urbanization of its public IS [DIS 12]. The urbanization approach led by the Inter-Ministerial Directorate for Digital Affairs and State Information and Communication System

(DINSIC – *Direction interministérielle du numérique et du Système d'information et de communication de l'État*) should thus bring transparency, agility, least cost and interoperability. To achieve this outcome, the DINSIC is promoting a long-term, ongoing process that is understood and accepted by all of the IS's stakeholders (operators, project managers, project owners). The DINSIC nevertheless intends to remain pragmatic and to prioritize project-related opportunities, rather than being universalistic.

In this urbanization context, a new role is emerging within the State's civil service function: the Functional Area Manager (RZF – *Responsable de zone fonctionnelle*). The RZF is a stakeholder, usually a management committee, a department or an operator, with responsibility for a clearly defined area of the LUP of the government IS. RZFs have overall responsibility for strategic project management within their functional area.

As such, more than 150 functional areas have been defined by a functional splitting of the government IS. These are divided into areas covering everything from transversal activities through all public services and areas covering the major operational areas of the various ministries and local communities.

This inter-ministerial approach to urbanization establishes the principles constituting the general doctrine to be applied by all stakeholders, inventorizes the activities of the IS department, the project manager and the operators, and consolidates the knowledge base of various IS components, based on an industrial process for knowledge maintenance. Within this knowledge, the issue of data processed and shared by all State actors is the key.

Armed with this understanding, it becomes possible to contemplate reuse of these data by breaking down the silos into which, traditionally, each ministry and each community has been organized. "Reference data" are thus identified, and specific IT tools known as "data repositories" are set up to manage these data over time and across operational areas. But it is not automatic. France's data protection agency (CNIL – *Commission nationale de l'informatique et des libertés*), which is responsible for ensuring that IT is at the service of every citizen, reminds us that data sharing has not necessarily been authorized by public service users at the time of being recorded. However, this user authorization is obligatory. This issue tends to make the front page of the newspapers whenever a crime is committed. With hindsight, we discover that one section of the administration was aware of a risk, but another section did not have access to this information and thus was not able to take timely action.

Test your skills

1) What are the differences between the urbanization of the government IS and the urbanization of the IS of a commercial business?

2) Why does the government publish its IS urbanization strategy and focuses online?

3) What might be the advantages and disadvantages for the various stakeholders of the information sharing to be introduced by the urbanization of the government IS?

6

Urbanizing the Inter-organizational IS

THE FUNDAMENTALS.–

1) Inter-organizational territory is complex because of the multitude of stakeholders involved.

2) Inter-organizational ISs can be either extended or cooperative ISs.

3) Inter-organizational urbanization directly addresses issues to do with shared protocols, free software, standardization and collaborative working.

6.1. Inter-organizational territory

As seen in Chapter 4, a territory implies the existence of borders. These borders are regularly called into question by transformations of the territory and by transformations of neighboring territories. Consequently, the spatiality of territory is generally perceived as a build-up of multiple levels, local or global. Thus, ongoing globalization processes call for a review of territorial boundaries and levels.

Territory is called into question by the development of networks. People, organizations, materials and capital are thus becoming increasingly mobile. This mobility reduces the scope of the concept of a territory with specific resources. However, borders have not completely disappeared. They are coming back in a more aggressive way, because borders are becoming the territory's one remaining institutionalized element. Consequently, a territory can become a guarantor of identity. As such, movements in the territory are supposed to be checked at the border. At the same time, differences within a territory are eliminated for the sake of unity. Thus, territories and their boundaries become geometrically flexible according to the times and the glances [JAI 09].

Power struggles are therefore no longer limited to within an inner territory delimited by corporate boundaries, but these struggles are increasingly extending beyond organizational boundaries. These struggles contribute to justifying the form an organization takes. This form may no longer depend solely on the quasi-automatic regulations linked to transaction cost in relation to its environment [WIL 98]. This is how an organization's identity changes.

The territorialization process of companies [AME 88, GAF 90] is becoming weaker, since businesses are interacting increasingly globally. Territorial trajectories are more uncertain, because the stakeholders who shape these trajectories are more mobile and less attached to (and dependent on) a certain territory. Large companies consider themselves global players and choose their territories and locations on a global scale. Thus, the company's territory goes from a status of fact and confinement to a status of internalized parameters and strategic choices. These continuous reconfigurations upset the territorialized actors who do not have the same flexibility. These territorialized actors must then work directly to attract organizations and more specifically large groups and investors. Mesoeconomic theories combine with micro-economic theories to explain this new situation and put forward operational guidelines.

6.1.1. *Inter-organizational territories and the value chain: the sectorial chain*

Development of the definition of a territory and structure of the production operations of the firm generate tensions between the logics incorporated in the processes, found in the firm's IS, and in particular in its software packages, and the logics of the external partners. These tensions are often resolved by redesigning the business processes of several organizations together. It is in this context that Porter [POR 85] puts forward the value chain model.

The starting point of the value chain, according to Porter, is the company's business units. At this level of analysis, the value chain is thus all the steps that determine the capacity of a business unit to gain a competitive advantage. These activities are divided into main and support activities. The main or primary activities contribute to the material creation and sale of the product, such as inbound logistics, marketing, sales and after-sales services. In addition to the primary activities, there are support or transversal activities. These support the main activities and include the company's infrastructure, HR management, research and development, purchasing, etc.

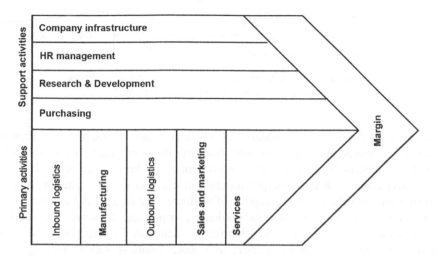

Figure 6.1. *Porter's value chain*

Competitive advantage is defined as all the characteristics or attributes of a product that gives the business an edge over its immediate competitors. This edge, also called the "value", translates in concrete terms into how much customers are prepared to pay for the product. As it is difficult to know of customers' inclination to pay, companies often content themselves with the selling price, as an indicator of value. Subtracting all the costs, to accomplish primary activities such as support activities, from the selling price, gives the margin.

In this perspective, the value chain becomes an instrument for the company to build a competitive advantage. This construction depends on the company's ability to keep the activities that create the most value in-house, while costing less than the value created, and outsourcing the other activities. The quality and sustainability of the created competitive advantage depend on the choice of activities kept in-house. These have an impact in terms of cost (if the company is pursuing a price leadership strategy) or quality (if the company is aiming for a differentiation strategy).

Compared to other companies involved in the chain of transforming raw materials into finished products, these choices to keep activities in-house or outsource result in a particular positioning of each company in the sector. The sector therefore becomes the inter-organizational territory of sequences of Porter's value chains, of a multiplicity of organizations.

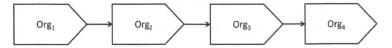

Figure 6.2. *The business sector as an inter-organizational territory of a series of Porter value chains*

The value chain helps us understand the importance of internal coordination within the company and external coordination with the other organizations involved, from the extraction of raw materials to consumption of the finished product. It is a sector-driven approach that emerges through an analysis of the value chain. This calls into question the classic perception of territory. The sector can be defined as a set of products or services and its producers, competing to serve one market. Globalization, and especially the significant reduction in transport costs and transaction costs, is resulting in more and more business sectors making their arrangements on a worldwide scale. Production processes become fragmented, with the companies involved constantly making choices between internalization and outsourcing of production and between integration and spatial disintegration. Porter [POR 85] shows that there is no reason why all activities should be carried out by the same company and he confirms the end of the vertical integration logic of multi-divisional companies.

6.1.2. *Inter-organizational territories and the value chain: the ecosystem*

The tensions that lead to business process redesign in multiple organizations can lead to the birth of business ecosystems [PAC 06; PAC 93]. The business ecosystem describes intensive production and inter-business communication resulting from the proliferation of industrial cooperation agreements. With the rejection of the integrated vertical, hierarchical vision, new horizontal and non-hierarchical structures based on the notion of districts or local networks are gaining ground. The idea is to build peer-to-peer networks (between equals) based on cooperation and information sharing. Even though companies have no structural links between them, they all contribute to the development of the same territory. This contribution has been theorized in the stakeholder concept [FRE 10a, 10b] which recognizes the existence of interdependent relationships between the company and the various groups that constitute its environment, and with which it interacts. Unlike the supply chain, where a certain main flow is unidirectional from the raw material to the finished product, the ecosystem is characterized by a network of interactions and interdependence without a precise beginning and end. The value emerges from the network and each participant appropriates a part of it.

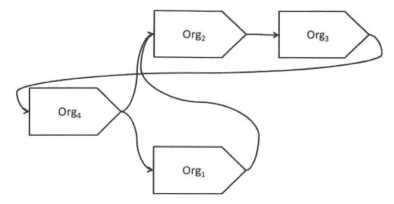

Figure 6.3. *The ecosystem as an inter-organizational territory in the value network*

These organizational networks should make the entire territory competitive, and thus should potentially be able to generate cumulative growth dynamics. In the absence of full mobility of people and capital, certain activities cluster together on territories that offer specific advantages. In competition, the ecosystems apply the same strategies as companies: price strategies, differentiation strategies and/or focus strategies.

Analysis of the benefits generated by business ecosystems has been facilitated by the value network theory [CHR 16]. Going beyond the value chain, the value network is an analysis framework for economic activities that defines the distribution of resources both within and across organizations. The nodes in the network are individuals, businesses or organizations, and these nodes exchange tangible deliverables (e.g. physical goods) or intangible deliverables (e.g. knowledge) between themselves. The network approach helps us to appreciate the interdependence of the stakeholders in a network. Seeing the full picture helps explain the value of products and services provided, and thus to go beyond the logic of the value chain and its linearity [STA 98].

Allee [ALL 00] gives the example of a pharmaceutical company's value network. This pharmaceutical company communicates with patients to inform them about the marketing of its new drugs and asks patients in return about their needs and wishes for changes in drugs.

This same pharmaceutical company must provide regulators with data that proves the qualities of the new drugs and the compliance of manufacturing with set standards. The regulator retains the possibility of inspecting the pharmaceutical company and authorizes (or not) the marketing of its drugs. The pharmaceutical company is in constant contact with health professionals.

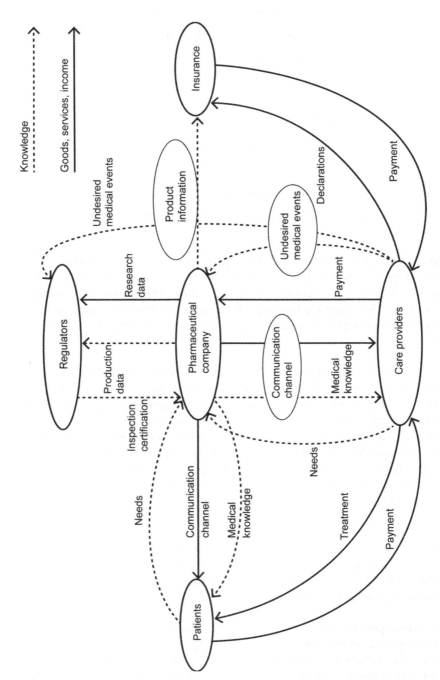

Figure 6.4. *Value network of a pharmaceutical company, adapted from Allee [ALL 00]*

Much like for patients, the pharmaceutical company disseminates new medical knowledge about its drugs to healthcare professionals, who, in turn, can communicate their drug needs, buy the drug and keep the manufacturer informed of any adverse reactions, during administration of the drug. The pharmaceutical company also informs the health insurance companies about the products for their correct reimbursement. In this network, key exchanges escape the pharmaceutical company. The health professional treats the patients and the patients pay for this care. If the patients do not pay, then the insurances are responsible for paying upon receipt of declarations of care. Finally, health professions inform the regulator of adverse effects.

6.2. Inter-organizational territory of the IS

The way we view the IS changes with this new perception of the territory. The IS no longer has to only ensure links between organizational functions and hierarchical levels. In addition to this linkage, globalization also leads ISs to create a new linkage of functions and of external partners [CAR 10].

The IS can no longer be viewed as exclusively internal (represented by MIS and OIS forms) or external. It is both at the same time. The micro-economic theories in Chapter 4 are compounded by mesoeconomic theories which identify two new IS categories: the extended IS and the cooperative IS [ALB 96]. In total, this taxonomy of ISs, along two axes (economic theory [DEB 89] and organizational theory [LEM 90]), provides a typology with four categories of business ISs [ALB 12].

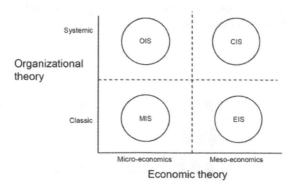

Figure 6.5. *A taxonomy of business ISs, according to "classic functional" and "systemic procedural" organizations, and, "micro-economics" and "mesoeconomics" [ALB 12]*

6.2.1. *The extended IS*

The extended information system (EIS) is the IS at the crossroads of mesoeconomics and classic functional theory. It principally comes from the work of Coase [COA 37] and Williamson [WIL 98], who accepted the need to re-examine the principle of pure and perfect market competition between companies. This re-examination includes the introduction of a new concept: interfirm strategic relationships. These strategic relationships are conceived as quasi-automatic adjustment mechanisms within a market, which are triggered in line with transaction costs. Strategic relationships thus reduce transaction costs. The firm can establish both strategic and market relationships: certain activities are outsourced without losing operational and strategic control. In addition to reducing transaction costs, these strategic relationships create a new territory, a third arena of resource allocation, beyond the two classic arenas of micro-economics: the firm and the market. The IS expands into this new territory, quasi-automatically, translating the strategic relationships that form. This is the extended information system (EIS). The EIS responds to new requirements for inter-organizational alignment, adjustment and coordination [ALB 12]. The EIS would be seen as the operational translation in IS terms of the economic need to outsource certain activities without losing operational and strategic control.

Electronic Data Interchange (EDI) is an example of an EIS where companies can communicate automatically, such as placing orders, invoicing, settling and resolving the outsourcing of their activities in a space where control is maintained. This control also comes from the use of proprietary standards, which allow the automation of two-way flows in real time between two different companies; however, one of the two decides how.

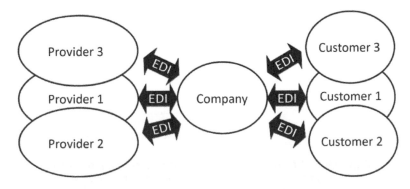

Figure 6.6. *EIS, taking up the logic of the sector*

The EIS appears as the ISM of a new mesoeconomic territory going beyond that of the micro-economic firm, but where each firm retains its autonomy and its control in a centralized manner. This EIS is reminiscent of a hub and spoke with a central point from which several connections are established.

Uberization comes from the name of the company Uber, which develops and operates mobile applications for putting users in contact with drivers providing transport services. Uberization refers, more generally, to the phenomenon allowing professionals and their potential customers to get in direct contact, almost instantaneously, through the use of ICT. In this case, ICTs support the creation of a platform for linking, debiting commissions on transactions, payment of the service provider and cross-assessment of the service.

The company Uber gave the name to this phenomenon because it popularized the organization of a regular commercial activity of selling services (in its specific case, car drivers) as if it was an occasional activity. This overturned the traditional social and regulatory framework by replacing wage labor with the free entrepreneurial initiative of service providers. While the customer often finds a direct advantage through a reduction in the cost of the service, better quality, ease of access to the service and immediacy, the professional faces more complex situations. The professional often has a status of self-employment worker, losing everything that labor law provides to employees, in various areas such as working hours, social security or paid leave. However, this entrepreneur is, in fact, completely dependent on the platform put in place. We find this trend in other collaborative economy platforms: the IS of these platforms is a kind of EIS that the platform owner makes available to service providers and customers, and exacerbates competition between service providers, by promoting the creation of an electronic market place connecting multiple service providers and multiple customers.

Box 6.1. *The uberization of firms, an IS and the impact at territorial level*

6.2.2. *The cooperative IS*

The cooperative information system (CIS) is the IS of mesoeconomics and the systemic theory of organizations [ALB 96]. The CIS is a double departure from the classic functional organization theory and micro-economic theories.

For Aoki [AOK 86], the principles of perfect competition in the market and economic calculation are not sufficient to understand the motivations of stakeholders and the configurations observed on the ground. The issue of outsourcing cannot be reduced to an economic calculation that could be resolved simply by market mechanisms, but needs an additional element. Aoki calls this a relational rent. Aoki defines this relational rent as the surplus value created by two or more stakeholders who cooperate to reduce the problems of asymmetry of information in an uncertain universe.

In other words, the value chain can be accomplished in a long-term industrial cooperation network with other firms to reduce uncertainties and information asymmetry [COH 90]. In this perspective, the company is seen as an open socio-technical system where strategy is founded upon industrial cooperation agreements, on the structuring of networking organizations and the joint pursuit of a productive project.

The Japanese form (J-form business) is given as a model for the networked business [AOK 92]. J-form is an alternative to, and contrasts with, the American form (A-form) and within which Aoki includes the unitary form (U-form) and the multi-divisional form (M-form). The J-form firm is particularly characterized by an extension of its territory, resulting from the phenomena of interfirm cooperation in the implementation of business processes. The J-form offers a hybrid form of firm, resulting from strategic relationship strategies [ARL 87] based on the principle of a value creation network that does not necessarily belong solely to one firm. Paché [PAC 93] and Alban [ALB 96] took up the Aokian concept of a network company and introduced, for the first, and developed, for the second, the concept of V-Firm (Vertical Network Firm) and H-Firm (Horizontal Network Firm). Thus, these industrial cooperations are constitutive of network companies organized by mainly vertical or horizontal relationships.

Relationships are vertical when a leading company develops a network with partner companies, mainly upstream and downstream of its activity. However, the main company retains control over the composition of the final product and the value-creating improvements. It benefits more than others from successful products. In general, there are high capital requirements to create, produce and distribute the final product, and the network mainly pursues efficiency improvements.

Relationships are horizontal when the company develops a network with members of the same industrial sector in a complementary way and is pursuing a common goal, without a proven leader. The interdependence between the participants is therefore stronger to the point that helping other companies strengthens the helping company. When a product is successful, all participants can benefit equally from its success. Capital requirements are reduced since these requirements are distributed across the network and other companies can own some of the assets to create, produce and distribute the final product. More than efficiency, the network pursues flexibility and the risks are then reduced by optimizing the network's flexibility [AOK 86].

Translating this theoretical proposal into the IS leads to the creation of a cooperative IS (CIS). The CIS resembles an "OIS" of a new mesoeconomic territory that exceeds that of the micro-economic firm.

For example, several companies, members of the same network, can concretely design software applications to share their knowledge. This sharing constitutes a common knowledge heritage with a view to solving complex problems that would be beyond the reach of each company individually. Complex projects, such as the construction of a metropolitan line and space rockets, take advantage of these inter-company sharing spaces. Other examples of CISs can be found in computer-aided design and engineering systems (CAD), videoconferencing applications and computer networks when they are shared between different companies. Each company becomes a node in the network, the exchanges are automated, multidirectional, in real time, peer-to-peer, and without central and dominant control. Several technologies for automating exchanges between applications are used: EDI, eXtended Markup Language (XML), WebService, Application Programming Interface (API), Virtual Private Network (VPN). The lack of domination is also marked by the preference for open standards and free software, instead of proprietary standards and packaged software. Several initiatives associated with Industry 4.0, such as the Internet of Things or RFID radio-identification technology, are part of this perspective.

The CIS can also justify itself in terms of the objectives of the information society:

> We recognize that building an inclusive Information Society requires new forms of solidarity, partnership and cooperation among governments and other stakeholders, i.e. the private sector, civil society and international organizations. Realizing that the ambitious goal of this declaration both at national and international level – bridging the digital divide and ensuring harmonious, fair and equitable development for all – will require strong commitment by all stakeholders, we call for digital solidarity, both at national and international levels [ITU 04].

Indeed, ICTs require heavy capital investments to be mastered and the importance of the necessary investments creates and accentuates inequalities of access, processing and recording of information. We see that digital divides are multiplying at all scales. There is a great imbalance between those who hold the information and the means to process it, and those who only use it. The question of social equality therefore deserves as much attention as the ecological question.

IS development has mainly adopted the functionalist paradigm for a long time. The main focus is therefore on improving IS performance with a focus on financial performance. Negative externalities on society are hardly taken into account. The functionalist vision sends IS users back to the status of resources that need to be exploited. It is therefore not surprising that the IS is often experienced by users as an instrument of oppression and alienation at work (even of social exclusion when computerization results in job cuts).

If, in the dominant models, people are considered as a resource, the social and environmental transition invites us to consider individuals as the purpose and therefore to promote their emancipation and social equality. Concerning emancipation, an example of IS design by integrating this purpose is Wikipedia. Among other functionalities, the wiki environment enables free discussions between the co-authors of the same article, according to a peer-to-peer logic. Regarding social equality, the implementation of e-government solutions has a favorable impact on the reduction of poverty and social inequalities, and facilitates social elevation.

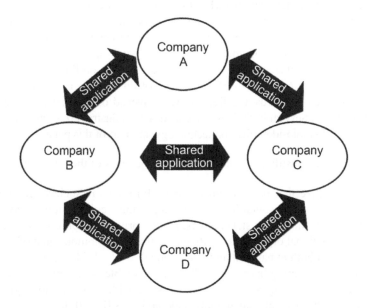

Figure 6.7. *A CIS based on an ecosystem logic*

Collectives characterized by a large number of stakeholders are becoming increasingly common. Their spread is a response to the need to take responsibility for global cross-disciplinary issues that call for broad collaboration. [LAT 07, ORL 10, DEV 15]. These groups operate on a multilateral logic that tends to promote participation by all stakeholders and to view users as co-creators. These collectives have an astonishing ability to come up with completely new solutions. The main issue for these collectives lies in managing to maintain an often-fragile balance between conflicting contingencies. These collectives need areas that facilitate dialog between stakeholders and stimulate social interaction. These areas are called "third-party spaces" [OLD 99]. A third-party space can be defined as being in-between, a neutral place, offering open access, whose purpose is to facilitate dialog and stimulate social interaction. A third-party space is thus a place where temporary proximities are formed.

In the MÉLIBIO project, the third-party space took the form of a cooperative IS, via a collaborative platform. MÉLIBIO is a project led by the association *Pôle Agriculture Biogique Massif Central* (Massif Central Organic Agriculture Center – PABMC), launched in 2012. The aim of the project is to assemble around the farmers a large number of institutional and scientific stakeholders, in the absence of a hierarchical link, to provide a relevant collaborative response to the global challenge posed by climate change. Stakeholders include the *Institut national de recherchepour l'agriculture, l'alimentation et l'environnement* (INRAE), the chambers of agriculture, agricultural teaching institutions, agricultural technical institutes, agricultural experts and farmers' unions.

The goal of this broad and open cooperation is to find the best methods (agricultural, and also organizational) to strengthen farmers' resiliency against the vagaries of the weather by planting meadows of varied flora and fodder crops suited to the climate constraints and objectives specific to each farmer. Managing a complex, long-term project involves a great deal of discussion between participants and regular meetings. Then, there is the issue of deciding on frequency, scope, nature and locations. Specialized meetings risk causing fragmentation in the collective. Assembling all of the participants poses the twin problem of mobilizing all stakeholders for a long meeting during which their expertise is sought only occasionally, and finding dates and places to bring the entire collective together.

Faced with this situation, the MÉLIBIO group very quickly stated its need for a collaborative space that would be permanent and capable of keeping the stakeholders connected between meetings; they reduced the entry cost for each meeting. At the participants' request, online tools were used. The first was an online project management tool, provided by a private operator. The online project management software led to the formalizing of working subgroups and the appointment of publication officers. Since then, members of the Group have made lively, creative contributions to the space.

However, while the online project monitoring platform was initially envisaged as a place for debate and for the storage of working papers, it has proved able to take on other roles. For example, one of the group members who was in charge of a seed test on a planted plot noted the presence of a parasite. This person took photographs and published them on the platform. An online discussion then started about the identity of the parasite and how to eliminate it. The computer tool has, to some extent, moved away from its primary function to become an extension of the reality on the ground by offering the group members enriched reality. This project management tool has created a common space that was necessary and anticipated by the group.

These results were sufficiently encouraging for the association to decide to subsequently invest in a platform based on free software, in order to gain independence from commercial solutions and to develop online solutions in line with its needs. The collective took ownership of these computer tools to turn them into its third-party space, to respond to the major challenges of managing a multi-partner project [DUC 07; WAT 15].

Box 6.2. *The CIS as a third-party space. Reworking of a text written by Philippe Eynaud and Julien Malaurent, "Une plateforme collaborative pour matérialiser la coopération d'un collectif hétérogène" (A collaborative platform to actualize cooperation in a heterogeneous cooperative), published at the AIM 2016 conference [EYN 16]*

Territory	Organization				IS	
Economic theory	Micro-economics				Mesoeconomics	
Organizational structure theory	Class functional	Systemic procedural	Classic functional	Systemic procedural	Class functional	Systemic procedural
Typology	Functional	Systemic	MIS	OIS	EIS	CIS
Elemental component	Function	Process	Business application	Integrated application module	Electronic Data Interchange (EDI)	Network node
Architecture	Functional per silo	Cross-disciplinary per process	Standalone applications	Integrated modular application	Hub-and-spoke	Peer-to-peer
Referent	Function mapping	Business process mapping	Applications mapping	Access mapping	Value chain mapping	Value networking mapping
Formalization	Procedure	Process	Program	Configuration	Proprietary standard	Open standard
Dissemination mechanism between units	Hierarchy	Process manager	Inter-dependence delayed monodirectional flow	Automation monodirectional real-time flow	Automation bidirectional real-time flow	Automation multidirectional real-time flow

Table 6.1. *A perspective of the territories of the organization and of the IS, inspired by [BID 06]*

6.3. Alignment and representation of the inter-organizational IS territory

With these changes in the territories of the organization and the IS, the question of alignment is reiterated. We are entering the territory of mesoeconomics.

Within the framework of classical functional organization theory, IS alignment here regards the linkage between the internal (firm's) network and the external partners.

This alignment broadly reflects the questions asked in the context of micro-economics, since every company has full control across the scope of its IS.

The question of alignment takes on a different aspect with regards to the theory of systemic procedural organization. The IS issue is no longer centered on a standalone system, but is designed and created to be in constant interaction with its ecosystem. Consequently, the interoperability issue becomes central. Territorial representations become more complex, because the company integrates items into them that exceed their borders and are controlled by other organizations. More people are involved and the choice of common rules and a common language for communicating about the IS has to be discussed and resolved.

6.4. Urbanization of an inter-organizational IS

In Chapter 5, we presented the urbanization of the IS as a process used in organizations to act as a framework for the transformation, rationalization and improvement of the business IS. With the increasing pervasiveness of multistakeholder debates and initiatives, IS urbanization must also move forward.

Classic urbanization changes and urbanism along with it. A city becomes increasingly populated, but due to a seesaw effect, the city becomes increasingly dependent on other territories that supply it with new arrivals and reabsorb the flow of leavers. As cities expand, neighboring towns intertwine to form conurbations. In addition to the urbanism plans that cover the municipal territory, there are other instruments such as, in France, the Territorial Coherence Program (SCoT – Schéma de Cohérence Territoriale). This document is created by several independent municipalities, which form a union to agree on a territorial plan covering several municipalities with the aim of coordinating all policies relating to housing, mobility, business development, environment and landscape.

This is no longer a simple process aimed at creating an IS capable of informing and supporting the company's strategy, but rather a process aimed at creating a number of ISs capable of informing and supporting the strategies of several companies in extended, distributed, cooperative organizational frameworks – or in other words open frameworks. In this inter-organizational perspective, IS governance takes on new meaning because there is no longer a single company's general management in charge, but several partners who must jointly manage the urbanization of their IS. This complexification of the urbanization project must also be counterbalanced by the opportunities it reveals. It is, in fact, by continuously confronting the change in norms and standards and the improvement proposals of its network's actors, that urbanization can promote the establishment of an application, information, interoperable and agile structure.

The top-down approach to urbanization loses in efficiency since there is no longer a company executive that can easily impose a strategic direction plan on all stakeholders. The bottom-up approach becomes relevant, since this is based on pooling and sharing, and involves dialog with companies' internal and also external stakeholders.

The chief objectives of the urbanization of an inter-organizational IS remain the same as those of the urbanization of an organizational IS. Nevertheless, some specificities stand out. In order to develop an understanding of the existing IS, the repository will be inter-organizational and cover several ISs belonging to several organizations. Similarly, the mapping will give a visual representation of several ISs of different organizations. In these contexts of inter-organizational urbanization of ISs, representations may have coarser IS granularity. Rather than focusing on functions and function blocks, the mapping will be more oriented towards the representation of functional districts and functional areas.

In terms of defining the target IS and associated trajectory, the target IS is no longer that of one company but the IS of several companies. Consequently, the trajectory must emerge from a convergence of the strategies of several organizations. The various organizations must reflect separately and together in order to decide how the IS's SI can serve the strategic objectives of each company in synergy with the other companies, and how the inter-organizational IS can facilitate the pursuit of these objectives. As in an internal urbanization process within an organization, the quest for rationalization and simplification of the IS's structure will be pursued in the inter-organizational urbanization process. However, in this case, rationalization and simplification must be measured at the wider territorial level, which can mean sub-optimal local solutions for the sake of maximum global optimization.

The two main rules of IS urbanization, weak links and strong ties, still apply in the inter-organizational context. Nevertheless, with regards to the functional flows, planners must integrate function blocks coming from other organizations. They must also recognize that each company's function blocks should be able to effectively and simply communicate with those of the other companies.

Faced with the exponential growth in the number of stakeholders, IS planners play an increasingly central role in building a common space for cooperation. The planner must indeed respond both to internal issues, concerning the interoperability of their application base, and to external issues related to the network stakeholders interacting with the company. It is not a simple extension of the perimeter, but additional capacities to interact with new interlocutors from other organizations and therefore potentially with other strategic objectives, professions and cultures.

Concretely and pragmatically, the planner must network with other planners or IS management stakeholders to engage in open innovation-type perspectives. They must seek to find room for maneuver not in the proximity of interest with publishers but regarding community perspectives (types of user clubs and communities of practice) and alliance strategies (around technological or strategic choices).

The development of technology, especially cloud computing, IT standards, blockchains, free software and open data, has done a great deal to support and contribute to the opening up of companies to their stakeholder networks.

6.4.1. *Cloud computing*

Cloud computing changes the IS territory and classic approach to IS urbanization, where all the ISs have been installed on premises.

Cloud computing is the use of the computing and storage capacity of remote servers via the Internet, on demand and on a self-service basis. Usage is agreed by subscription between the provider, who arranges access to the servers, and the customer who uses the service. From the customer's point of view, this service is ready (or nearly ready) for use as soon as the subscription is taken out, regardless of the size of the request and the service selected from the provider's catalog. The client pays, generally, a regular subscription to the service, usually in line with usage requirements. This is calculated and forecast from the number of users, the computing capacity needed, the volume of storage used, the bandwidth occupied, the service reliability level, etc.

Providing the service over the Internet ensures a significant opening up of the service. This is reinforced by the use of international standards and protocols and a wide range of devices and networks. The provider, on their side, has the advantage of being able to pool their IT resources. Thus, the same server can potentially be used by several customers at the same time in line with fluctuations in demand. In contrast, if demand increases, the provider can use multiple servers in parallel to meet the requirements of one customer, in a way that is transparent and instant for the end customer.

These common features are then offered in different packages, according to target group:

– Public cloud is the service made available to the general public.

– Private cloud is the service made available for the exclusive use of a particular organization. This organization will have more room for maneuver in handling resources made available by the provider.

– Community cloud is the service made available to a group of organizations, by the same group of organizations, as part of a pooling of resources.

– Hybrid cloud is the service that combines both private and public cloud in order to perform different functions.

Another important difference in the package is which main service category it falls into:

– Infrastructure as a Service (IaaS). This means the provision of access to virtualized computers on which customers can install an operating system and applications.

On premise model	Infrastructure as a Service (IaaS) model	Platform as a Service (PaaS) model	Software as a Service (SaaS) model
Business application	Business application	Business application	*Business application*
Data	Data	Data	*Data*
Database software	Database software	*Database software*	*Database software*
Operating Systems	Operating Systems	*Operating Systems*	*Operating Systems*
Virtualization layers, platforms and internal networks	*Virtualization layers, platforms and internal networks*	*Virtualization layers, platforms and internal networks*	*Virtualization layers, platforms and internal networks*
External partners and networks	*External partners and networks*	*External partners and networks*	*External partners and networks*
Legend: Organization's responsibility (normal text) *Shared responsibility (italics)* **Supplier's responsibility (bold)**			

Table 6.2. *The various cloud computing models compared to on premise*

– Platform as a Service (PaaS). This means the provision of access to computers on which an operating system chosen by the client has already been installed. Based on this operating system, the customer can install applications.

– Software as a Service (SaaS). This means the provision of direct access to specific applications, with the supplier being responsible for managing the computers and the operating systems required to run the application.

Small- and medium-sized companies especially have the option of gaining access to services previously reserved for large companies because of their traditionally high entry cost. However, these benefits have to be offset against, for instance, the difficulties frequently encountered in getting out of a cloud computing contract that generates customer dependency on the service provider.

This introduction to cloud computing gives an insight into its impact on the IS territory and on its urbanization. The territory of the IS is indeed changed, because traditionally the company's servers used to be within the company (on premise) and its IS management directly controlled their operations. With cloud computing, the IS territory moves further away to the leased remote servers. However, it is difficult to find a clear answer to make questions: where exactly these servers are; which servers, among the thousands housed in the same data center, process and store which company data; what happens at the service provider's premises; what a service provider does with the company's data; who has access to these data; what would happen if the service provider were to go out of business; which country's law applies or what security is in place to protect the data.

Consequently, IS urbanization is impacted by cloud computing. As we have seen, the urban planning of a city steers the construction of various public facilities and private buildings, and their development over time. The urbanization of ISs picks up this logic and applies it to IS design and development. However, cloud computing conceptually changes the object of IS urbanization. With cloud computing, there is a shift from a logic of property, purchase and ownership of hardware to a service logic, which is part of a broader and deeper tertiarization of the economy. For the IS planner, cloud computing leads to the vacating, in part at least, of certain levels of the ISs, depending on the category of services subscribed to, from the lowest, the hardware.

6.4.2. Computing standards

Like between humans as in computing, establishing a dialog between several partners requires the use of a common language and common rules. With the expansion of telecommunications, multinationals and international trade, the need to create shared languages and rules for ISs has led to the progressive development of several IT standards. Since the late 1960s, American companies have been looking for a way to make better use of their computer equipment and telecommunication networks. These companies set up the Transportation Data Coordinating Committee, whose findings formed the basis of what was to become today's EDI. The American National Standards Institute (ANSI) then established its Committee X12, responsible for establishing inter-industry standards for the EDI, to extend the Transportation Data Coordinating Committee's outcomes to other economic sectors. The ANSI X12 standards were published in 1985 and purported to be applicable to all business sectors.

In parallel, the US joined with their European partners (in France, for example, the retail sector had developed the EAN standard and the automotive sector had developed the GALIA/ODETTE standard) to create a set of international standards. The international standards EDIFACT (Electronic Data Interchange For Administration, Commerce and Transport) was released in 1987. EDIFACT offers a set of standards and guidelines for the electronic exchange of structured data between independent ISs.

ISO standard number	Topic covered
ISO 2709	Information exchange format (ISO/DIS 2709)
ISO 7498	Open Systems Interconnection (OSI) standard for communication between computers in seven layers
ISO 10303	Standard for the exchange of product model data
ISO 14048	Formats for electronic data interchange
ISO 15504	Framework for process evaluation
ISO 19005	Portable Document Format (PDF) designed for long-term archiving of information
ISO 19503	Data exchange standard based on XML
ISO 21127	Benchmark ontology for the exchange of cultural heritage information
ISO 26300	Open Document Format for Office Applications data format for office applications
ISO 29500	Office Open eXtensible Markup Language (XML) format for office applications

Table 6.3. *Indicative (but non-exhaustive) list of ISO standards for IS standardization*

A great many standards have been created since the early 2000s to standardize formats and for the exchange of data between ISs. The International Organization for Standardization (ISO) plays a large role in defining interoperability standards for the development of ISs at the international level. These standards must continually evolve to keep up with technological developments and business practices. The recognition of new technologies and new practices such as ISO standards has significant economic repercussions. For example, every office suites user is impacted by standards relating to file saving formats (doc, docx, odt, rtf, etc.), because they are also derived from ISO standardizations.

ISO standards have also contributed to the development of the Internet. The EDI's origins lie in the business environment, while the origins of the Internet are more military and academia-based, notably at America's Defense Advanced Research Projects Agency (DARPA). First, in the 1960s, the original intention was to design a computer network within the agency, the ARPANET. In the 1970s, the IT protocols Transmission Control Protocol/Internet Protocol (TPC/IP) were designed to enable other IT networks to connect to ARPANET, thus introducing network interoperability and the creation of a network of networks: the Internet. In the 1980s, more institutions, universities and research centers in the United States adopted TCP/IP protocols and linked to ARPANET. In the early 1990s, the network was opened up to commercial traffic. It was in the 1990s again that the Web, written in HyperText Markup Language (HTML), and its base protocol, HyperText Transfer Protocol (HTTP) were developed. The EDI has also developed and attached itself to Internet standards and protocols.

Layer	Examples of protocols
Application	HyperText Transfer Protocol (HTTP), Telnet, File Transfer Protocol (FTP), Simple Mail Transfer Protocol (SMTP), Trivial File Transfer Protocol (TFTP), Domain Name System (DNS), Internet Message Access Protocol (IMAP), Post Office Protocol (POP), Secure Shell (SSH)
Transport	Transmission Control Protocol (TCP), User Datagram Protocol (UDP), Stream Control Transmission Protocol (SCTP), Real-Time Protocol (RTP)
Internet	Internet Protocol (IP) version 4 (v4), IPv6, Internet Control Message Protocol (ICMP), Internet Group Message Protocol (IGMP), Routing Information Protocol (RIP), Address Resolution Protocol (ARP), Reverse Address Resolution Protocol (RARP), Exterior Gateway Protocol (EGP)
Network access	Ethernet, Global System for Mobile communications (GSM), Universal Mobile Telecommunication System (UMTS), Token-ring, Point-to-Point Protocol (PPP), Digital Subscriber Line (DSL)

Table 6.4. *Examples of Internet protocols*

Finally, hundreds of different protocols exist today. They can be grouped according to the domain, or layer treated. The Application layer allows different applications to communicate. The Transport layer manages how communications are routed from one point of the Internet to another. The Internet layer enables the addressing of communications. The network Access layer is required to connect to the Internet. While web services are surely the most used protocols, many others are necessary, in parallel, to date, to interconnect actors and applications evolving in distinct environment but contributing to the realization of shared processes.

6.4.3. Blockchain

The blockchain is a distributed information storage and transmission technology without a central supervision and control system [LEL 17]. When used, the blockchain is automatically enriched with new blocks. A distributed control system validates transactions and information, in already validated blocks and becomes impossible to modify. Each validated block is attached to the previous block chain; as the recorded transactions increase, the blockchain gets longer, hence the name blockchain.

The first uses of the blockchain were in the financial field and in particular for the creation of bitcoin, an electronic currency, whose creation rules are recorded in the bitcoin software's source code, which is public and its use distributed. The open source code makes it possible to know how money is created and therefore to know the existing and future money supply. Distributed operation prevents an individual or organization from changing the system in its favor. Bitcoin has demonstrated its competitiveness against banks and traditional money transfer services, such as MoneyGram.

Figure 6.8. *Western Union versus bitcoin. Author: unknown according to Coindesk, attribution: public domain*

If the price paid by the user is a few cents, the cost of the transaction to reward the various participants who ensure the global operation of the blockchain's distributed network for bitcoin, does not exceed 10 US$[1]. This cost is the reward to participants for validating a transaction in a block on the chain. In the case of bitcoin, the user does not pay this amount because the participants involved in validating transactions in the blocks of the chain are remunerated through the creation of new bitcoin currencies.

The functioning of blockchains is very interesting, in several other fields beyond its first field of application. For example, the state of Georgia uses blockchain to certify real estate titles. Artists publish their works and content via a blockchain for better management of copyright and distribution rights, and better compensation for creators.

This extension of blockchain application domains is part of a larger idea of a decentralized Web, which gave rise to the term Web3 or Web 3.0. This Web 3.0 succeeded Web 2.0, linked to the creation of content facilitated by electronic social networks. Web 3.0 is distinguished by its decentralization, in contrast to the successful centralization by Google, Amazon, Facebook, Apple and Microsoft (GAFAM). Web 3.0 also makes it possible to better manage the confidentiality and integrity of data and stakeholder authentication.

6.4.4. *Free software*

As we saw in Chapter 2, free software is software that can, technically and legally, be used, inspected, modified and disseminated via copies [STA 10]. These rights may simply be available if the software is in the public domain (such as the SQLite database management system), or if these rights are protected by a license that is itself governed by copyright law (like the GNU/Linux operating system). Free software is a cooperative alternative to proprietary software in that it promotes the freedoms to use, inspect, modify, copy and disseminate developed solutions.

Open source, i.e. making the software source code available, is a necessary condition for software to be regarded as free software, but open source is not in itself sufficient to make it free software. It is more a method of development through the reuse of the source code, than a piece of software itself. Free software is not necessarily free either, but only gives the right to use the software without monetary compensation. Software can be shared (shareware), but without giving the rights to read the source code and modify it. Finally, a lot of software does not agree to study the source code, modify it and copy and distribute it freely. These are called proprietary software [STA 10].

---

1 See: https://blockchain.info/charts/cost-per-transaction.

		Type			
		Free software	**Freeware**	**Shareware**	**Proprietary**
Rights	**Use**	Yes	Yes	Limited by license	Limited by license
	Inspection	Yes	No	No	No
	Editing	Yes	No	No	No
	Copying and dissemination	Yes	Yes	Yes	No

Table 6.5. *Differences in rights between the main types of licenses*

Intensified development of free and open-source software is both an indicator and a facilitator of this collaborative movement towards shared spaces, where stakeholders are less and less constrained by interoperability problems. Free software is now widespread within organizations, especially charities and government departments. Many government projects have in fact supported the development and distribution of free solutions, such as the compilation, by the government, of a catalog of free software used and recommended for French administrations.

Beyond software, hardware can also be "open", meaning that its design itself becomes freely accessible. You can then theoretically make it yourself, adapt it, modify it, improve it and redistribute it once improved. For example, the Open-Source Hardware (OSH) movement aims to make it easier for everyone to access the details of computer hardware design. In order to promote the manufacture of equipment, the manufacturing processes and the components chosen are standard and easily accessible.

One example of free software development is the "OpenMairie" (Open City Hall) project[2]. This project provides a suite of free software to support the shared development of territorial activities. The applications are developed according to the interoperability standards of ADULLACT (Association of Developers and Users of Free Software for Administrations and Local Authorities). The platform provides an IS covering all of the local activities[3] of a municipality such as administration and communication, nuisance reports, local associations, town plans, sanitation and elections.

Box 6.3. *OpenMairie*

---

2 See: http://www.openmairie.org/.
3 See: demo.openmairie.org/.

6.4.5. *Open data*

The CIS has certain limitations relating to the difficulty of protecting data and information in line with copyright – and more generally in line with intellectual property rights – because data are not considered to be original creations. IS managers therefore prefer not to disseminate them so as not to allow certain competitors to benefit from them. This inaccessibility of data can limit the dissemination of knowledge in society and our understanding of the reality around us, and impair the right of citizens to be informed.

However, the legal protection for databases was introduced in Europe through the Directive 96/9/CE of March 11, 1996, and was transposed into French legislation in the law of July 1, 1998. It is a sui generis protection of the investment that the owner of the database had to make in order to structure the database, fill it with content and make it externally presentable. Databases are thus protected for 15 years after their creation. Consequently, the author of the database may prohibit unauthorized extraction and/or reuse of the contents of a database that would be contrary to the legitimate economic interests of the author of the database. In practical terms, the data available on websites can be used on a one-off individual basis, but the extraction of all the data stored in the database feeding the website is not permissible. Similarly, an obligation to open up the data comes from the right to information. This right generally refers to freedom of access to public authority documents (Law No. 78-753 of July 17, 1978) and of the duty to inform the consumer about the nature of goods for sale (art. L 111-1 and L-221-1-2 of the Consumer Code).

Some administrative bodies have thus implemented an IS enabling access to data collected by public services and to information resulting from the processing of collected data (e.g. the French government through the www.data.gouv.fr website). In the private sector, some organizations have veered towards opening up their data (e.g. the company Uber via through the Uber Movement website). Even one of the world's four largest audit and consultancy firms, Deloitte, is inviting companies to open up their data to developers and to the public, because this creates opportunities for innovation [BRA 11]. Finally, many individuals share their data, such as those concerning the weather (via the Weather Underground website).

6.5. Exercise: AGK

The AGK Group was born out of the recent merger of two brands of interior furniture, one French and the other Swedish, with a consolidated company turnover of 1 billion euros. The "business" strategy has three major focuses:

– to acquire a "creative" image, follow the latest trends;

– to be attentive, responsive and "in tune" with the end consumer (not only distributors);

– to elevate the quality of service, both in terms of its production processes and in terms of sales support (rapid delivery, guarantees on furniture purchased, etc.).

The existing distribution model makes AGK too reliant on its distributors, both in the definition of its offers and in their presentation. The distributors mask consumers' reactions and prevent AGK from accessing market and competitor information. Restocking times are felt to be too long for the present day. Some distributors complain that this loses more than one sale in two from customers who are interested in the catalog offers, as they are put off by the timescales quoted. These delays are partly attributable to the factories' limited capacity, and partly to the scheduling process based on the forecasting data that is too often unreliable. Many sales are also lost due to sizes and colors not matching the living environment of interested customers.

AGK sees its operational processes evolving as follows. Distributors will no longer be treated as "resellers" (in the sense of furniture dealers), but as "exhibitors" paid commission on sales. New forms of collaboration can therefore be established, so as to optimize or even adjust the offer displayed in each location, depending on context and local appeal. New methods of promotion, based on a direct relationship with AGK, will be developed for the specifiers, who are interior designers and decorators. There are no plans to open an online sales channel for consumers, as they will continue to make their purchases from local distributors.

Despite the efforts made to overhaul an IS, finding information remains a nightmare. The introduction of a new ERP has had virtually no effect, because the information is still very much structured in a layout specific to each individual's view or understanding. It is said that you can only manage what you can measure; however, at AGK, when you have measured something, you no longer have time to manage it.

The company executive intends to drive the transformation of the group and a program that directly concerns the IS supporting distribution. The program that involves distribution aims to develop shared technical infrastructures to unify and protect the exchange infrastructures between all parties involved, both internal and external. A major business issue in this program is to open up the decision-making processes to partners through collaborative processes. Specifically, the establishment of an EDI with distributors is proposed. The growing power of the distribution chains' IS systematizes the use of the EDI as the quasi-exclusive mode of communication for logistics relationship and sales administration materials. Failure to comply with this constitutes a handicap that is reflected in the discount rates agreed upon. The estimated investment figure is 1.5 million euros, recoverable in two years.

Test your skills

1) What are the boundaries of the company's IS?

2) Does EDI technology seem to you to be the best solution to meet the company's needs and objectives?

3) Is the EDI aligned to the corporate strategy?

4) What value can be created by the EDI according to Porter's value chain?

5) What alternative or complementary IS could be considered?

6) What value could potentially be created by the alternative or complementary IS you are considering?

PART 3

Project Alignment

Introduction to Part 3

The third part of this work tackles an open-ended issue: the alignment of the IS and its projects on the general strategy of an extended organization. This is a constantly returning issue due to the strategic shifts the organization has to make in response to changes in the competitive environment and technological developments that make the solutions quickly obsolete, once implemented. While alignment is the responsibility of the strategist, it is nonetheless a day-to-day issue that must be under continual revision. To guide and direct this strategy, it is important to link the concepts of alignment and governance, on the one hand, and of alignment and urbanization, on the other hand.

In doing so, the strategic manager's main concern is to ensure that their choices are consistent with the operating procedures of the IS stakeholders, on the one hand, and the territorial occupation patterns, on the other hand. While the concern for alignment equates to organizational consistency in the dynamic context of project management, we could also say that it leads on to methods of managing change. For our part, we advance a continuous improvement model (proposed by Deming under the name of PlanDoCheckAct), which allows it to be put into operation. To further clarify our proposals, we will conclude this part with a case study that will explain the different parameters to be reconciled when considering this approach.

7

IS Project Management

THE FUNDAMENTALS.–

1) IS projects include formal governance mechanisms, based on defined processes and structures, and also informal mechanisms that emerge as a consequence of the organization's values and culture.

2) Agile development methodologies put the developer and the user at the center of the IS project.

3) DevOps, in an extension of software agility, enables links to be made between IS developments and the IS department.

7.1. Strategy of IS projects

The IS strategy sets objectives that are then defined by the modalities of IS governance. The strategy helps define how the IS should contribute to value creation for the company and clarifies the role of the various stakeholders.

The development of an IS represents significant investment that must be managed (projects, programs, transformations). Steering is an important aspect of governance, since its effectiveness contributes to achieving payback on the digital investment made.

The IS department's strategy can be centered around five axes.

7.1.1. *The strategic plan*

This is an integral element in the creation of the company's strategic plan and involves making the best use of staff and resources to respond to the main issues:

– ensuring the strategic alignment of the IS with the business strategy;

– delivering priority business needs;

– achieving and maintaining an exemplary level of service to customers and users;

– improving the overall performance of the IS to free up room for maneuver.

The strategic vision of the IS department is defined on a half-year basis by the CIO.

7.1.2. Business department's strategy

In a context where the IS department must continue to innovate while at the same time maintaining the quality of service of the IS, reducing its costs and development cycle duration, it is essential to have an effective departmental strategy that is appropriate to the business context. The IS department should adopt a business model that reflects its existing resources and anticipates changes in IT jobs and skills and in its strategy (make and/or buy). It must adapt its existing operations and provide training and support for the target activities and skills (cybersecurity, automation, etc.). Implementation of an outsourcing strategy can make it easier to adjust capacity to needs and to optimize the positioning of resources and internal expertise in strategic and/or sensitive areas.

7.1.3. Operational project governance

Within a mature IS department, IS management governance is organized around business function projects (finance, marketing, sales; each business department is represented). Carrying out an IS project equates to implementing an IS solution that is necessarily in response to a business function project. The key factors in good governance are:

– being able to liaise with departmental staff, towards achieving the project's major objectives: departmental commitments, planning and budget;

– ensuring that service quality is maintained throughout iterations and improves from the users' and operators' point of view;

– aligning projects with the long-term aspirations of renovation and urbanism;

– ensuring that project leaders have clear responsibilities and the associated levers.

To do this, operational governance uses three levers.

7.1.3.1. *Project decision-making mechanisms*

The ISM department bases its management on decision-making mechanisms appropriate to the various project stages, for example:

– validation of investment;

– validation of project milestones;

– validation of user needs.

7.1.3.2. *Performance management*

The meeting of commitments (deadlines, costs, quality of service, etc.) made by the IS department to departmental management is regularly monitored through KPIs reviewed by the ISM department. IS management and departmental dashboards are established with sequenced updates.

7.1.3.3. *The tools*

ISM stakeholders use tools to help them monitor the activities:

– end-to-end monitoring of business function projects;

– monitoring of IS activities;

– production of the various monitoring and management reports.

The use of best practices and project management tools (such as PERT or the GANTT chart) is recommended.

These tools assist with designing, scheduling and updating the management of complex projects by facilitating the visualization over time of the various project tasks.

7.1.4. **Budget management**

Managing the IS budget involves prioritizing projects with the departments. The economic relevance of projects is studied in terms of payback and is validated by investment committees. Business reviews at different levels are arranged to assist project managers.

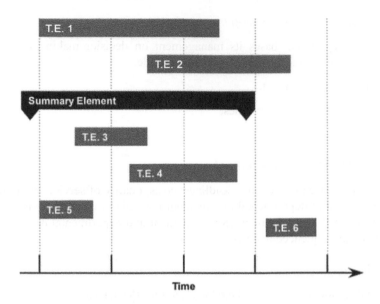

Time

Figure 7.1. *Example of a GANTT chart with units of time on the abscissa and the various tasks on the ordinate (T.E. = Terminal Element). For a color version of this figure, see www.iste.co.uk/alban/information2.zip*

7.1.5. *Quality system*

The quality system brings together all the information linked to quality management to the information management department. It includes all documents relating to the operations, procedures and methods deployed to achieve quality. It must be accessible to everyone and can draw upon best industry practices, such as CMMI for processes, ITIL for exploitation of IS's quality of service, PMBOK or PRINCE2 for IS project management or simply ISO 9001 covering the continuous improvement philosophy.

7.2. Roll-out of a traditional IS project

7.2.1. *Defining, researching and initializing the project*

It is necessary to clearly define need with the department, with the emphasis on simplicity. This definition phase should lead to identifying potential solution scenarios. These avenues will subsequently be refined and the various scenarios will be evaluated (comparison of costs, timescales, IS simplicity/complexity, compliance with application targets). Together with all the project stakeholders (business owner,

IS, department, etc.), area-specific tactics must be decided upon: the use of open source, quantifying license costs (at infrastructure and departmental levels), ad hoc market consultations or request for proposals (RFP), relationship with software companies (budgets, contracts, conflicts), outsourcing, etc.

By the end of the initialization phase, the IS project team will have explored every avenue and studied the various scenarios. A scoping meeting with management will lead to the project being given the "GO" or "NO GO". This meeting is an opportunity to validate project parameters (from additional features to the wider transformation program), costs and deadlines with all partners, and also the commitment made by all of those involved in the project.

Once the project manager gets the go-ahead from stakeholders, they prepare their project management plan, i.e. their project strategy (production model, test strategy, production strategy, roll-out strategy, etc.).

7.2.2. Developing and building the IS solution

By the end of this first phase of the study and maturation process, the project manager knows their parameters, the solution they have to build, the budget available, the associated deadlines and costs and the identified risks. They can now move on to the development of the solution. This is often the most substantial task in an IS project: whether V cycle or agile, development lies at the heart of projects. During this phase, the project will build the entire solution.

That includes:

– conceptualization (design of the solution, software architecture, features to be implemented, etc.);

– development;

– testing and debugging: end-to-end integration testing of the IS solution (functional, nonfunctional, technical, etc.) and also tests that are purely department-focused (business process, customer journey, etc.) and will be carried out by users and department staff;

– today, many technologies make it possible to support developers: automated tools to check the consistency, security and quality of code, integrated production chains to facilitate updating, maintenance and use of code or the use of AI in the form of machine learning technology that can help write code by providing suggestions and examples of based on pre-trained models. AI can help reduce the time it takes to write code by providing reusable examples and code snippets. It can also help find solutions to common problems and reduce code errors by working as a spell checker in the embedded development interface.

7.2.3. Management and roll-out of the IS solution

It is good project management practice to carry out a pilot (i.e. a small-scale roll-out) on a selected website (often a sample of customers or users).

To test and improve the reliability of the IS solution, it is also possible to do a beta-launch. This means that it is implemented on a real website, but one that is isolated from downstream operations (its product flows and data are not used by the rest of the IS). This is often reserved for the first iteration of a new application or a major change in technical architecture and requires the old version to be kept in operation. Its purpose is to validate database initialization (configuration, data recovery, etc.), check the new functionalities and verify non-regression by checking consistency with results from the old version. For example, for the launch of a new invoicing application (or for a new version in preproduction and an old version in production), the reliability of the new invoicing application can be checked against the old version by comparing the results given.

At the end of all of these tests, a governance committee gives the go-ahead for market launch or dissemination of the solution to all users. The collective project is ready to be rolled out in phases or as a one-shot roll-out. What has to be done next is to fully deploy the IS solution and prepare the teams who will use and maintain the solution, as well as the teams that will handle user support.

7.2.4. Project assessment

Project assessments are a good practice of project management that show whether or not the project objectives have been achieved and enable learning from the difficulties encountered by the project teams. Attention is paid to whether the objectives were met:

– in project implementation (meeting schedule, deadlines, scope);

– after product launch (meeting financial and quality targets).

This ensures formal debriefing with the department and the IS on the success or failure of the business function project. It is the most effective way to capitalize on feedback from the experience (good practice, problem resolution, difficulties encountered, etc.). A review of these project assessments can identify areas for improvement to be taken into account in project management, both on the IS side and on the department's side. It also enables an evaluation of the successful achievement of the project's objectives especially at the level of a complete unit, such as at the departmental management level.

7.3. Agile IS projects: a development methodology, a process and a philosophy

The term "agile" can sometimes be a source of confusion, because it is often associated with the notion of speed, whereas what is being sought is, rather, flexibility, the ability to accept change during the development process.

For this, a short development phase is adopted to frequently deliver new, stable versions of the application. These frequent deliveries allow feedback from the department to be collected rapidly in order to adjust the application in line with project commitments. Equally, the way the team operates is reviewed at the end of each phase to make improvements in the next phase. It is, simultaneously, a methodology (a different way of carrying out developments), a process (redesigning hierarchical structures: developers have autonomy to estimate the timescale for implementing the features, are directly in contact with the business department, etc.) and a philosophy (restoring power to the "software craftsmen").

Let us take a look at the fundamentals of agility to see and understand the agile movement's key messages.

In 2001 in the United States, 17 software development experts held a meeting. These 17 imaginative, creative experts in development, inventors of development methods and exceptionally talented developers had complementary skillsets. They shared the same values, which they set out under their "Agile Manifesto", consisting of four core values and 12 core principles [AUB 13].

For [BEC 01], the agile philosophy promotes:

– "individuals and interactions over processes and tools;

– working software over comprehensive documentation;

– customer collaboration over contract negotiation;

– responding to change over following a plan".

The Agile Manifesto is underpinned by core principals [BEC 01]:

"Our main priority is to satisfy customers through early and continuous delivery of valuable work.

Welcome changing requirements, even late in a project. Agile processes harness change to strengthen the customer's competitive advantage.

Deliver frequent operational solutions, at intervals ranging from a few weeks to a few months, with a preference for shorter time scales.

The department or business managers and the people in charge of implementation must work together on a daily basis throughout the project.

Use motivated people to build projects. Provide them with the environment and support they need and trust them to get the job done.

Face-to-face discussion is the most effective and most economic way to give information to a production team and to exchange information within the team.

The availability of operational solutions is the main measure of progress.

Agile processes promote adherence to a sustainable pace for completed work. Specifiers, developers and users should be able to maintain a constant pace indefinitely.

Paying continuous attention to technical excellence and the quality of the design enhances agility.

Simplicity – the art of maximizing the amount of work not done – is essential.

The best architectures, the best specifications of needs and the best designs emerge from self-organized teams.

The team reflects at regular intervals on how to become more effective, then tunes and adjusts its behavior accordingly".

The agile movement's objectives are:

– to deliver the right business application, one that will make the business process more efficient;

– to rationalize IS costs by delivering the simplest IS solutions that will be 100% used by the business;

– to speed up initial deployment of a part of the application.

Box 7.1. *The agile manifesto*

7.3.1. *An empirical, iterative, incremental approach*

As shown in Figure 7.2, developments in agile mode are organized in sprints. Sprints are short iterations that tend to last between two and four weeks. Each sprint takes on board users' stories (functional requirements) which are specified, conceived, implemented and tested (SCIT) during these four weeks. Between each sprint, new ideas, originating from discussions with the business departments, may emerge.

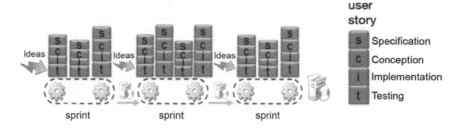

Figure 7.2. *Development in agile sprints, each containing the ingredients of a user need (specification, conception, implementation, testing)*

A sprint is a small, simple, clearly identifiable objective on which a commitment can be made, and at the end of which an operational increment of the product is delivered. Each increment of a sprint is completely finished such that it will not be revisited and can potentially be put into production. The product is permanently under test to ensure non-regression. Figure 7.3 shows a monitoring indicator in agile methodology: the business value of the developed product. Between two sprints, it is possible to adjust the functional scope and/or the functioning of the team to bring more value for the department (a more user-friendly product, meeting its needs in the most effective way). Development can potentially be halted at the end of a sprint, if the delivered product meets user expectations and generates sufficient ROI (return on investment).

Figure 7.4 shows the burn-up chart. This indicator helps focus each sprint's development efforts on achieving the business objectives. The challenge is to not spoil the development team's productivity and to optimize development cycles in order to deliver at the end of each sprint. The objective is to meet user need with a minimum of time and development effort (in a lean approach – see the exercise in Chapter 3: GreenNRJ).

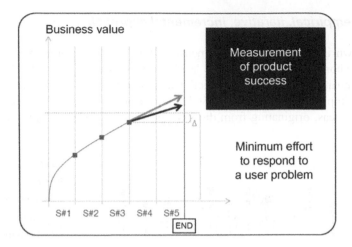

Figure 7.3. *Sprint objectives and measurement*

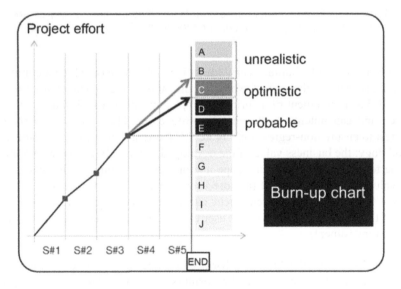

Figure 7.4. *Burn-up chart and measurement of sprint effort. For a color version of this figure, see www.iste.co.uk/alban/information2.zip*

7.3.2. *The conditions of success of agile projects*

Agile projects fail first due to human resources (where resource allocations are insufficient), poor communication between stakeholders and the corporate culture (through resistance to change and lack of support from management). The impacts of transition should not be underestimated nor should agile projects be created for the wrong reasons. Agile is often misunderstood: it is not a way to produce IS projects for less money and with no documentation or quality! The agile philosophy is disruptive. Developers have the power, are more independent and speak directly to business departments and users. This involves organizational and cultural change that will not suit every organization.

Before embarking on an application of an agile methodology, it is essential to first check the conditions of success for agility. These checks should be carried out jointly with the department/project owner: what are the business department's criteria for the success of the application? How will the department be able to say that the application is a success? How will it be able to say that during development? What are the acceptance thresholds? What is the first user problem that should be addressed? How will each iteration deliver a part of the application that is coherent from the department's point of view? What are the business department's criteria for the success of that iteration? How will end-users be engaged in the process of feeding back from the field on the iteration? With the business department/project owner, how will change be managed during development? How will feedback received be prioritized and integrated – while at the same time complying with the constraints defined at the start of the project?

Once the conditions for agile success have been shared and agreed with the department, the choice of agile methodology is made while taking into account the project context and the various stakeholders. Agile methods are intentionally minimalist so as to be potentially applicable to any context. All methods prioritize the empirical, iterative approach to software development, seeking feedback at the earliest opportunity and adapting the software accordingly. The idea is to add what is needed in the context to make the project a success.

End of iteration demonstrations can be replaced by demonstrations carried out as and when features are embedded in the iteration. This is an opportunity to get instant feedback from the departmental representative/project owner in order to quickly adjust development. The project team can suggest practical work at the end of each iteration in a dedicated environment. This is an opportunity to get real feedback from end-users as a result of a concrete hands-on experience of the application. The key to success is still to obtain feedback as early as possible.

7.4. DevOps: making the link between IS developments and IS department procedures

A company's IT department consists, on the one hand, of development units, whose mission is to create new functionalities and, on the other hand, of operational services, which are guarantors of system stability. Where the problem lies is that inevitably, while the development units are fine-tuning another new feature, the various phases of handover, delivery and roll-out generate instabilities. Thus, these two services find themselves each with conflicting missions, and the meeting of these two worlds can very easily become a source of conflict.

The DevOps philosophy (DevOps being a contraction of "development" and "operations") is an extension of the agile logic. Agile methodologies focus on the developers and business departments. But what about ICT procedures such as infrastructure management, bringing into production, implementation, software and hardware updates, changes, etc.? IT processes are often not a priority within the company. However, infrastructure-related incidents are extremely costly to companies and can cause severe disruption. AliYun, a subsidiary of the Chinese giant Ali Baba, paid the price in 2015, losing $12 million after one day's downtime at its Hong Kong data center. A lack of information on IT procedures and lack of business culture is too often the cause of costly mistakes, incidents and communication problems between developers and the IS project and between operators and IS teams responsible for system maintenance.

DevOps is an emerging movement within the profession, aimed at infrastructure maintenance and operation teams, and it seeks to strengthen collaborative working with business departments, users and the development team, based on quick iterations that systematically incorporate improvements to the production environment and the ICT infrastructure.

Amazon's motto "You build it, you run it" is particularly representative of this philosophy. It focuses on integrating development units and operational services, facilitating the exchange of skills, task automation and the collaborative culture.

DevOps:

– responds to the quickening demand for quality software products and services;

– recognizes the interdependence of the IS management functions;

– recognizes the need to change the culture and vision of IS management operations;

– supports and leverages agile methodologies and digital services management;

– encourages the use of automation.

The DevOps movement is based on four core pillars: culture, automation, measurement and sharing. The movement promotes a common culture between developers and operational maintenance and exploitation staff, through integrated teams and via agility. Automation is envisaged through continuous integration, automated testing and continuous delivery. Measurement encourages the collection of technical and departmental performance indicators, proactive detection of incidents and anticipation in order to better keep within budget, deadline and scope. Finally, the pillar of sharing underlines the importance of multi-disciplinary, business-focused collaborations.

DevOps offers major advantages such as speeding up production cycles, reducing delivery costs and errors and at the same time increasing the IS's reliability and the quality of service. IS management is based on agile projects, and DevOps is totally focused on business objectives and department needs.

Increasingly, organizations are adopting this new model to streamline the development process by combining several phases into a single automated process – which is the very essence of this approach. The major change is that all IT teams must work together from the outset in order to reduce product launch time. Whereas security used to be isolated and often put at the end of a project to verify the absence of risk before bringing to market, these days, the DevOps approach will integrate it from the start.

The idea that safety has no place within a DevOps team is a fallacy. The team must work to ensure that security is carefully applied throughout product and project development. However, DevOps team members must realize that they are not security experts. The environments in which these teams work are constantly changing. Each month, dozens of new services and applications are designed. The IS department must be able to support teams by making good security solutions available to them that will help them to control compliance with good practice. Among the action proposals, the first is to above all facilitate communication between DevOps and the security team. DevOps teams are a boon for security teams, who can implement their security policy from the beginning of the project. Everyone's place must be defined in order to be sure that the action plan will be followed while making use of the appropriate indicators. By providing comprehensive reports upstream, the team's task will be made easier.

In a complementary fashion, the DevOps teams should not overlook the important role of the security experts. Most DevOps team members are not security experts. It would be irresponsible on the company's part to reduce its security team under the single pretext that it is hiring DevOps teams, especially with the increasing numbers of vulnerabilities (more than 28 new vulnerabilities each day on average in 2016). This complementarity is needed so that everyone can raise their skill levels. A constant for DevOps teams is automation. This is also advantageous for security.

DevOps teams promote the technologies of the Cloud, containers and Big Data for their needs in automation and flexibility. They must therefore integrate a continuous monitoring solution so that they can continue to enjoy the benefits of automation. Throughout the project, DevOps teams and security teams will be able to analyze the test environment to address its weaknesses. The DevOps philosophy also calls for implementation of tailored security solutions. The speed of deployment brings the risk of bad configurations that hackers will exploit. DevOps teams, like the security team, must ensure that good security practices are enforced. To do this, it is recommended that market standards should be leveraged to reduce their risk level as far as possible.

Finally, communication with the CIO must not be forgotten. DevOps must be able to provide comprehensible indicators not only on the progress of their projects but also on the level of security of the services they are using. They are an integral part of the company and must be understood by management in order to successfully complete their mission.

The principles of agility and DevOps subsequently spread to other areas. FinOps, for example, is a term that was created to designate a set of practices to manage and optimize the costs of IT systems and cloud services. It includes strategies to monitor and control costs, identify possible optimizations and drive improvement initiatives. FinOps practices can be applied to any IT organization, regardless of the cloud service provider used.

Box 7.2. *What place does security occupy in the DevOps culture?*

7.5. Security in IS projects

Security in projects relies on implementing good practices throughout the life cycle of the IS solution. Implementation of security starts at the beginning of the project when the IS is studying the department's needs, with the risk assessment and the risk analysis. It continues with the design and development phase, through designing security features, secure development and testing. Then, it carries on with the deployment and the life of the solution, which require monitoring and updates.

7.5.1. *Risk parameter assessment*

This assessment is conducted on the basis of the data and functions contained in the IS solution, for example, if the IS solution is accessible to surfers, or if it contains business-sensitive data such as company know-how, intellectual property, personal data, bank card information, financial data, direct debit mandate data or competition-related data, etc.

To protect data, the following criteria must be observed: authenticity, availability, integrity, privacy and traceability.

Authenticity is the property of a user being identified with certainty by the IS, especially for the management of a permissions service.

Availability is the property of elements being accessible to authorized users when required. These elements can be functions or information. The availability of a function ensures the continuity of processing services and the absence of problems related to response times in the wider sense. The availability of information ensures access to data and the fact that information cannot be totally lost as long as an archived version of the information exists.

Integrity is the property of elements being accurate and complete. If the element is a function, then integrity ensures compliant processing in accordance with specifications and the absence of incorrect or incomplete results from the function. If the element is information, integrity ensures the accuracy of the totality of the data from the point of view of errors in manipulation or unauthorized uses and the non-alteration of information.

Confidentiality is the property of elements being accessible only to authorized users. Confidentiality of a function involves (a) protection of management rules and results (the disclosure of which to an unauthorized third party would be prejudicial) and (b) the absence of disclosure of any processing or mechanism of a confidential nature. Confidentiality of information involves (a) protection of data, access to which or use of which by an unauthorized third party would be prejudicial and (b) the absence of disclosure of data of a confidential nature.

Traceability is the property of logging and identifying access to elements, again whether function or information. For a function, traceability ensures visibility of use and prevents modification of a process (or mechanism) and the absence of unregistered or unidentified use of a process. For information, traceability ensures historical logging of changes and guarantees that the information has not been modified or accessed by unauthorized users.

Box 7.3. *Data protection criteria*

7.5.2. Risk analysis

When conducting a risk analysis, project managers should identify the essential items to be protected, list threat scenarios, assess their likelihood/probability and identify and quantify the risks by combining the probability of the threat and severity of the impact. Based on risks listed on a probability/impact matrix, projects can take informed risks and avoid or refuse risk. Thus, by not doing the project or by doing it differently, we can transfer the risk to a third party via an insurance policy or a contract. Security objectives can also be defined through measures to be implemented at the design stage. The IS project manager assesses the cost of security measures and has the solution approved by the department in the same way as they have risk cover approved at the level of decision-making defined by the project governance.

SolutionSI system contains employee pay data. These data require high confidentiality: the disclosure of employee pay data has a critical impact, because it would be a breach of personal data protection. As per the European standards established in Regulation (EU) 2016/679 of the European Parliament and of the Council of April 27, 2016, noncompliance can cost up to 4% of the company's global turnover.

Threat scenario: an external tester discloses wage information from data used in test sets. This scenario is classified as "probable". The impact is critical for the company. Since the test sets are identical to the production data, the attack is not very complex for one to perform, the external tester who naturally has access to these test data. The combination of probability and criticality categorizes this risk as high risk.

Recommendation: probability can be reduced by making the service provider aware and informing them of the risks in the event of data disclosure, leveraging the terms of the agreements or contracts signed with the service provider. The impacts can also be moderated by anonymizing the test data. Once security risks have been identified and security measures put in place for major risks, the project must have the residual risks validated by functional specialists.

Box 7.4. *Example of risk analysis*

7.5.3. *Security in development*

IS project managers must identify the security requirements to be put in place. Requirements may be of a technical nature, such as the implementation of firewalls, the protection of physical access to the infrastructure and buildings, traceability of activity on production data, regular anti-virus updates or setting up real-time 24/7 supervision on sensitive applications to detect early symptoms of intrusion and take appropriate action (Security Operations Center).

Requirements can be of the application type, in the form of carrying out checks on the integrity of financial flows and stream or data encryption or development to protect against the most common cyberattacks. The organizational aspects are also important. Requirements of an organizational nature include password policy and permission management and the anonymization of production database copies used for testing.

Industry best practice recommends the use of development standards such as the Open Web Application Security Project (OWASP) or the recommendations of the SANS Institute and Common Weakness Enumeration (SANS/CWE). Development teams should be given training on these standards, and where development is outsourced, the standards should be passed on to the service provider and their integration made a prerequisite.

To develop secure code, i.e. code that has no security vulnerabilities, the use of code verification tools is recommended. Static analysis tools can analyze the code statically at the time of writing, and other tools can analyze it dynamically by analyzing the software in operation. Code reviews can also be implemented. Although these are usually more expensive than using tools, they very often prove more effective.

Before going into production for the first time, it is important to test what the developers have implemented. A security audit with intrusion tests will detect potential security flaws. If the flaws are too major, the projects committee may call a halt and declare the IS solution's implementation "NO GO".

7.5.4. Security for putting into production and deployment: towards a permanent watch

Before going live, projects make sure that production activity is safe. This involves the following practices: making secure the procedures for going live and reversal, backups, process planning, setting up technical support channels, operating instructions, disaster recovery plan (DRP), supervision, including security supervision, audit of components and configuration management in production, compliance of infrastructure components with security policy, etc. Throughout the application's lifecycle, it is the IS's job to monitor and anticipate the emergence of new vulnerabilities.

The first version of SolutionSI enables the company's customers to connect online to view their bills. Going live on the Internet raises all intrusion threats linked to online apps, but the impact of an intrusion remains minimal (what would anyone do with their neighbor's bill?) The company has implemented a weak authentication solution based on the customer's phone number and the total of their latest invoice.

In the new version of the application, the developers are introducing an order function. The risk management teams are carrying out the risk analysis, which highlights the fact that the impact on the customer of an intrusion becomes much more critical. The project manager decides to implement secure development; planning a security audit and reinforcing authentication solution with password management.

When the business department wants to further develop an IS project, such as adding features, it is the CIO's duty to act as "consultant" and to clarify the risks and the security of the projects. New problems can emerge, making it necessary to put in place incident and crisis management procedures; also, a process to monitor vulnerabilities and new threats. Security reviews of the solution are essential and are a particularly important best practice. Internal meetings and meetings with service providers are an opportunity to discuss security, set up common action plans if necessary and monitor indicators to be fed back to management, such as the number of security incidents, number of vulnerabilities detected and resolved, etc.

Box 7.5. *Example of risk monitoring and follow-up*

7.6. Exercise: cybersecurity in projects, managing tomorrow's threats

Sixty percent of digital businesses will suffer major service disruptions in the years to come due to the inability of IT teams to manage cyber threats. Gartner proposes five tips for successful future-proofing.

Improve leadership and governance

"Improving leadership and governance is probably more important than developing tools and technology skills" in dealing with cybersecurity issues. "The decision-making process, prioritization, budget allocation, measuring, reporting, transparency and accountability are key attributes of an effective program that balances the need to protect and the need to manage the business" [POT 16].

Adapt to developing threats

Information systems security officers (ISSOs) must see past the notion of preventing all threats. It is difficult to accept, but perfect protection is not achievable. Gartner anticipates that 60% of the cybersecurity budgets of companies will be earmarked for early threat detection by 2020 [PRO 16]. This was less than 30% in 2016. "Organizations must detect and respond to malicious behavior and incidents because even the best preventive controls cannot prevent all incidents" [PRO 16].

Align cybersecurity with business speed

Businesses that go digital have a faster pace of development and R&D than traditional businesses. Therefore, following this logic, traditional security no longer works. ISSOs must evaluate and transform their programs to become facilitators of digital transformation, rather than obstacles to innovation.

Search for new contours of cybersecurity

Earlier, it was perhaps easier to protect data: it resided exclusively in data centers. New technologies bring an overflow of data which is now on the outside, via cloud computing and mobility, for example. In 2018, 25% of corporate data traffic will directly come from mobile to cloud computing, bypassing the company's security controls [POT 16]. "Organizations must now respond to cybersecurity and risk issues on technology and items that they no longer own or control" [PRO 16].

Initiating change in processes and culture

With the acceleration triggered by digitization and the power that technology gives to individuals, it is necessary to change the behavior and commitment of employees and customers. Cybersecurity must meet people's needs through changes in processes. A people-centric cybersecurity strategy, centered on individuals, gives each person greater autonomy in using data and digital devices.

Test your skills

1) How can security leadership be improved? What organizational, managerial and hierarchical measures would you, as CEO, put in place to facilitate security governance?

2) Is security compatible with the speed of a project developed using agile methodology? Compare the values upheld by the agile movement with the objectives of cybersecurity and highlight the similarities and the potential conflicts.

3) What new risks are posed by bring your own device and the use of mobile and cloud computing? What are the advantages of the Cloud for DevOps projects?

8

Technology, Alignment and Strategic Transformation

THE FUNDAMENTALS.–

1) The alignment of stakeholders, territories and projects is based on a co-construction between the business and IT.

2) The IS and technology create new business opportunities and play a central role in the business's value chain.

3) A strategic transformation program may be necessary to align the IS and the business.

What is a business strategy? This question could provide sufficient material for an entire MBA course. For the purposes of this chapter, we will summarize our answer in few sentences. A business strategy is a vision, a strategic intent [CAM 91]. This includes the long-term objectives, the policies and the resource allocations necessary to achieve the strategic intent [HAM 90]. The much more operational question that follows the strategic vision question is often: how do I compete with my competitors and exceed them in my markets? How can the top management implement the strategic transformation necessary to attain the strategic objectives and achieve the strategic intent?

First, we will describe the alignment between business strategy and IS strategy. Next, we will focus on the contribution of the IS and new technologies to the strategy and the IS's transformative contribution both to operational excellence and to new business opportunities. Finally, we will list the characteristics of a strategic transformation linked to the IS and new technologies.

8.1. The alignment of stakeholders, territories and projects

At the beginning of this book, we saw that an organizational IS is mapped like a group of stakeholders (firms and their agents, upstream, downstream and lateral partners and end customers), territories (the extended business) and projects (cooperation agreements, partnerships, e-business and e-commerce). Organizational management focuses on these three aspects. It is about the system to be instrumentalized by the CIO. We could say that this is what is "given" to the CIO, the strategy implemented in the Mintzberg sense at a time *t*, the system to be aligned [MIN 94].

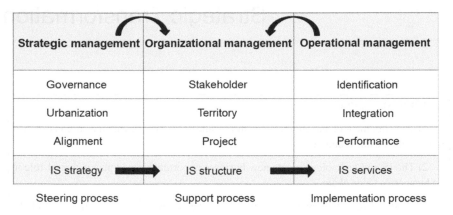

Strategic management	Organizational management	Operational management
Governance	Stakeholder	Identification
Urbanization	Territory	Integration
Alignment	Project	Performance
IS strategy	IS structure	IS services
Steering process	Support process	Implementation process

Figure 8.1. *Alignment of the systems and processes of organizational management [ALB 12]*

As shown in Figure 8.1, organizational IS management is framed by two processes: a steering process for strategic management and an implementation process for operational management. The structure is a result of the strategy and enables delivery of IS services, at the right time and to the right person, to a customer for whom it leads to value creation.

Operational management of the IS involves identification of the stakeholders (including the "CIO" stakeholder), territorial integration and project performance. As for the IS strategic management process, this focuses on stakeholder governance, territorial urbanization and project alignment. Apart from the vertical analysis in Figure 8.1, as summarized above, studying this table gives a grasp of the role of the decision-making system, IS and operation system within IS management. In short, in this context, "decision-making" involves governing and identifying the

IS stakeholders in order to co-define their informational needs. "Informing" involves urbanizing and integrating IS territories so as to meet the co-defined needs. "Operating" relates to aligning and performing IS projects to create value.

8.2. Strategic alignment

The theme of strategic adjustment is a relatively new concept in management sciences. The theoretical referential that quickly became dominant is that of the Strategic Alignment Model (SAM) [HEN 93]. This model establishes correlations between business strategy, ICT strategy, organizational and management processes and ICT infrastructure. Alignment is reckoned to happen on two levels: the external level, creating the strategic "fit", involves making the organization's strategic activities consistent with its choices of technology deployment and the internal level harmonizes the organizational processes with the ICT infrastructure. The SAM-type strategic alignment model is based on its co-construction with the organizational and operational model.

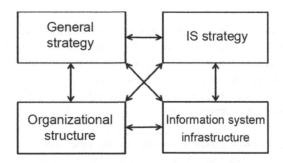

Figure 8.2. *Co-construction between the organizational and operational models*

In doing this, the SAM model suggests a certain number of deployment pathways for strategic alignment in an organization. The general strategy can thus lead to a change in the internal organizational structures, which brings with it a reorganization of the IS infrastructure. It is also conceivable that a new IS strategy would validate the implementation of a new IS infrastructure which will have an impact on the organization's structural models. These top-down visions of strategic alignment have been supplemented by bottom-up approaches. In all cases, the four-area model has positioned itself as a tool for the understanding and deployment of a strategic alignment process.

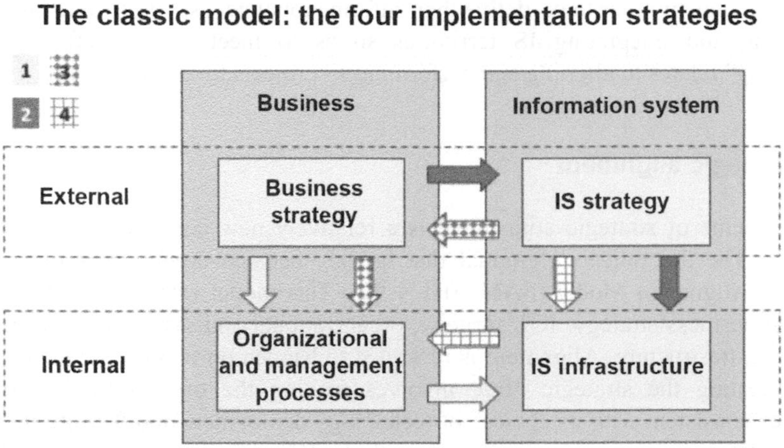

The classic model: the four implementation strategies

Figure 8.3. *Methods of implementing the alignment. For a color version of this figure, see www.iste.co.uk/alban/information2.zip*

Depending on the case, business strategy is conceived as the driver of IS strategy (case 1) or of IS operations (case 2), in the fairly classic hierarchical top-down perspective. In other cases, it is the IS which enables the redefinition of managerial operations (case 4) or indeed a corporate strategy (case 3). With new trends in technology, such as the use of chatbots and artificial intelligence, the IS is increasingly emerging as a driver of business strategy and operations.

The systemic approach makes it possible among other things to recognize, in IS management, both a management system and a system to be managed. From this dual nature, we can deduce another method of approach to strategic alignment.

Alban [ALB 12] came up with the idea of using the continuous improvement loop along with the type Plan Do Check Act (PDCA) by offering the IS manager a more dynamic model consisting of a mapping of the system to be managed, the IS (which implements the *Do*), and a three-stage management system consisting of a steering system (*Plan*), a monitoring system (*Check*) and a continuous improvement system (*Act*)

The steering system is the first level of the management system and provides strategic, organizational and operational management of the IS with a view to creating value for the organization.

Value creation is measured both in the long term, by strategic alignment and effectiveness, and in the short term, by operational performance and efficiency. Accordingly, it can be seen that within this framework, the CIO sets out a blueprint and an action plan. This is a guarantee of development of the system to be managed and is a tool that can be used to analyze disparities between expectations and achievements.

The monitoring system can be seen as the second level of the management system offered to the CIO. At this level, the IS audit plays a vital role. Benchmarks can be leveraged to ensure regulatory compliance and performance of strategic and operational management compared to good practices and other standards. The use of benchmarks will determine the corrective items, thus opening up the potential for improvement over time.

The continuous improvement system is the third stage and the last level of management system we are offering to the CIO stakeholder. This involves activating the feedback loop and making the CIO aware of the elements for evaluation and improvement across the entire management process.

Box 8.1. *A dynamic model of strategic alignment*

8.3. Competition, technological revolutions and new strategies

The business objective is to create value and to generate a competitive advantage via this value on the market. Porter [POR 85] describes three different strategy typologies that can be implemented in relation to competitors in a given market:

– operational excellence that suggests being a price leader;

– differentiation that implies being a product leader;

– a focus that enables maximum proximity to a market segment or a certain type of customer in order to offer the best value.

For Porter, ICT lies at the heart of each of these three strategies. In fact, the IS can bring the operational efficiency necessary for a price-oriented strategy. Think, for instance, of the use of RFID chips to facilitate the daily deliveries of thousands of containers or the use of drones to deliver packages, as proposed by Amazon.

The IS can also provide the keys to a better strategic focus. Through business intelligence tools and an analysis of Big Data, a travel company may, for example, aggregate airline flight information, data provided by tourist offices on tourists' country of origin, places visited and destination and mobile geolocalization data. Using that, it can put out targeted packages with high added value for these tourists in the form of special offers on local excursions or recommendations for tours and shopping.

Finally, the IS can also be at the heart of differentiation, by bringing a unique value to the business strategy and turning this into a strategic advantage. This is the case, for example, for Netflix, which, thanks to a powerful artificial intelligence (AI) engine and a gigantic database of usage data, manages to provide its users with extremely well-tailored and accurate recommendations on future series they may enjoy.

D'Aveni suggests an alternative vision of competitive advantage, more in line with current turbulent, dynamic, open organizational contexts, the explosion of new business models and technologies [DAV 10]. D'Aveni does not believe it is possible to maintain a competitive advantage in the context of new markets or dynamic industries.

Technology is not necessarily standardized. Therefore, there are not necessarily any rules and the company can use these technologies to achieve a temporary strategic advantage. Think, for instance, of the use of the "Internet of Things" (IoT), which is waging a standardization war and which has not yet been regulated.

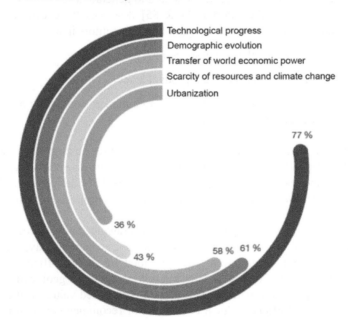

Figure 8.4. Survey of directors [PRI 16]: CEOs feel that technology is the factor that will have the greatest impact on their business in the future. For a color version of this figure, see www.iste.co.uk/alban/information2.zip

In this context, investment in the IoT is still very risky, because there is no clear visibility as to which technology will become standard between Long Range (LoRa) Sigfox or Long-Term Evolution for Machines (LTE-M). An equally uncertain situation exists in terms of robots, physical for industry and virtual for services (such as chatbots). Regulators and opinionists are showing an interest in robots. In an interview published on February 16, 2017, even Microsoft's founder, Bill Gates felt that "a robot that destroys a job should be taxed", in order to finance social policies [COM 17]. Companies that use robots are using this technology pending the lawmakers' decision. Similarly, some shops in France have started to accept bitcoin in spite of legislative uncertainty.

D'Aveni's proposal is pertinent. Indeed, these new technologies and market disruptions (fed by ISs) allow only temporary competitive advantages to be built.

---

1) Artificial intelligence

Artificial intelligence (AI) has long since left the domain of science fiction to facilitate, accelerate and indeed take over tasks formerly done by humans. Nowadays, algorithms are capable of taking our places in activities as varied as they are specialized: decision-making, translation, voice and visual recognition, etc. AI is what is called an "umbrella" concept; in other words, it encompasses a great variety of subcategories. AI is by its nature constantly "learning", and thus, increasing in power and competency. Machine learning techniques are being used more and more by companies today, such as deep learning (a machine learning technique based on the neural network model: tens or even hundreds of layers of neurons are stacked to bring greater complexity to the establishment of rules).

2) Robotization: drones and robots

"The introduction of robots liberates man from tasks with low added value or conversely augments his activities" [PRI 16]. Robots, whether electromechanical or virtual agents, are becoming increasingly powerful and autonomous. While the myth of the robot as destroyer of jobs may still be very much alive in some minds, the inclusion of robots in the value chain of the business should be seen in perspective.

Drones are air or water robots, autonomous or controlled. They are causing disruption in all business sectors, from agriculture to the film industry, including insurance and transport. Today, the global market is estimated at more than $127 billion [PRI 16].

3) The Internet of Things

The Internet of Things, or IoT, is the term used for any "connected" device that is accessible via a network connection. These new tools are potential levers for generating data and thus playing a significant role in value creation for a business. We find them in all business sectors: industry, agriculture, leisure, automobile, etc.

4) Blockchain

Blockchain enables the storage and transmission of information with total transparency and security. It is a technology that first revolutionized banking transactions and which is expected to open up many opportunities for most business sectors.

5) Augmented reality (AR) and virtual reality (VR)

AR is designed to augment the quality of the user experience of a service or product in a confined space. This augmentation of reality is made possible through so-called "auxiliary" devices that allow information or visual effects to be added through the overlaying of images and/or sounds. Whether on packaging, on physical advertising material, in retail or even in architecture, augmented reality is a way of enhancing the user experience.

Unlike augmented reality, VR can find its place in any space on the one condition that it has been predefined. It is a computer simulation of a three-dimensional image or a complete environment, most often involving the use of a helmet. Concrete applications have already been developed in many areas such as health, property and aeronautics.

6) 3D printing

3D printing seems to be limitless, since after plastic and metal, it is now possible to print on glass and even wood! The principle of this machine is based on this simple concept: start from digital models and print them using successive layers of material.

7) Quantum computing

Quantum computing is based on the principles of quantum mechanics to enable computer processes to process data at much higher speeds and accuracy than conventional computers. Quantum computers are able to handle complex tasks faster and more efficiently and can be used to solve problems that are too complex for classical computers (e.g. "breaking" a military encryption algorithm or achieving in seconds calculations that would take decades for a conventional computer).

Through these new ICTs, the IS will be a driver of business strategy. The IS could create new business opportunities by, for instance, introducing AI into tourism, or virtual reality into a video game publisher. The IS would be in a position to rewrite the customer relationship (sales interaction, support and after-sales service) with virtual robots used as a sales force and supplied with customer data, linked to a machine learning engine. The IS would have the potential to enhance operational excellence, as Amazon does with its deliveries by drone. The IS would destroy jobs, but it would create new jobs and would require new talents, such as cognitive science experts to feed an AI engine and "robot management" experts. Finally, new regulatory frameworks are awaited for many technologies, such as, for example, artificial intelligence, robots, drones, blockchain and bitcoin.

Integration of these new technologies within an existing business model will not be achieved without major changes to existing processes. How can this type of transformation be managed?

Box 8.2. *Technology trends in 2030,*
by Pricewaterhouse Coopers [PRI 16]

8.4. Strategic transformation linked to ISs and new technologies

A new strategic intent can lead the company to opt for a radically different organization or to completely transform its IS. For example, the use of connected drones to effect deliveries will impact stakeholders, territories and business projects. Similarly, the use of a large integrated software package within a multinational (including orders, deliveries and invoicing) with robots (tasked with taking simple orders and replacing the myriad local systems) will have major consequences for the whole of the business. These are not minor projects. Strategic transformations are involved. These transformations alter the heart of an organization, its deep structure and its critical processes, often in a radical and abrupt manner. The transformation process is risky and uncertain.

There are several aspects to strategic transformation. Planning theories highlight the role of the Top Management Team (TMT) in steering the transformation along the predetermined steps and managing the change. Conversely, for emergence theorists, the strategy depends not on planning and maintaining objectives, but rather on developing priorities as they emerge over time. Change is seen as uncertain and unpredictable. The environment is chaotic and dynamic, making any planning difficult and requiring improvisation of new strategies, which, in this sense, "emerge". Within this notion of improvisation, transformation is seen as a widespread, spontaneous, unpredictable and constantly shifting phenomenon. Orlikowski and Hoffman [ORL 97] compare organizational improvisation to improvisation by a jazz band: the musicians agree on a theme, but they do not know exactly what they are going to play, unlike a symphony orchestra. During their performance, the musicians will improvise iteratively and opportunistically on each individual's explorations and jointly develop a creative composition. In the organizational context, the stakeholders will engage in DIY and over the course of the iterations will enable the emergence of new practices as an efficient and creative response to a local issue, new local practices that will contribute to organizational development and lead to the emergence of a new organizational structure [ORL 96]. Ciborra [CIB 92] uses the term "DIY" to describe the creative behavior of users who adjust their IT practices incrementally to changing needs via improvisation. Improvisation leads to developing new and better practices, to promoting the emergence and facilitation of knowledge creation within the organization, flexibility and organizational effectiveness [CIB 96]. In this vision, strategy is no longer the product of a TMT's carefully designed plan, but rather the result of an emerging and collective practice, collective DIY.

New challenges arise: the reconciliation of planning and emergence in the context of a strategic transformation process linked to the IS and new technologies, but equally, the effective management of this transformation, so that the disruption is short-lived. Besson and Rowe [BES 11] see the transformation process in four phases:

1) The *uprooting* phase, which corresponds to the Upheaval of Tushman and Romanelli's punctuated equilibrium model [TUS 85] or to the Unfreeze of Lewin's organizational model [LEW 51]. In this phase, the organization departs from its old model.

2) The *exploration/construction* phase, which corresponds to the Move phase of Lewin's model; it is in this phase that the new organization is built.

3) The *stabilization/institutionalization* phase of the new organization, which partly corresponds to the convergence of Tushman' and Romanelli's models and to the Freeze phase of Lewin's model.

4) The *optimization/routinization* phase of the new organization, which corresponds to the convergence of the punctuated equilibrium model, but it has no equivalent in Lewin's model.

Each phase is also linked to various transformation strategies, and stakeholders must choose the most appropriate strategic action.

An important element to take into account is the deep structure of the business. Gersick [GER 91, p. 15] defines the deep structure as "a set of fundamental choices an organizations system has made involving basic structural elements for reconfiguring organizational units and the basic activity patterns that maintain its existence". This deep structure is the submerged part of the iceberg that is the organization: a stable and implicit structure, difficult to grasp or understand, shaping management practices, monitoring mechanisms and strategic thinking, connecting beliefs, structures, values and systems. An attempt to transform the deep structure will cause both a certain drop in performance and a domino effect of dangerous positive and negative externalities, potentially causing the failure of the transformation. These characteristics of the deep structure explain why organizational transformations are difficult to plan and manage. Thus, the way in which the business units are connected will condition the domino effects related to the transformation. The strategic transformation will be slowed down according to the number of domino effects [HAN 07]. The more central the unit is to a node, the more we must anticipate major domino effects on units hierarchically linked to it.

Thus, we can expect domino effects in the context of a "flat hierarchy"-type interconnection to stop more quickly than those initiated in a "vertical hierarchy" type because of the units' parallel responses to the architectural changes. The longer an architectural change lasts, the more damaging it will be. The units will have to manage current practice, business as usual and the transformation at the same time. Means and resources will be consumed in changing roles and responsibilities, reallocating resources, etc. In fact, not only is strategic transformation linked to information expensive, but the performance of the organization will also suffer in the short term.

Very recently, a new integrative conceptual framework has emerged in biology. The Biodiversity Ecosystem Function Paradigm [NAE 02] highlights the importance of biodiversity in the functioning of ecosystems. This theory combines community, ecosystem and evolutionary ecology into a single holistic vision. Parisot and Isckia [PAR 13] believe that this theoretical progress in biology gives "the biotope an active role in the governance of environmental conditions" (p. 14) and that it could provide solid support for the ecosystem concept in management.

In this context, we can note a number of features of the ecosystem that are favorable to IS transformation: the heterogeneity of stakeholders (trade unions, business units, pressure groups, institutions, etc.), the stakeholders' interdependence and interactions within the ecosystem, co-evolution, coopetition and biological coupling, bringing positive and negative externalities. This aspect is of interest. Interdependent stakeholders in the transformation will come into conflict, generating coopetition, at the interface points between the old and the new organization. Changes of governance and strategic plan will result in positive and negative externalities, i.e. the domino effects mentioned above.

Managing this type of transformation calls for ambidexterity: "the ability to simultaneously pursue both incremental innovations and radical, discontinuous innovations [...] by setting up divergent and contradictory structures, processes and cultures within the same firm" [TUS 96, p. 24]. This ambidexterity provides for simultaneous exploitation and exploration. Exploitation is the use of existing capabilities, while exploration could be seen as "processes set up to improve existing capabilities" [ORE 13, p. 7]. Ambidexterity allows the company to adjust to disruptive technological change: it is a way to understand how the management team manages threats to the company's survival. Ambidexterity can, for instance, explain how the hardware manufacturer IBM became a software distributor and then a services company. According to circumstances, ambidexterity can be sequential, structural or contextual. Ambidexterity is sequential when structural development takes place over time. Ambidexterity becomes structural if two independent structures develop in parallel and simultaneously. Finally, it is contextual when ambidexterity is integrated into the organizational culture, creating people who themselves meet the conflicting demands between exploitation and exploration. In the general context of a transformation linked to the IS, we would first find the sequential approach as part of a design phase during which the organization swings between exploration and exploitation. Subsequently, the structural approach could occur as part of a pilot. We would thus have "two separate units for exploration and exploitation, aligned, but fostering different systems, controls, processes, incentives, skills and cultures" [ORE 11, p. 192]. However, these two units would be bound by a common strategic plan.

As part of the IS transformation process, these two activities of exploitation and exploration can be present in differing proportions according to the process phase – we can see the construction phase as involving a higher level of exploration activity, whereas the routinization/optimization phase would involve a greater proportion of exploitation. According to Hannan et al. [HAN 07], the informal culture of the organization is a key component of its deep structure, because it restricts future architectural choices and conditions the domino effects. Likewise, for ambidexterity theorists [ORE 13], the culture conditions the success of organizational ambidexterity – it enables the organization to tolerate the tensions of two paradoxical visions.

8.5. Towards a dynamic perspective of strategic transformation linked to the IS

We firmly take the standpoint of viewing the organization as an ecosystem: the stakeholders are heterogeneous but interdependent and are as apt to adopt competition strategies as cooperation strategies. Positive and negative externalities are linked to the way in which the units are interconnected and explain the stakeholder's strong resistance to change and their behaviors. These characteristics explain why organizational transformations are difficult to plan and manage.

Next, we consider organizational ambidexterity as a theory of the initiative and intentionality of strategic transformation linked to the IS [ORE 13]: the management will put in place divergent structures, processes and cultures to exploit the existing capacities while at the same time exploring the construction of the new organization. This approach shows strategic transformation as an initiative that is both planned and emerging. Following the ambidextrous approach outlined above, we could speak of the "combination" or "simultaneity" of these two paradigms (planning and improvisation). We could see a combination in a contextual approach to ambidexterity (where planning and improvisation are inseparable, linked, combined and become a composite material), but we could also see a simultaneity of these paradigms in sequential and structural approaches (where there is a dissociation of the two activities).

8.6. Exercise: TechOne: Big Data and the Cloud

Over half (51%) of those surveyed [PRI 16] stated that they use Big Data to map potential threats (both external hackers and malicious employees) and to identify incidents. Big Data, however, is a major challenge for many companies. It requires vast storage capacity and also experienced specialists to develop algorithms and sophisticated analytical applications. The shortage of cybersecurity specialists and also budgetary constraints can be the brakes to implementing advanced solutions in terms of Big Data.

TechOne's IS security manager, Alain Richard, believes that Big Data and intelligence on threats are needed to alert the top management of TechOne to risk and to help them understand the tactics and the operating mode of their adversaries. In fact, TechOne operates several patents in the field of biotechnology, and Alain Richard intends to rapidly implement a solution in order to better anticipate attacks and detect threats. He is thinking especially of Big Data and its ability to have a single source of correlated data across the company as a whole, which can be managed in real time. Alain Richard is thinking of hosting his Big Data solution on a public cloud (PaaS).

The computer power and storage of the cloud packages on the market (Amazon, Microsoft, etc.) will enable TechOne to monitor significant volumes of data, facilitating the identification of suspicious activities. The data are multiple: traces and logs from TechOne's IS applications, network probes, firewalls and supervision probes set up within the IT infrastructure. Big Data will make it possible to compare all network activities and evaluate them permanently, to some extent constituting an advanced SIEM (Security Information and Event Management) system. When a new threat is identified, data analysis enables prioritization of responses according to the impact on business data.

Test your skills

1) Does Big Data bring a competitive advantage to TechOne in this case? What is its contribution to the business?

2) Is the public cloud a safe place to store sensitive company data? What are the advantages and disadvantages of the solution proposed by Alain Richard?

9

Auditing ISs

THE FUNDAMENTALS.–

1) The audit is a function of the organization's governance model: it is the strong arm of governance.

2) However, there is the audit of the IS and the audit by the IS: the audit of an IS is often an input into the other audits.

3) The nature of the audit is complex: it enables better alignment, while, at the same time, setting constraints on the organization.

4) The audit is the linkage, internal or external, between alignment dynamics and IS governance.

9.1. What is an audit?

9.1.1. *A need for measurement: alignment by audit*

Alignment requires an objective, an outcome and a measurement. For this, a governance mechanism is necessary. To meet the economic and organizational realities of businesses, a governance policy must be defined.

The processes of alignment and governance must, however, be dynamic, while covering all of the stakeholders of an organization and its network. Given these organizational challenges, a great many audit processes and repositories, both internal and external, have appeared. In this chapter, we propose an analysis of IS alignment and governance by audit. This approach tends to demonstrate the importance of existing frameworks and repositories for the management of an open, multi-stakeholder territory.

As previously mentioned, the strategic alignment of ISs involves: ensuring business department issues have been understood, taking into account process developments, mapping an urbanized target IS, defining the technical architecture and infrastructures to support the target applications, breaking the target IS down into projects, defining the route map to reach the target, prioritizing projects and highlighting interdependencies.

To accomplish these multiple objectives, organizations have progressively set up audit structures and repositories to ensure that their IS is aligned to strategic IS governance and also to the organizational structures in which the ISs are anchored [VAN 09].

Auditing has a long history. The etymological origin of the word comes from the Latin verb *audire*, meaning "to listen". The Romans were already using this word to refer to the monitoring exercised by the Imperial power over all provinces. The audit as we know it these days is, however, a modern invention.

Internationally, the audit became officially recognized in 1941, with the formation of the Institute of Internal Auditors (IIA). The French equivalent of this organization is the *Institut français des auditeurs et contrôleurs internes* (IFACI), established in 1965, which, between 2001 and 2009, produced its *Guides pratiques*, the French version of the Global Technology Audit Guide (GTAG). The IS audit made its first appearance in the banking and insurance sector, and then developed in industry, services and transport. The 1990s were a turning point in the development of IS auditing, with the publication of important standards and repositories such as Control Objectives for Information and related Technology (COBIT) by the Information Systems Audit and Control Association (ISACA). This progress has been reinforced and confirmed by the IS elements of the 2002 U.S. regulations, the Sarbanes–Oxley Act (SOX) and its French equivalent in 2003: *La loi de sécurité financière (LSF)*.

In its traditional form, the audit is a set of monitoring, verification and advisory exercises, the aim of which is to make a comparison between an object and a benchmark framework. Thus, it is a mission of expertise and assessment on a management system. Audits have a cost, which means that not everything can be audited. Accordingly, the audit is linked upstream to a decision as to its purpose and the level of detail needed. The audit has two requirements: to give visibility to the organization's internal mechanisms and to establish communication between them, the auditees and the Executive. An audit is driven by the need for clarification on scope and budget, performance measurement and alignment, and reassurance on certification and approvals.

9.1.2. *IS auditing practices*

The IS audit adopts the general audit process to evaluate the IS through the added value it brings to the organization. IS auditing is unique because of the IS's central structuring position within an organization. Consequently, an IS is unquestionably strategic in nature and appears as a pivot and tool for continuous improvement. However, at the same time, the integration of the IS into the overall control framework requires specific projects to be managed in line with:

– Implementation of the Public Company Accounting Oversight Board (PCAOB) rules internationally and of the *Haut conseil du commissariat aux comptes* (H3C) rules in France.

– Compliance with the requirements of SOX, the European directives or the *Loi de sécurité financière* (LSF).

– Compliance with requirements relating to confidentiality, availability and integrity of data, in relation to the Data Protection Act and the European data protection regulations.

Therefore, the IS has a double commitment: one is to adapt to quality or reliability requirements, deriving from the performance audit, and the other is to meet regulations whose aim is to correct specific organizational deficiencies, deriving from the regulatory compliance audit. Separate elements emerging from the IS audit can be mentioned, such as the framework audit for the business continuity plan (BCP), whose primary objective is to protect the organization from an IS failure, or an IT security audit, designed to test the IS's resistance to intrusions and attacks via a vulnerability assessment.

For a long time, the IS was regarded as a neutral factor in terms of the production of information for audit purposes. As such, it was not subject to any special procedures. The development of international standards and the application of the regulatory dictates deriving from SOX changed the situation. ISs must now be held accountable. As such, they are subject to their own audit. In a sense, auditing the IS gives an assurance as to the quality of data collected for the other audits. The audit is a way to combat internal fraud, as well as to protect the IS from external cyberattacks.

This puts the IS in a central position in terms of auditing. In the 1990s, responsibility for conducting the IS audit was mainly given to external providers, but the 2000s saw the creation of audit departments in major corporations as part of their IS management. This reflects the importance attached to the IS audit in general management deliberations.

One of the major problems in the fight against cybercrime is the rapid spread of new hacking techniques, the reduction in cost of criminal activity and finally, the reduction in knowledge required to become a cybercriminal. Indeed, the barriers to entry have never been so low: the services provided by cloud computing platforms can be abused to launch spam campaigns at minimal cost, crack passwords and increase the power of a botnet.

There is no longer any need to be an IT expert to become a cybercriminal: black-hat hacker communities market crimeware-as-a-service [RIC 13a], software that enables its users to launch cyberattacks with no technical skills. Online cybercriminal communities contribute to the growth in cybercrime, providing tips, techniques and turnkey tools; and in some cases, they even offer tutorials for beginners who want to become cybercriminals.

New money laundering techniques increasingly involve the use of cryptocurrencies, and, in particular, bitcoin. Bitcoin is a decentralized currency and uses screen names – in other words, it requires no identification as such, unlike a traditional bank that needs to know exactly who you are. However, a user's identity can be traced from their posts, which are displayed publicly in the public ledger recording bitcoin transactions, and this is accessible to all on the Internet. These methods involve the use of "electronic money-laundering services", platforms that will camouflage tracks in the public ledger, sometimes referred to as "layering", enabling criminals to use bitcoin without fear of detection. Each time a member of a money-laundering service makes a bitcoin transaction, that transaction will be merged at random with a transaction made by another of the money-laundering service's users. The more members the money-laundering service has, the more difficult it will be for investigators to trace the flows of dirty money.

The task will be harder if the cybercriminal uses a number of bitcoin money-laundering services to cover their tracks with even more layering. Other money-laundering methods involve the use of virtual currencies from massively multiplayer online role-playing games (MMORPGs or MMOs) such as Second Life or World of Warcraft. Cybercriminals buy virtual gold coins on the black market with their dirty money and arrange meetings via a video game, in which their online alias will retrieve the gold coins. They then immediately resell them to other players in exchange for genuine real money –and the other players find themselves quite involuntarily involved in a money-laundering operation [RIC 13b]!

In this context, auditing and monitoring play an increasingly important role. Some MMORPG platforms implement monitoring tools to inspect sudden and suspicious gains by players (the buyers) and to detect players who suddenly win and lose large amounts of gold coins on a regular basis (the sellers, moving the gold pieces through their accounts). These gaming platforms can subsequently conduct investigations (audits) to determine whether the money has been acquired legitimately (a reward following the completion of a quest in the game) or illegitimately (an external purchase). This satisfies both internal mechanisms (to keep the game balanced and prevent cheating) and external mechanisms (to provide assurances to the financial markets that the game is not being used to commit fraud). Investigations use End-User License Agreements (EULA) as the audit repository; an EULA lists the rights and commitments of players in the context of the game (these are, in a way, the rules of the game). Following the investigation, a decision may be taken to suspend a player temporarily or even to permanently ban them from the game.

Box 9.1. *Money laundering, cryptocurrencies and virtual gold coins*

9.2. The IS and auditing

Reconciling the concepts of alignment and governance entails drawing parallels between the notions of evaluating and monitoring the IS and leads to consideration of an audit of the IS, which has major implications for the governance of a computerized organization. IS auditing raises many questions, because it involves a large number of internal and external stakeholders. To a large extent, the IS audit has been developed and structured at the international level, with the Institute of Internal Auditors (IIA), the Information Systems Audit and Control Association (ISACA), the Public Company Accounting Oversight Board (PCAOB), and on the French national level with the *Institut français de l'audit et du contrôle internes* (IFACI), the *Association française de l'audit et du conseil informatiques* (AFAI) and the *Haut conseil du commissariat aux comptes* (H3C). Thus, its interpretations and the standards on which it is based are also multiple: Global Technology Audit Guides (GTAG), Control Objectives for Information and related Technology (COBIT) and Auditing Standard 2 (AS2).

As mentioned above, the repositories available are potentially in competition and sometimes redundant. The auditor must therefore be capable of seeing the bigger picture, as this will help confirm wise use. They must also be able to apply them so as to meet the legal and organizational obligations of the IS. To do so, the auditor must be able to refer to an analysis grid. This may be based on a breakdown into operational versus strategic audit and on a redistribution of competences between stakeholders, territories and projects. The various auditors must also be capable of comparing their findings and extracting from them similar analyses [HAM 81b].

As with the majority of management activities, the various stages of the IS audit can involve the use of Computer-Assisted Audit Techniques (CAAT).

9.2.1. *IS internal audits*

Internal audits are most often part of the regular monitoring of compliance and risk management. As such, the internal audit team specializing in ISs or ICT is there to meet requests for ongoing monitoring made by the General Management or by third parties: legal or regulatory responses, requests from shareholders or customers. When the General Management is the originator of the audit request, it sets targets and produces a mission list to answer its own questions relating to IS management. In this case, the internal audit traditionally focuses on the business activities and the specialist functions of the IS department: architecture, quality, methodology and security. An internal audit can also be carried out at the request of the IS department itself for purposes of legitimization or reassurance. Finally, an audit can be requested by the internal or external customers of the IS management. It is then in the IS management's interests to position itself as a high-quality provider, leveraging transparency and partnership.

An internal audit can cover the entire group, one subsidiary or one business activity. Thus, there could be a decision to change the scope of the audit and to move from a global IT audit to an audit of one particular subset: country and region. Requests are addressed to internal experts, who usually become involved upstream of an external audit, for example, during an accreditation process. We also talk about "mock audits". In all cases, IS audits cover compliance and risk management with reference to best practices. IS risks are identified and addressed. Otherwise, they are pending identification and in that case they pose a threat.

In large organizations, internal audit teams dedicated to the IS management must be provided with sufficient resources and clear procedures to successfully carry out their assignments. Indeed, issues relating to conflicts of interest may soon arise if roles and resources are not clearly defined. It is therefore important that the internal audit manager should report directly to the General Management on the findings from their work.

9.2.2. *IS external audits*

These are audits conducted by an external provider. This is the most common audit and the one which historically was the first to make its appearance. The advantage of an external audit is that it can leverage the cutting edge expertise of major specialist practices. Apart from the assumed reduction, according to the transaction costs theory, bringing in an external provider offers the advantage of greater legitimacy in communicating the findings of the audit. An external auditor has greater autonomy with regards to the IS department than the person in charge of an internal audit.

With regards to external audits, the Executive is usually seeking reassurance on complex topics and challenges such as ICT processes and IS project management. Therefore, having confidence in the expertise of an external provider will lead to the triggering of this type of audit.

In the latter case, it can be assumed that the findings reported will receive recognition from all stakeholders and everyone involved. In the field of IT production, for example, there are recurrent issues that must be addressed: the IS's response time in relation to the number of workstations and users, processing time (historically referred to as batch processing), the frequency and duration of downtime, etc. In the field of project management, the issues that crop up regularly are more to do with costs, deadlines and quality expectations.

Directors also ask for external audits on topics which they feel are not being dealt with adequately and that they do not know how to manage. Certain gaps have been reported, but no solution has been proposed. For example, the General Management may have noticed a lack of transparency and problems in coordinating IS strategies between the group and its branches, when implementing a CRM application. The external audit will then address the ICT issues between the group and the local entity (the branch). In this context, the external audit will be an explicit request for recommendations on how to structure and steer governance.

As regards audits carried out at the request of the IS department, these are mainly external audits. They have an operational and/or strategic focus, for example, a budgetary issue. If the IS management feels the budget that has been allocated to it is unrealistic, it will look to the external auditor for arguments it can use in renegotiating the budget with the General Management in the short term and/or resources to effect cost savings in the medium and long term.

The external audit market is regulated by a number of international and national institutional actors. It is controlled within the regulatory framework established by private operators who have developed expertise that now crosses national borders.

Do you know Watson? Watson is a language analysis engine, the world's first acknowledged cognitive system. In 2011, IBM's artificial intelligence made the headlines by winning $1 million on Jeopardy!, competing against the two greatest champions in the history of the game. Watson was capable of reading sentences (words and letters) and analyzed questions syntactically, grammatically and semantically. It then buzzed to offer its hypothetically most viable answers, all in under three seconds. Prior to this, Watson had ingested 200 million pages of natural language (including Wikipedia) so as to be able to find the answers. The different version of GPT arrived much later.

Some people see AI as the beginning of a new world, while others are afraid of the massive volume it represents. One thing is for sure: Big Data is at the heart of current thinking. The ecosystem in which we live, full of personal devices (smartphones, tablets, etc.) and connected objects, is causing an exponential increase in data volume, to the point where, these days, human intelligence alone is no longer capable of processing it.

In terms of cybersecurity, this raises questions. Knowing that a computer attack is generally fragmented and dispersed across a number of sources, how can we expect these nexuses of information to monitor large data flows in real time? Would not artificial intelligence, which is now able to review and process massive quantities of data, be a solution to identify the full range of weak signals relating to a threat?

The same question arises for audits. During a technical audit of an IS, the auditor can collect a lot of data, such as extracts from system logs, access logs and databases. How can we ensure end-to-end system security? AI can be of great assistance by correlating this mass of data to detect weak signals, indicating vulnerabilities in the IS being audited.

The contribution that AI makes these days is the technological capacity to review a massive amount of data and filter out the noise to extract weak signals, and in doing so, make connections between them to produce new significance, new information, which is more highly synthesized and thus more understandable to humans. All in all, it emerges as the cure for data saturation, which is typical of the information age.

AI is spreading pretty much everywhere, surpassing human performance in the challenges of image analysis, for instance. It opens the potential to automate (thanks to powerful computers) information processing in record time. The issue of its application to cybersecurity, particularly within Security Operation Centers (SOC), or the department responsible for operational security within an organization, has never been more relevant.

Intelligent conversational agents (for example, chatGPT) could also be described as decision support tools, guiding humans in the event of a computer crisis, feeding on log data to issue diagnoses and suspicions of root cause to investigate in order to solve the problem. The following conversion is very close to reality in 2023: "I analyze the millions of logs in real time: it seems that there is a problem in the core network … At the same time, these IS applications are out of service, while they are on the faulty node. I suggest two avenues of investigation […]"

Box 9.2. *Artificial intelligence to the rescue of cybersecurity and auditing*

9.3. The audit process

The audit process is based on very strict methodology and working practices, which enable the definition and sequencing of the various activities to be carried out [HAM 81a]. While specialist audit firms use many repositories, there are a number of recurrent and important steps that can be noted:

– *Defining the audit parameters*: as explained above, the audit has a cost, and this will inevitably limit the scope of the investigation. Moreover, the requirement specified by the person making the request will determine the scope of the domain to be audited. For instance, in the case of a request initiated by the General Management, the audit may be strategic in nature and focus on the IS's place within the organization and its degree of alignment. If the request was initiated by a departmental manager, the audit may be more operational in nature and may aim to assess the security attached to an application or the quality of a delivered service covered by a Service-Level Agreement (SLA). These two examples show how the nature of the requester will determine the focus of the audit and, consequently, its scope.

– *Planning the audit process*: during this phase, the auditor will determine the audit's objectives and priority themes, individual responsibilities (of the stakeholders and the auditor), the preliminary analyses and feasibility studies, the competences needed in terms of the number of people in the audit term and their experience, the methods to be used (according to the type of repositories used) and the provisional completion schedule, which is normally short, less than two months. During this stage, a number of documents – such as tracking sheets, specifications and the results of preliminary studies – are produced and passed on to the audit committee and the requester.

– *Conducting the audit*: the process will be different according to the nature of the audit to be carried out. In every case, however, it will begin with data collection, using specific tools, evaluation grids and maintenance grids and will proceed with data analysis: reprocessing of raw data and analysis of deviations from good practice.

– *Audit outcomes*: the purpose of this stage is to deliver an assessment on the domain under audit. This assessment will be driven by the drafting of action plans for improvement designed to demonstrate to the requesters the reasons for deviations noted and corrective action that could be taken to solve them. Based on this initial work, the auditor will prepare to follow up on the recommendations. The purpose of this second document is to set out the re-evaluation period chosen, which we call "periodicity of audit", the number of criteria to be re-evaluated and the impact of the corrective measures proposed. Moreover, following up the recommendations usually means considering a new contract with an external provider to undertake and implement the corrective measures.

9.3.1. *Structuring an IS audit project*

An IS audit project is structured around a number of essential stakeholders, among whom are, for instance, the requester, those being audited, the audit team and the audit committee [CHA 03]. The requester includes the actors who can claim to be at the origin of an IS audit, and there are potentially many of them. It can be the General Management, the IS department, a department manager or an end-user. It can also be a request from shareholders, the government or an accrediting body. We must therefore distinguish between an external requester and an internal requester, because they each have different needs and expectations.

Those under audit are not only the IS management, as project manager, but other stakeholders too: the end-user and the department manager. When the IS department has signed outsourcing contracts, the audit will extend to external service providers involved both in project management and in project owner support. The auditor will thus ask for details of the outsourcing scope negotiated by the IS department.

The composition of the audit team is directly related to the request by the person asking for the audit. The number of people involved and their level will depend on the size of the structure to be audited and the scope of the audit: how many processes, applications and stakeholders are involved and the nature of the technical architecture. The audit team, including the junior auditors performing the basic operational checks and the senior auditors supervising them, is under the charge of an assignment supervisor, manager or associate. This at least is the type of organization that predominates in large audit firms.

The audit committee's objective is to bring together representatives of all the stakeholders involved in the audit process within the organization, such as the Executive and the General Management in terms of the internal IS audit. The audit committee plays a watchdog role, to ensure that the requirements of transparency and communication, essential to the correct implementation of an audit, are well insured throughout the process. Article 14 of Ordinance No. 2008-1278 of December 8, 2008, transposing directive 2006/43/EC of May 17, 2006 relating to the statutory auditors, sets out the duties of this committee in terms of monitoring the process of preparing accounting and financial information. This ordinance also specifies that the audit committee is under the exclusive and collective responsibility of the Executive or the Supervisory Board.

Grade	Experience	Role
Junior auditor	Less than two years and CISA-qualified (Certified ISAuditor)	Works as part of a team on all or part of the auditing tasks: implements the audit program specified by their firm, participates in information-gathering, carries out most of the operational checks
Senior auditor	Three to five years	Supervising, organizing and coordinating tasks delegated to the junior auditors, supervising teams on assignments, customer relationship management, reporting to management
Assistant manager, Senior manager	Five years +	Managing teams, participating in in-house training and recruitment, business development, mandate management
Associate	Has a diploma in accounting	Managing the practice, business development

Table 9.1. *Levels of responsibility within large audit firms [NOË 08]*

9.4. Scope of the audit

To define the scope of the audit, it may be useful to refer to the typology adopted by the Public Company Accounting Oversight Board (PCAOB). The European directives are directly based on this.

There are three families of IS controls: Company Level Controls, Application Controls and General Controls.

Audit level	Content	Objectives
A company or entity	Strategy and action plan, policies and procedures, risk assessment, training, quality assurance, internal audit	Organizational scoping
Application	Comprehensiveness, precision, existence and approval, range of information to be provided	Functional scoping
Computing in general	Development of applications, changes to applications, access to data and programs, computer processing	Integration of monitoring within the IT function

Table 9.2. *Audit typology*

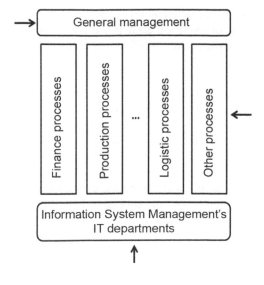

Figure 9.1. *Audit configurations*

Figure 9.1 illustrates the structure and its audits. At General Management level, audits will be carried out at the scale of the entity (this is organizational scoping). At the level of the IS management's IT services, general audits will be carried out at the scale of the IT function. Finally, at the process level, application audits will be carried out (functional scoping).

9.4.1. *Domains and processes audited*

An IS audit may involve: IS management, an IS project, an IS study, the IS infrastructure and IS planning. An audit of the IS management has the widest scope, because it sets out to give an audit of the positioning and structuring of the whole IS management. It is therefore necessary to identify management roles in steering the IS, to check the definition and quality of the standards and procedures used, to determine the positioning of the management stakeholders within the IS, and to check the existence and reliability of an analytical accounting system.

Auditing IS projects involves checking the existence of a project management methodology and compliance with the various phases required in the implementation of delivered IS services. It is necessary to audit the deviation between actual management practice and the management standards adopted. The audit should also enable an analysis of project risks and an assessment of the steering affected.

Auditing the studies aims to assess compliance with standards in terms of documentation and quality of deliverables. In terms of good practice, studies must be linked to the entire lifecycle of each project (analysis of needs, challenges, production, reception, implementation follow-up). The audit involves checking this link.

Auditing IS infrastructures carry out an inventory of the network and telecommunications infrastructures and the exploitation and management of resources. This audit aims to highlight the potential risks associated with the choice of standards and protocols used, to take stock of incident management and to analyze resource management.

Auditing IS planning involves checking the existence and quality of an IT plan and blueprint. This audit focuses on the coherence between the objectives expressed in these documents and the organization's strategy.

9.5. Audit repositories

At the international level, the Institute of Internal Auditors (IIA) is an American expert on internal auditing. As regards control procedures, the IIA has published the Global Technology Audit Guides (GTAG). The IIA has also developed a code of ethics that aims to promote an ethical culture within the internal audit profession.

The Information Systems Audit and Control Association (ISACA), whose motto is "Trust in, and value from, information systems" is an organization whose role is to promote IS governance, control, security and audit through the publication of repositories, such as Control Objectives for Information and related Technology (COBIT), Val IT, Risk IT and IS audit standards.

The Information Systems Audit and Control Association (ISACA) also advocates the use of methods and techniques to improve stakeholder skills. This takes the form of certifications in three major areas: internal IS auditing, Certified Information Systems Auditor (CISA), IS security, Certified Information Security Manager and IS governance and Certified in the Governance of Enterprise IT. In 1998, the Information Systems Audit and Control Association (ISACA) set up its own research unit, the Information Technology Governance Institute (ITGI). This institute develops standards and norms and offers advisory guides.

The repository Control Objectives for Information and related Technology (COBIT) has now attracted a great many stakeholders for its relevance in terms of IS audits, having received endorsement from the Institute of Internal Auditors (IIA).

In France, for instance, there are two organizations that it is important to be aware of. These are the *Institut français de l'audit et du contrôle internes* (IFACI), which is the French equivalent of the Institute of Internal Auditors (IAA), and the *Association française de l'audit et du conseil informatiques* (AFAI), which is the French equivalent of the Information Systems Audit and Control Association (ISACA).

At the European level, the Commission produces guidelines designed to provide a framework for IS auditing. These European directives have been transposed into French law under law number 2008-649 of July 3, 2008, which precisely defines a frame of reference for internal IS audits, and by the Ordinance of December 8, 2008, which establishes an audit committee.

Among the regulatory bodies, we should mention at the international level the Public Company Accounting Oversight Board (PCAOB), author of Auditing Standard 2 (AS2) or Audit of Internal Control over Financial Reporting Performed in Conjunction with an Audit of Financial Statements, and, in France, the *Haut conseil du commissariat aux comptes* (H3C).

Acronym	Name	Repository	Scope
IIA	Institute of Internal Auditors	Global Technology Audit Guides (GTAG) and practical IT audit guides adopted by the *Institut français des auditeurs et contrôleurs internes* (IFACI)	IS audit taking the traditional internal audit approach
ISACA (ITGI)	Information Systems Audit and Control Association (Information Technology Governance Institute)	Control Objectives for Information and related Technology (COBIT) Adopted by the *Association française de l'audit et du conseil informatiques* (AFAI)	External, specific audit, legal versus contractual
PCAOB	Public Company Accounting Oversight Board	Auditing Standard 2, i.e. Audit of Internal Control over Financial Reporting Performed in Conjunction with an Audit of Financial Statements (AS2)	Financial audit complying with the Sarbanes-Oxley Act (SOX)
H3C	*Haut conseil du commissariat aux comptes* (statutory auditors)	Repository based on AS2	Financial audit
CE	Commission européenne	8th directive (206/43)	IS audit

Table 9.3. *Audit types*

9.6. Towards an approach via the risks of strategic alignment?

The approach via the risks of strategic alignment was developed as an extension of the COBIT standard (integrating RiskIT and ValIT), chiefly in the English-speaking world.

The aims of this approach are to align the ISs, to bring benefits to the IS stakeholders and to manage IS risk. In terms of aligning the IS to business needs, the IS must be able to provide correct and relevant information, ensuring integrity, to the right users, ensuring confidentiality, at the right time for the business, ensuring availability, relative to the tangible benefits to the IS's stakeholders, projects and territories. This is possible through improving business process operations. It enables efficient and effective use of resources, maximization of the IS's usefulness to users and also a reduction of the IS's usefulness to unauthorized users who may succeed in breaking into the system. On the subject of managing risks related to the IS, this approach makes it possible to measure their impact on business departments (plan), to safeguard the company's strategic assets (do) and to constantly evaluate the performance delivered by the IS in order to improve it and make it more resilient (check and act).

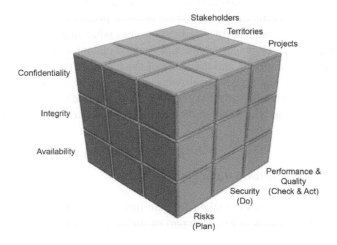

Figure 9.2. *An overview of information assurance (adapted from the model of [MCC 04])*

Alignment should be seen as situated at the crossroads of a number of business activities: risk management, resilience, IS security and business continuity. However, while this method does address security issues, it sees them at a strategic and organizational level. Thus, the issues addressed will remain within the field of security governance.

Implementation of this method is based on identifying the business's critical assets and strategic advantages to be protected, assessing threats to these assets and evaluating vulnerabilities. Thereafter, it will study the potential and severity of each risk scenario and roll out a plan to manage strategic risk that will be visible to management. IS audits can be carried out and, through successive iterations, the risk management plan will be incremented by new threats on new assets.

9.7. Conclusion

IS audits present a strong organizational aspect and a clear link to the "traditional" activities of audit and management. Their distinguishing feature lies in leveraging and advocating standards to provide a framework for the audit. An audit can be seen first and foremost as a comparative analysis process of what currently exists against a frame of reference. The only value of an audit is that it can determine the triggering of sanction mechanisms in the event of non-validation. Ultimately, an audit is only of value because of what preceded it, i.e. the analysis of a dysfunctionality or a request for clarification, and what follows it, in the form of corrective actions, development plans and organizational adjustments. It should enable the auditee to improve, and the value of the audit is thus measured by what it brings to the auditee. The audit's focal point in economic terms is naturally seen as the implementation timescale and the cost. As such, the audit is correlated with the setting of the budget, in which the amount of budget allocated to the audit itself will be borne in mind.

9.8. Exercise: an auditor's view

The following comments are taken from an interview with an external IS auditor (who must evaluate aspects of the IS as part of the annual audit of accounts):

> What is an audit? How is the success of an audit determined? I see an auditor as a trusted third party, a partner. As auditors, our mandate with a company often lasts for several years. We develop a trust-based relationship. With every company we experience high points, resulting from strategic decisions and technology choices. A strong relationship between auditor and auditee gives the auditor a better understanding of the company's challenges, its projects, its management, its practices and its strengths. The human and interpersonal aspect of the audit is always present. However, it is because this is a lasting relationship that the auditor is able to really act as an independent and legitimate third party. The purpose of the audit is to give an opinion on the financial and operational health of the business: we communicate honest and trustworthy information to the market. [...]
>
> You could say that the auditor acts as a critical friend. In a sense, a friend who has no qualms in telling you home truths and coming straight to the point. "Trust" does not mean "collusion". Criticism is not intended to damage the business; the auditor is not in opposition to the business. On the contrary, this critical friend wants to help the

business. The auditor gives positive, relevant and constructive criticism. This leads towards continuous improvement.

For sure, the auditor is working in the interests of the business being audited. Notwithstanding his or her independence, the auditor is a cornerstone of the governance of the business, contributing to external audits and improve internal audits. That is how (s)he builds trust and confidence, making the business's activities more robust, and giving his or her opinion on its conformity with the regulatory environment.

Test your skills

1) What are the benefits of a good relationship with the customer in the context of an audit?

2) According to this auditor, what place do compliance and adherence to standards occupy?

3) How can adopting the stance of critical friend, as advocated by this auditor, impact the quality of the auditor's judgment?

4) How independent can a trusted third party be?

Conclusion

Management of Information Systems in its Complexity

For the purposes of analysis, the previous parts have looked separately at three key concepts of IS science: governance, urbanization and alignment.

We have seen how IS governance seeks to define the structures and modalities of decision-making by IS stakeholders, be they internal or external to the organization. We have linked IS governance to organizational theory via the stakeholder figure. The stakeholder has thus been recognized as the crucial element in being able to design governance, because the stakeholder is the source of value creation. The issue for strategy makers is therefore to govern the stakeholders.

We have presented IS urbanization as the approach to a representation of the IS, in its different facets, in order to design and provide tools for the continuous development of ISs.

We have linked IS urbanization to organizational theory via the concept of territory. Territory is thus the operating field where the IS is deployed, with a correlation between the multiplicity of territorial levels and multiplicity of IS representations. Planning the IS's urbanization is thus the management role that is strategically central to territorial urbanization.

We have covered IS alignment, showing the importance of evaluating the IS's capacity to make a significant contribution to organizational strategy and acting to increase its strategic contribution. IS alignment encourages mobilization of the project concept, favored by organizational theory. The project is thus a specific implementation of strategic alignment of the IS, and the management of the IS project portfolio defines the path towards the target IS. The project director must confirm the links between the formulation of the organization's overall strategy and the development and agility of the organization's IS.

However, this analytical separation of the concepts of governance, urbanization and alignment may seem arbitrary. The day-to-day work of IS managers is such that these three aspects are inextricably linked for most of the time. Therefore, it is necessary to coordinate these three notions in a process focused on transversality and reflexivity. One way to meet this requirement is to link the concepts two by two. We can thus consider the model's areas of confluence and study the links connecting governance to stakeholder, urbanization to territory and alignment to project.

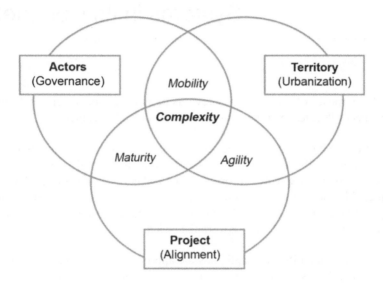

Figure C.1. *The complex vision of IS management*

Mobility: the meeting between stakeholders and territories raises the consideration of increased stakeholder mobility in an organizational context where the organizational boundaries are significantly pushed back or even broken down. This mobility takes four different forms and stems from multiple causes. Of their own free will or by force of circumstance, workers change jobs within the same organization and also change employers more frequently, generating internal and external mobility. The work structure requires more and more business trips, remote working and also working with remote colleagues and partners. Territories are stretching and borders are more permeable to stakeholders. IS management should therefore grasp this mobility to enable its organization to extend its territory by populating it with its mobile stakeholders, while maintaining remote contact via information and communication technologies. In particular, mobility is facilitated by the miniaturization of devices (smartphones, tablets, connected objects) and the widespread dissemination of digital technologies.

Agility: we analyze the meeting between territories and projects through the development of an agility made necessary by new expectations of customers, operators and users. These new expectations call for a review of organizational strategy, and thus, the projects to develop an IS aligned to strategic needs. IS managers have to anticipate the adjustment and spatio-temporal development of organizations at a time when collaborative software is widely extended, beyond organizational boundaries. It is therefore necessary to develop scalable, agile strategies where information and communication technologies should make it possible to respond to current needs while opening up opportunities for the future.

Maturity: the meeting between stakeholders and projects calls for a search for organizational maturity. Organizational maturity is largely the result of developments of norms, standards and benchmarks for IS management. In order to manage the maturity and scalability of the IS, its management must take ownership of these norms and standards, comply with them and audit its IS to identify deviations and areas for improvement. Stakeholders must be trained in project management and more generally on the benchmarks. Stakeholders should also be able to participate proactively in improving these management tools, so that they continue to be the tools that support stakeholders and agile strategies and not burdens that fossilize the organization.

A second way of meeting the need for transversality is to focus on the point of confluence of confluences, or in other words, the precise spot where mobility, agility and maturity coincide. The intersection of issues of governance, urbanization and IS alignment can be a site of complexity management.

C.1. The thought of complexity

First, "complex" does not mean "complicated". The etymological origin of the word is clear: *complexus* means "something that is woven together". It is therefore important to include, within the decision-making focus, complementaries and extensions of the various facets of world reality. Complex thinking rejects the *Ceteris paribus* (other things being equal) concept – where variables are fixed in relation to each other for the purposes of the analysis – in favor of seeking a comprehensive approach where variables are perceived in the fluidity of their interactions.

Complexity has its roots in many disciplines and research streams: cybernetic complexity [WIE 48], with the idea that dynamic systems are capable of feedback; the complexity of networks, dynamic systems and chaos theory [AUB 02]; Kolmogorov's algorithmic and mathematical complexity [LI 14]; and the system-cybernetic approach, with the work of Atlan and Morin [ATL 79; MOR 13]. Complex systems are capable of actions and feedback internally and in interaction with the environment. Informational feedback loops are managed by the system via regulation mechanisms seeking homeostasis: balance in the middle of the vortex of dynamic forces. In this vortex, dialogisms appear – contradictory dynamics that come into conflict, but are complementary and at the same time participate in the co-creation of value [MOR 13].

Complex systems are characterized by their self-organization. Complexity [MOR 82; MOR 13] is valuable in giving some clear principles of analysis. Thus, complex systems are characterized by:

– the diversity of their components;

– the adaptation of their components;

– their multiple connections;

– their mutual dependence.

Edgar Morin states that "complexity does not only involve quantities of elements and interactions that challenge our computational capacities; it also involves uncertainties and indeterminacies; random phenomena. Complexity, in a sense, always has to do with chance" [MOR 13].

C.2. Complexity and IS management

At a time when ISs occupy a central place in organizational transformation, it is important to have a method to understand arrangements that are a mixture of human and materiality, ultra-localization and globality, standardization and agility. The functionalist and utilitarian vision of ISs does not allow for such tensions to be taken into account. It remains a prisoner of technological determinism, leaving little room for studying the human element in the utilization and ownership of systems. In response to this movement, complex thinking offers great scope for the study of ISs. Indeed, it allows us to overcome dichotomy, decontextualization and linear causality [MOR 08] and to focus instead on the study of contingencies, contradictions and their dynamics.

The link between Edgar Morin's complexity and the analysis of ISs was made by Jean-Louis Le Moigne [MOR 99]. Complexity theory implies that every system (defined as the combination of various elements) is complex by nature since it is open to its environment and that systems are empirically embedded in a plurality of interdependent processes. We find this particularly illuminating in understanding how ISs are technological and at the same time procedural and cultural. Thus, the complex approach suggests various unpredictability factors associated with user behavior in organizational contexts, with mobile technologies, etc. Developing a complex view of ISs therefore implies leveraging the founding principles of the complexity theory. Among these, we would highlight openness, nonlinearity, uncertainty, self-organization and autopoiesis.

Openness requires that every system interacts with its environment. This is the case for ISs. Every IS should be analyzed and understood in its extent and its capacity to provide operational bases for an extended organization or business [IDB 06].

Nonlinearity is present in a system when causes are not directly proportional to effects. Therefore, it is necessary to accept and anticipate every magnification (and reduction) rationale of events that may seem insignificant (or major) when studied in isolation. These elements of nonlinearities occur repeatedly in ISs and cannot be ignored.

Uncertainty concerns ISs that take unexpected paths, resulting from technological, human and cultural configurations arising from interaction between elements. For several decades, information and communication technologies have been undergoing astonishing growth, which puts uncertainty at the heart of innovation.

Self-organization is present insofar as today's ISs are mainly distributed and open to multiple interactions; they develop unpredictable capacities for self-organization. The growth of the collaborative economy is the strongest proof of the significance of self-organization in the growth rationale of ISs.

Autopoiesis is the property of a system being able to create itself, permanently and in interaction with its environment and thus maintain its structure despite changes in its components. When Maturana and Varela study the characteristics of what they call "living machines" and formulate a theory based on the dynamics of the recursive relationship between closed systems, subsystems, components and the environment [MAT 80], they are envisioning autopoietic systems. An autopoietic system (from the Greek *auto*, "self", and *poiesis*, "production, creation") is organized as:

a network of production processes of components that (a) continually regenerate the network through the transformations and interactions that created them, and that (b) constitute the system as a concrete unit in the space where it exists, specifying the topological domain where it fulfills itself a network [MAT 80].

Building mature, mobile, agile ISs thus means developing auto-regulating systems, via self-learning practices, repositories and stakeholders [VAR 92].

C.3. Action principles on ISS

Le Moigne proposes an organizational model [LEM 90] within which the information and the organization interact: the information gives structure to the organization, which in return structures the development of information. The IS is conceived by Le Moigne as an organizational subsystem positioned at the interface between the decision-making system and the operational system. Thus, the IS shapes and steers production management and can supply qualified data to management for decision-making.

Organizational model
Decision-making system
Information system
Operation system

Table C.1. *The organizational model*

In relation to this perception of the organizational model, we propose a complex approach to the IS itself in its capacity to be a subsystem of the organizational system, in other words, an organizational IS in Le Moigne's sense. Taking the Stakeholder/Territory/Project approach, we can identify within the IS the Decision/Information/Operation aspects put forward by Le Moigne.

Organizational IS model
Stakeholder/governance/*decision*
Territory/urbanization/*information*
Project/alignment/*operation*

Table C.2. *The organizational IS*

Faced with these theoretical elements, we propose to adopt a cross-disciplinary approach in order to manage and anticipate the complexity of ISs in their organizational contexts. This involves taking the technological factor into account through careful attention to the collective aspect of the action, the history of the organization, its corporate culture, its social dimension and the ethical implications of data processing. The questions to be asked are simple, but they need to be asked together. How was technology introduced into the organization? Where does it come from? Who created it? Who is steering it? Does it have self-organizational potential? Does it allow transparency and ownership of its processes? How are users connected to it? What are the current controversial issues? How big a factor is uncertainty? How can it be addressed? How can environmental constraints be met? Where are the available resources to establish seamless and sustainable development of the IS?

Behind these questions, we find the principles mentioned above, and in particular the concept of autopoiesis. In a changing and competitive environment, it is increasingly vital for organizations to seek a dynamic balance in the face of technological challenges and to know what they must change in order to maintain their identity and their autonomy. We believe that this kind of framework allows designers, developers, managers and also users to grasp the most relevant issues through a global approach that includes the IS's stakeholders, territories and projects.

In this panel, our intention is to take stock of the implementation of this framework of analysis, derived from the theory of complex thinking, in research carried out for the headquarters of a French multinational company specializing in electricity transmission and distribution, and particularly the acquisition of an ERP by its Chinese entities.

This global leader in the energy sector established itself in China in 2000 through a network of joint ventures with the major local electricity supplier. It had 10,000 employees worldwide and 3,000 employees in China. In this context of expansion, it was decided by Head Office to implement a global ERP, not progressively, but in a radical switchover from the old system to the new one.

In the face of this transformation, flaws soon appeared. Several months after the switchover, many employees were in fact still using the old ISs for the greater part of their activities, merely integrating some of the data – the strict minimum – into the new ERP to satisfy their managers. This practice was killed off. The implementation of this new ERP had not actually sparked much protest, but users had adopted this strategy to express, silently, their rejection of a tool which they felt did not meet their needs.

Since the ERP training delivered by Head Office to the Chinese teams had proved inadequate to become proficient with the tool, the teams operated an informal learning process that directly led to the emergence and development of workarounds. To take one of many examples, one of the workarounds was to add an extension to the supplier code to identify second-tier suppliers, a status that was missing in the newly implemented ERP.

In the light of the theoretical framework presented in this chapter, we focused our analysis on the mechanisms of the ERP workarounds by its users, namely:

– *contradictions inherent in the IS* (between the initial design and the user needs) in terms of its features, its ergonomics and the organizational culture associated with it;

– *experimentation aimed at overcoming these contradictions*: namely, modifications developed by its users relating to data, processes and the use of third-party solutions outside the ERP (e.g. spreadsheets);

– *the organizational consequences of these experiments* that could be classed as: harmless, disruptive or critical.

This analysis enabled us to identify 64 workaround practices, including 36 modifications to data, 19 modifications to procedures and nine modifications using third-party solutions. Eight of these workarounds were deemed harmless, 29 disruptive and 27 critical. To take the example of data modification: the short-circuiting of payment deadline monitoring. While the management insisted on paying suppliers within 90 days, the parameter set in the ERP, it was customary for the Chinese entities to pay suppliers twice a year. From this point of view, the new IS introduced a major change. The staff did not want to comply with these instructions, fearing it would destabilize supplier relationships. In this case, the inappropriateness of the ERP was cultural in nature.

We found certain elements specific to the complexity theory particularly enlightening in analyzing the situation of this company and its IS:

– *Nonlinearity*: even though the system designers had liaised upstream with operators to standardize management procedures before implementing the ERP, it was naive to think that this unifying effort would have only the intended consequences. The complexity with which the IS's components merge internally and externally provides no predictability.

– *Uncertainty:* ISs take unpredictable paths due to interactions between users, the IS and environmental pressures.

– *Auto-organization*: contrary to the expectations of the mother company, the global ERP proved to be decentralized, with unforeseen practices of the Chinese users. The scale of the system left scope for innovation and initiative.

To cope with the challenges of a project of this nature to transform an IS, a cross-disciplinary approach is useful:

– *A collective approach*: it became evident that the trialing of workarounds was a collective practice and not the result of isolated initiatives. Thus, informal meetings were an opportunity to share best practices, advice and "tips and tricks".

– *A historical approach*: the history of this business's presence in China for almost 15 years, the strategies it had used to form partnerships and joint ventures with local stakeholders, etc. were all essential factors in understanding the adoption of the ERP by its Chinese users.

– *Contradictions and deviations, drivers of change*: the contradictions between the initial blueprint for the global ERP and the Chinese entity's local needs triggered major rationales for organizational and informational transformation.

– *The trialing of solutions coming from the field*: all of the practices designed to address the contradictions and unsuitabilities of the system emerged from users in the field.

– *Continuous agility*: the ERP must, at all times, be kept in perspective with the particularities of doing business in China, the power balance between the Chinese entities and the mother company, the economic context, the legal context, etc.

Box C.1. *Illustration of complex thinking*

Glossary

Actor network: a concept used in actor–network theory (ANT) to refer to the imbrication of humans and objects in a world regulated by techniques.

Agile methods: a set of practices for planning and carrying out projects, more pragmatic than traditional development methods. Agile methods claim to be closer to the end-user and aim to build the project by iterations and increments in line with user need.

American form (A-form): an organizational structure that includes unitary form and multi-divisional form.

Business function: a set of activities performed by a structure within the company designed to achieve a specified result.

Business to administration (B2A): a technical and informational environment enabling direct communication between a business and its contact persons in administrative bodies.

Business to business (B2B): a technical and informational environment enabling direct communication between businesses.

Business to consumer (B2C): a technical and informational environment enabling direct communication between a business and its customers.

Business to employees (B2E): a technical and informational environment enabling direct communication between a business and its employees.

Capability maturity model integration (CMMI): a repository of good practices developed to measure the quality of software suppliers.

Chains of translation: concept used in actor–network theory (ANT) to refer to the imbrications between humans and technical objects that facilitate an understanding of the world and interactions.

Client/server: a computing environment that combines two approaches: customer-centric (where resources are managed locally) and server-centric (where resources are centralized).

Cloud computing: leveraging the processing power and storage of remote servers via the Internet, on request and on a self-service basis.

Confidentiality, integrity and availability (CIA) criteria: criteria used, in IS security, when looking at the protection of confidentiality, integrity and availability of information.

Control objectives for information and related technology (COBIT): a repository of good practice focusing on IS governance.

Cooperative information system (CIS): an IS in the mesoeconomics system, where inter-business relationships are conceived as collaborations that generate relational rents.

Decision support systems (DSS): an IS at the management level that provides basic information to department managers so that they can take decisions on medium-term policies.

Ecosystem: a set of relationships (vertical, horizontal and transverse; direct and indirect; formalized and unformalized) between heterogeneous actors steered by the promotion of a common resource and an ideology that leads to the development of shared skills.

Electronic data interchange (EDI): computerized exchange of data regulated by standardized communication protocols between two organizations (often a business and its supplier). This exchange of information has the dual purpose of data fluidification and cost reduction.

Enterprise resource planning (ERP), integrated management software (IMS), enterprise systems (ES): management application that meets the needs of the whole of the business, with modules for the various departments: accounting, finance, production and procurement, etc.

Executive information systems (EIS): ISs at the executive level that provide highly synthesized information on the business' macroactivities but with the potential to go into greater detail on specific elements using aggregated data, to support strategic decision-making.

Extended information system (EIS): an IS in the mesoeconomics system, where inter-business relationships are conceived as quasi-automatic adjustment mechanisms within a market, activated in line with transaction costs.

Extranet: a computer network based on public Internet protocols giving access to its services to the partners of a private organization.

Free software: software giving the freedom to execute the program, inspect its functioning, adapt it to need, distribute copies, improve it and share the enhancements. To do this, access to source code is assured by a public license.

Functional silo: a strong separation between the functions of an organization, each with its own set of rules for apportioning authority, tasks, controls and the coordination of an organization.

Gantt chart: a tool to assist with planning, scheduling and updating complex project management by enabling real-time visualization of the various project tasks.

Global technology audit guide (GTAG): a repository relating to the IS for setting up internal audits.

Hardware structure: physical components, in the form of a technological base and infrastructure, supporting the software applications.

Hierarchy: a social structure that establishes relationships of subordination and graduated levels of power, position and responsibility.

Horizontal network firm: an organizational structure whose organizational territory is extended through inter-organizational cooperation in carrying out business processes, with no recognized leader firm and pursuing a common objective.

Host-centric: a computing environment where work stations act as slaves to a central computer that hosts centralization.

Information asymmetry: a situation where some participants have access to information that others do not. For example, corporate governance is characterized by directors who have privileged access to accounting and financial data that is not shared with shareholders.

Information content: basic descriptions of realities recorded, in the wider sense, by the organization and that is available to it.

Information Technology Infrastructure Library (ITIL): a repository of good practices for IS management focusing on the improvement of IT services.

Infrastructure as a service (IaaS): a commercial solution accessible on a remote server. The service provider provides access to a machine and manages all the technical processes associated with this service. The client is responsible for installing their operating system, middleware and software.

International Organization for Standardization (ISO) 27000: the IS security standard, published by the International Standards Organization.

Internet: a worldwide network, accessible to the public, connecting private information networks with many key services like messaging, the World Wide Web, social networks, etc.

Internet of Things (IoT): the Internet of Things refers to a set of technologies that enable interconnection between the Internet and connected objects. The resulting digital identity of objects opens up new opportunities for assets and physical environments to be managed and maintained.

Intranet: a computer network based on public Internet protocols, giving access to its services to the members of a private organization.

IS function: a set of activities available in a defined IS, giving a specified result.

IS planner: a function whose aim is to ensure that the complete IS develops consistently in line with the corporate goals, the functional domain, external and internal constraints and to exploit technical opportunities to the full.

IS security: a field of activity that includes technical, behavioral, managerial, philosophical and organizational approaches addressing protection against and mitigation of threats to informational assets.

IS territory: an arrangement of material and symbolic resources capable of structuring the practical conditions of the existence of an IS.

IS urbanization: a process that provides a framework of analysis for rationalizing, transforming and improving the IS.

IT framework for management of IT-related business risks (RiskIT): a repository relating to IT risk management.

IT scorecard: a dashboard to align is management to the rest of the organization.

IT standard: a common, documented repository to harmonize IT activities.

Japanese form (J-form): an organizational structure whose organizational territory is extended through inter-organizational collaborations in carrying out business processes.

Key performance indicators (KPI): indicators to monitor the performance of services included on the list of facilities management contracts.

Managed services: the handing over of all or part of the IS to a specialist subcontractor.

Management IS: an IS linking the organizational functions and the hierarchical levels of a hierarchical–functional territory.

Mapping: the process of creating a graphic representation.

Mesoeconomics: a branch of economics, between macroeconomics and microeconomics that models the behavior of small clusters of economic actors, in the same business sector, the same industry or the same region.

Microeconomics: a branch of economics that models the behavior of economic actors (consumers, households, businesses, organizations, etc.).

Middleware: third-party software, the purpose of which is to enable the exchange of information between different applications. The EDI is an example of middleware.

Multi-divisional form (M-form): an organizational structure where control is shared by business units.

Network-centric: a computing environment where organizations interact by means of complex interfaces. The development of this kind of environment is linked to Internet usage.

On premise: management and production of computer services internally within an organization. On premise is the opposite of software as a service (SaaS).

Open-source data: electronic data that allows users free access and use.

Organizational boundary: a border that determines the organization's territory.

Organizational chart: a blueprint of the organizational structure showing its various elements and also the relationships that exist between them.

Organizational IS: an IS of a business system incorporating a multitude of processes.

Organizational structure: a set of rules for apportioning the authority, tasks, control and coordination of an organization.

Organizational territory: an arrangement of material and symbolic resources capable of structuring the practical conditions of the existence of an organization and, conversely, informing this organization of its own identity.

Platform as a service (PaaS): a package providing access to virtualized computers with the operating system already installed, upon which customers can install applications.

Process: a set of sequenced operations, designed to achieve a specified result.

Production chain: a set of production process phases that enable the progression from raw materials to finished product sold on the market, including all the processing stages.

Program: a strategic effort aimed at business transformation. It requires the coordination of many interrelated projects. Envisioning a program as one large project often leads to failure.

Project: a temporary system aimed at completing a specified task at a fixed cost in a fixed timescale. IS projects are considered more complex than traditional projects, involving a diverse range of stakeholders and various layers (infrastructure, software and human aspects).

Project management: brings together the functions that deal with the organizations' computing services projects.

Project management body of knowledge (PMBOK): a repository of good practices focusing on project management.

Project manager support: the stakeholder who supports the project manager in the definition of the project owner's needs and of the specification sheet.

Project owner: brings together the functions that deal with the organization's core business activity and defines the needs and expectations that the project manager will work on.

Project owner support: the stakeholder who supports the project owner in defining their needs and writing the specification sheet for the project manager.

Proprietary software: software that does not legally or technically allow execution of the software for any purpose, or inspection of the source code, or distribution of copies or any modifications and thus enhancements to the source code.

Protocol: specification of several rules for a particular type of communication.

Service-level agreements (SLA): agreements that establish a link between service levels and the expectations of the IS's customer.

Service-level management (SLM): management of IS service levels.

Service-level requests (SLR): requests in terms of requirements and service levels.

Software: the applications installed on the hardware and each application's incoming/outgoing information flows.

Software as a service (SaaS): a commercial solution accessible on a remote server. The service provider provides access to a machine and manages all of the technical processes associated with this service. The customer uses the software without having to worry about the infrastructure or the operation of the service.

Territory: an arrangement of material and symbolic resources capable of structuring the practical conditions of the existence of an individual or a social collective and, conversely, informing the individual or collective of their own identity.

Total cost of ownership (TCO): a method perfected by the Gartner Group to approach the total cost of ownership of computer infrastructures.

Transaction cost theory: a theory developed by Coase to explain the existence of businesses. This theory posits that certain transactions on markets can lead to punitive costs for economic operators who then resort to the use of a hierarchical organization.

Transaction processing systems (TPS): an IS at the operational level of an organization that integrates execution procedures and records transactions.

Unitary form (U-form): an organizational structure where control is shared by functions.

Urbanism: the study of the urban phenomenon, the action of the urbanization and the arrangement of the city and its territories.

Urbanization: a historic movement defining the increase in the numbers living in the city relative to the general population.

Value chain: all of the steps in determining the capacity of a strategic business unit (SBU) within an organization to gain a competitive advantage.

Value information technology (ValIT): a repository for IS management, with a risk window and a performance window.

Value network: economic activities and resources distributed within and across organizations, with organizations as nodes and interactions between them as links.

Vertical network firm: an organizational structure whose organizational territory is extended through inter-organizational cooperation in carrying out business processes, with a leader firm that develops a network with partner firms upstream and downstream of its business activity.

Web 3.0: describes the third phase of the World Wide Web. The first phase allowed the Internet user to access the content of web pages in read-only mode. The second gave the user the power to create content (blogs, wikis). Web 3.0 refers to the interaction between machines and data around shared semantics.

World Wide Web (WWW): a service that can be accessed on the Internet using a web browser. It works with a multi-media offering and is based on a hypertext-type navigation mode.

References

[AKR 06] AKRICH M., CALLON M., LATOUR B., *Sociologie de la traduction. Textes fondateurs*, Presses des Mines, Paris, 2006.

[ALB 96] ALBAN D., Organisation du système d'information et stratégies d'entreprise étendue : les systèmes d'information coopératifs, IAE de Paris, Université Paris 1 Panthéon-Sorbonne, June 1996.

[ALB 09] ALBAN D., EYNAUD P., *Management opérationnel du système d'information*, Hermès-Lavoisier, Paris, 2009.

[ALB 12] ALBAN D., "Management du système d'information au moyen d'un modèle projectif : approche heuristique du pilotage et du contrôle du système d'information des organisations", *Congrès de l'AIM*, Bordeaux, 2012.

[ALL 00] ALLEE V., "Reconfiguring the value network", *Journal of Business Strategy*, vol. 21, no. 4, pp. 36–39, 2000.

[AME 88] AMENDOLA M., GAFFARD J.-L., *La Dynamique économique de l'innovation*, FeniXX, Paris, 1988.

[ANT 65] ANTHONY R.-N., *Planning and Control Systems: A Framework for Analysis*, Harvard Business School, Boston, 1965.

[AOK 86] AOKI M., "Horizontal vs. vertical information structure of the firm", *The American Economic Review*, vol. 76, no. 5, pp. 971–983, 1986.

[AOK 92] AOKI M., "Decentralization-centralization in Japanese organization: A duality principle", in KUMON S., ROSOVSKY H. (eds), *The Political Economy of Japan*, vol. 3, pp. 142–169, 1992.

[AOK 01] AOKI M., *Toward a Comparative Institutional Analysis*, MIT Press, Cambridge, MA, 2001.

[AOK 10] AOKI M., *Corporations in Evolving Diversity: Cognition, Governance, and Institutions*, Oxford University Press, Oxford, 2010.

[ARC 98] ARCHER M., BHASKAR R., COLLIER A. et al. (eds), *Critical Realism: Essential Readings*, Routledge, London, 1998.

[ARG 78] ARGYRIS C., SCHÖN D.-A., *Organizational Learning: A Theory of Action Perspective*, Addison-Wesley, Reading, 1978.

[ARL 87] ARLANDIS J., "De l'alliance stratégique à la stratégie d'alliance", *Revue d'économie industrielle*, vol. 39, no. 1, pp. 228–243, 1987.

[ARR 69] ARROW K.J., "The organization of economic activity: Issues pertinent to the choice of market *versus* non-market allocations", *Analysis and Evaluation of Public Expenditures: The PPP System*, vol. 1, pp. 47–64, 1969.

[ATL 79] ATLAN H., *Entre le cristal et la fumée : essai sur l'organisation du vivant*, Le Seuil, Paris, 1979.

[AUB 02] AUBIN D., DALMEDICO A.-D., "Writing the history of dynamical systems and chaos: Longue durée and revolution, disciplines and cultures", *Historia Mathematica*, vol. 29, no. 3, pp. 273–339, 2002.

[AUB 13] AUBRY C., *Scrum : Le guide pratique de la méthode agile la plus populaire*, Dunod, Paris, 2013.

[BAL 06] BALANTZIAN G., *Le plan de gouvernance du S.I.*, Dunod, Paris, 2006.

[BAL 10] BALANTZIAN G., *Co-gouvernance des S.I.*, Dunod, Paris, 2010.

[BAL 12] BALIN P., BERTHOUD F., BOHAS A. et al., *Les impacts écologiques des technologies de l'information et de la communication*, EDP Sciences, Paris, 2012.

[BEC 01] BECK K., BEEDLE M., VAN BENNEKUM A. et al., The agile manifesto, available at: http://agilemanifesto.org, 2001.

[BEL 18] BELKHIR L., ELMELIGI A., "Assessing ICT global emissions footprint: Trends to 2040 & recommendations", *Journal of Cleaner Production*, vol. 177, pp. 448–463, 2018.

[BER 67] BERLE A.-A., MEANS G.-C., *The Modern Corporation and Private Property*, Harcourt, Brace and World, New York, 1967.

[BES 11] BESSON P., ROWE F., "Perspectives sur le phénomène de la transformation organisationnelle", *Systèmes d'information & management*, vol. 16, no. 1, pp. 3–34, 2011.

[BID 06] BIDAN M., "Systèmes d'information et territoires de l'entreprise (SITE). Cartographie, cohérence et cohabitation à la lumière d'un projet d'intégration du système d'information de gestion", *Management & Avenir*, no. 9, pp. 17–43, 2006.

[BIH 14] BIHOUIX P., *L'Âge des low tech. Vers une civilisation techniquement soutenable*, Média Diffusion, 2014.

[BLO 13] BLOEMMEN M., BOBULESCU R., NHU-TUYEN L., et al., "Slow management and accounting for a socio-ecological transition: The case of agro-ecology", *European Conference on Ecological Economics*, Lille, 18–21 June 2013.

[BRA 11] BRANCH D., LEWIS H., Unlocking growth, A Deloitte Analytics Institute Paper, Deloitte, London, 2011.

[CAI 22] CAIL, O., Nomenclature des profils métiers du SI, CIGREF, p. 278, 2022.

[CAL 15] CALDER A., WATKINS S., *IT Governance: An International Guide to Data Security and ISO27001/ISO27002*, Kogan Page Ltd, London, 2015.

[CAM 91] CAMPBELL A., YEUNG S., "Brief case: Mission, vision and strategic intent", *Long Range Planning*, vol. 24, no. 4, pp. 145–147, 1991.

[CAR 10] CARMES M., "Le territoire organisationnel à l'épreuve des pratiques socio-numériques des salariés sur Internet : éléments d'une controverse", *Actes du XXIe Congrès AGRH*, Saint-Malo, 18–19 November, available at: https://archivesic.ccsd.cnrs.fr/sic_00550166/document, 2010.

[CAR 17] CARPENTIER J.-F., *La gouvernance du système d'information dans les PME : pratiques et évolutions*, Éditions ENI, Saint-Herblain, 2017.

[CER 12] CERCLE SIRH, *Le SIRH – Enjeux, projets et bonnes pratiques*, Vuibert, Paris, 2012.

[CHA 77] CHANDLER A., *The Visible Hand: The Managerial Revolution in American Business*, Belknap Press, Cambridge, 1977.

[CHA 03] CHAMPLAIN J.-J., *Auditing Information Systems*, John Wiley & Sons, New York, 2003.

[CHO 22] CHOHAN U.W., Web 3.0: The future architecture of the internet?, available at: https://ssrn.com/abstract=4037693 or http:// dx.doi.org/10.2139/ssrn.4037693, 2022.

[CHR 16] CHRISTENSEN C.-M., *The Innovator's Dilemma: When New Technologies Cause Great Firms to Fail*, Harvard Business Review Press, Boston, 2016.

[CIB 92] CIBORRA C.-U., "From thinking to tinkering: The grassroots of strategic information systems", *The Information Society*, vol. 8, no. 4, pp. 297–309, 1992.

[CIB 96] CIBORRA C.-U., "The platform organization: Recombining strategies, structures, and surprises", *Organization Science*, vol. 7, no. 2, pp. 103–118, 1996.

[CIG 04] CIGREF, MCKINSEY & COMPANY, Dynamique des relations autour des systèmes d'information dans les équipes de directions des grandes entreprises françaises, White book, Cigref, Paris, 2004.

[CIG 11] CIGREF, IFACI, Gouvernance du système d'information, Guide d'audit, Paris, 2011.

[CIG 15] CIGREF, Nomenclature RH – Les métiers des SI dans les grandes entreprises, Paris, 2015.

[COA 37] COASE R.-H., "The nature of the firm", *Economica*, vol. 4, no. 16, pp. 386–405, 1937.

[COD 08] CODDE, *Analyse du cycle de vie du téléphone portable*, Moirans, France, 2008.

[COH 90] COHENDET P., LLERENA P., "Nature de l'information, évaluation et organisation de l'entreprise", *Revue d'économie industrielle*, vol. 51, no. 1, pp. 141–165, 1990.

[COM 17] COMPAGNON S., "Bill Gates veut taxer les robots... comme Benoît Hamon", *Le Parisien*, February 2017.

[DAV 10] D'AVENI R.-A., *Hypercompetition*, Simon & Schuster, New York, 2010.

[DEB 89] DE BANDT J., "Approche méso-économique de la dynamique industrielle", *Revue d'économie industrielle*, vol. 49, no. 1, pp. 1–18, 1989.

[DEL 80] DELEUZE G., GUATTARI F., *Capitalisme et Schizophrénie 2. Mille Plateaux*, Éditions de Minuit, Paris, 1980.

[DEV 15] DE VAUJANY F.-X., *Sociomatérialité et information dans les organisations. Entre bonheur et sens*, Presses Universitaires de Laval, Laval, 2015.

[DIS 12] DISIC, Cadre commun d'urbanisation du SI de l'État français, Direction interministérielle des systèmes d'information et de communication, Paris, 2012.

[DOS 84] DOSI G., *Technical Change and Industrial Transformation: The Theory and an Application to the Semiconductor Industry*, Palgrave Macmillan, Basingstoke, 1984.

[DUC 07] DUCHENEAUT N., MOORE R.-J., NICKELL E., "Virtual "third places": A case study of sociability in massively multiplayer games", *Computer Supported Cooperative Work (CSCW)*, vol. 16, nos 1/2, pp. 129–166, 2007.

[DWI 12] DWIVEDI A., *End-User Computing, Development, and Software Engineering: New Challenges*, Idea Group Publishing, Hershey, 2012.

[EYN 16] EYNAUD P., MALAURENT J., "Une plateforme collaborative pour matérialiser la coopération d'un collectif hétérogène", *Colloque de l'AIM*, Lille, 18–20 May 2016.

[FAY 99] FAYOL H., *Administration industrielle et générale. Le texte fondateur du management*, Dunod, Paris, 1999.

[FLÜ 17] FLÜRY-HERARD B., DUFAY J.-P., Le déploiement du compteur Linky, Report no. 010655-01, Ministère de l'Environnement, de l'Énergie et de la Mer, 2017.

[FRE 10a] FREEMAN R.-E., *Strategic Management: A Stakeholder Approach*, Cambridge University Press, Cambridge, 2010.

[FRE 10b] FREEMAN R.-E., HARRISON J.S., WHICKS A.C. et al., *Stakeholder Theory: The State of the Art*, Cambridge University Press, Cambridge, 2010.

[GAF 90] GAFFARD J.-L., "Stratégies de mobilité et formes organisationnelles : quelques repères analytiques", *Revue d'économie industrielle*, vol. 51, no. 1, pp. 226–237, 1990.

[GAR 09] GARNIER DE LABAREYRE F., MOISAND D., *CobiT. Pour une meilleure gouvernance des systèmes d'information*, Eyrolles, Paris, 2009.

[GEO 09] GEORGEL F., *IT Gouvernance. Management stratégique d'un système d'information*, Dunod, Paris, 2009.

[GER 91] GERSICK C.-G., "Revolutionary change theories: A multilevel exploration of the punctuated equilibrium paradigm", *Academy of Management Review*, vol. 16, no. 1, pp. 10–36, 1991.

[HAL 13] HALLEPEE D., *La gouvernance des systèmes d'information*, Les écrivains de Fondcombe, 2013.

[HAM 81a] HAMILTON S., CHERVANY N.-L., "Evaluating information system effectiveness – Part I: Comparing evaluation approaches", *MIS Quarterly*, vol. 5, no. 3, pp. 55–69, 1981.

[HAM 81b] HAMILTON S., CHERVANY N-.L., "Evaluating information system effectiveness – Part II: Comparing evaluator viewpoints", *MIS Quarterly*, vol. 5, no. 4, pp. 79–86, 1981.

[HAM 90] HAMEL G., PRAHALAD C.-K., "Strategic intent", *McKinsey Quarterly*, vol. 2, pp. 36–61, 1990.

[HAN 07] HANNAN M.-T., POLOS L., CARROLL G.-R., *Logics of Organization Theory: Audiences, Codes, and Ecologies*, Princeton University Press, Princeton, 2007.

[HAN 09] HANSEN S., BERENTE N., LYYTINEN K., "Wikipedia, critical social theory, and the possibility of rational discourse", *Information Society*, vol. 25, no. 1, pp. 38–59, 2009.

[HAY 13] HAYES B., *Bring Your Own Device*, Elsevier, Amsterdam, 2013.

[HEN 91] HENDERSON J.-C., VENKATRAMAN N., "Strategic alignment: A framework for strategic information technology management", in SCOTT MORTION M.S., MCDONALD H., (eds), *The Corporation of the 1990s*, Appendix E, Oxford University Press, New York, 1991.

[HEN 93] HENDERSON J.-C., VENKATRAMAN N., "Strategic alignment: Leveraging information technology for transforming organizations", *IBM Systems Journal*, vol. 32, no. 1, pp. 472–484, 1993.

[HIL 05] HILTY L.-M., SEIFERT E.K., TREIBERT R. et al., *Information Systems for Sustainable Development*, Idea Group Publishing, London, 2005.

[HIR 70] HIRSCHMAN A.O., *Exit, Voice, and Loyalty: Responses to Decline in Firms, Organizations, and States*, Harvard University Press, Cambridge, MA, 1970.

[HÖL 16] HÖLZLE U., We're set to reach 100% renewable energy – and it's just the beginning, available at: http://www.blog.google:443/topics/environment/100-percent-renewable-energy/, 2016.

[ITU 04] ITU, SMSI: Déclaration de principes, available at: http://www.itu.int/net/wsis/docs/geneva/official/dop-fr.html, 2004.

[IZA 17] IZAMBARD A., "Ransomware, DDoS... Comment les cyberattaques menacent les entreprises", *Challenges*, available at: https://www.challenges.fr/high-tech/ransomware-ddos-comment-les-cyberattaques-menacent-les-entreprises_450028, 2017.

[JAI 09] JAILLET M.-C., "Contre le territoire, la "bonne distance"", in VANIER M., DEBARBIEUX B., TURCO A. et al. (eds), *Territoires, territorialité, territorialisation : controverses et perspectives*, pp. 115–121, Presses universitaires de Rennes, Rennes, 2009.

[JOF 99] JOFFRE P., KOENIG, G., *Gestion stratégique. L'entreprise, ses partenaires-adversaires et leur univers*, Éditions Management et Société, Caen, 1999.

[KHA 17] KHAN E., MARTINI A., *Le baromètre de la cyber-sécurité : sondage Opinionway pour le CESIN*, Opinionway, Paris, 2017.

[KUM 96] KUMAR K., VAN DISSEL H.-G., "Sustainable collaboration: Managing conflict and cooperation in interorganizational systems", *MIS Quarterly*, vol. 20, no. 3, pp. 279–300, 1996.

[LAT 07] LATOUR B., *Changer de société, refaire de la sociologie*, La Découverte, Paris, 2007.

[LEL 17] LELOUP L., *Blockchain. La révolution de la confiance*, Eyrolles, Paris, 2017.

[LEM 86] LE MOIGNE J.-L., "Vers un système d'information organisationnel ?", *Revue française de gestion*, vol. 6, no. 3, 1986.

[LEM 90] LE MOIGNE J.-L., *La modélisation des systèmes complexes*, Dunod, Paris, 1990.

[LEV 13] LEVY J., LUSSAULT M. (eds), *Dictionnaire de la géographie et de l'espace des sociétés*, Belin, Paris, 2013.

[LEW 51] LEWIN K., *Field Theory in Social Science: Selected Theoretical Papers*, Harper & Brothers, New York, 1951.

[LI 14] LI M., VITÁNYI P.-M.-B., *Kolmogorov Complexity and its Applications*, Springer, New York, 2014.

[LON 09] LONGEPE C., *Le projet d'urbanisation du SI. Cas concret d'architecture d'entreprise*, Dunod, Paris, 2009.

[MAR 58] MARCUSE H., *Le marxisme soviétique*, Gallimard, Paris, 1958.

[MAR 13] MARKESS INTERNATIONAL, Optimiser la gestion des processus RH pour contribuer à la performance de l'entreprise – Solutions et tendances, Résumé, MARKESS International, 2013.

[MAT 80] MATURANA H.-R., VARELA F.-J., *Autopoiesis and Cognition: The Realization of the Living*, Springer, Berlin, 1980.

[MCA 09] MCAFEE A., *Enterprise 2.0: New Collaborative Tools for Your Organization's Toughest Challenges*, Harvard Business School Press, Brighton, MA, 2009.

[MCC 04] MCCUMBER J., *Assessing and Managing Security Risk in IT Systems: A Structured Methodology*, CRC Press, Boca Raton, 2004.

[MID 12] MIDLER C., *L'auto qui n'existait pas. Management des projets et transformation de l'entreprise*, Dunod, Paris, 2012.

[MIN 94] MINTZBERG H., "The fall and rise of strategic planning", *Harvard Business Review*, vol. 72, no. 1, pp. 107–114, 1994.

[MIR 93] MIRA S., "Le rôle effectif du système d'information dans l'entreprise industrielle", *Revue française de gestion*, no. 95, pp. 36–43, September–October 1993.

[MOE 13] MOELLER R.-R., *Executive's Guide to IT Governance: Improving Systems Processes with Service Management, COBIT, and ITIL*, John Wiley & Sons, Hoboken, 2013.

[MOR 82] MORIN E., *Science avec conscience*, Le Seuil, Paris, 1982.

[MOR 90] MORIN E., *Introduction à la pensée complexe*, Le Seuil, Paris, 1990.

[MOR 99] MORIN E., LE MOIGNE J.-L., *L'intelligence de la complexité*, L'Harmattan, Paris, 1999.

[MOR 13] MORIN E., *La méthode : la nature de la nature*, Le Seuil, Paris, 2013.

[NAE 02] NAEEM S., "Ecosystem consequences of biodiversity loss: The evolution of a paradigm", *Ecology*, vol. 83, no. 6, pp. 1537–1552, 2002.

[NOË 08] NOËL-LEMAITRE C., CHEMANGUI M., "Les cartes conceptuelles comme outil de représentation du rôle des auditeurs dans la fiabilité de l'information financière : une exploration des différences liées à l'expérience", *Systèmes d'information & management*, vol. 13, no. 2, pp. 5–31, 2008.

[OLD 99] OLDENBURG R., *The Great Good Place: Cafes, Coffee Shops, Book-stores, Bars, Hair Salons, and Other Hangouts at the Heart of a Community*, Marlowe & Company, Berkeley, 1999.

[ORE 11] O'REILLY C.-A., TUSHMAN M-.L., "Organizational ambidexterity in action: How managers explore and exploit", *California Management Review*, vol. 53, no. 4, pp. 5–22, 2011.

[ORE 13] O'REILLY C.-A., TUSHMAN M-.L., "Organizational ambidexterity: Past, present, and future", *The Academy of Management Perspectives*, vol. 27, no. 4, pp. 324–338, 2013.

[ORL 96] ORLIKOWSKI W.-J., "Improvising organizational transformation over time a situated change perspective", *Information Systems Research*, vol. 7, no. 1, pp. 63–92, 1996.

[ORL 97] ORLIKOWSKI W.J., HOFFMAN J.D., "An improvisational model for change management: The case of groupware technologies", in MALONE T.W. LAUBACHER R. SCOTT MORTON M.S. (eds), *Inventing the Organizations of the 21st Century*, pp. 265–282, MIT Press, Cambridge, MA, 1997.

[ORL 10] ORLIKOWSKI W.-J., "The sociomateriality of organisational life: Considering technology in management research", *Cambridge Journal of Economics*, vol. 34, no. 1, pp. 125–141, 2010.

[ORT 90] ORTON J.-D., WEICK K.-E., "Loosely coupled systems: A reconceptualization", *Academy of Management Review*, vol. 15, no. 2, pp. 203–223, 1990.

[PAC 93] PACHE G., PARAPONARIS C., *L'entreprise en réseau*, Que-sais-je ?, Paris, 1993.

[PAC 06] PACHE G., PARAPONARIS C., *L'entreprise en réseau : approches inter et intra-organisationnelles*, Les éditions de l'ADREG, Bordeaux, 2006.

[PAR 13] PARISOT X., ISCKIA T., "Metaphor in organization theory: The case of the business ecosystem concept", *22nd AIMS International Conference*, Clermont-Ferrand, 10–12 June 2013.

[PAR 17] PARKER G.-G., VAN ALSTYNE M.-W., *Platform Revolution: How Networked Markets are Transforming the Economy and How to Make them Work for You*, W.W. Norton & Co, New York, 2017.

[PIC 08] PICKERING A., GUZIK K. (eds), *The Mangle in Practice: Science, Society, and Becoming*, Duke University Press, Durham, NC, 2008.

[PIE 00] PIECES ET MAIN D'ŒUVRE, Accueil : pièces et main d'œuvre, available at: http://www.piecesetmaindoeuvre.com/, 2000.

[POR 85] PORTER M.-E., *Competitive Advantage. Creating and Sustaining Superior Performance*, Free Press, New York, 1985.

[POT 16] POTTER K., BUCHANAN S., Metrics and planning assumptions required to drive business unit IT strategies, available at: https://www.gartner.com/doc/3289120/metrics-planning-assumptions-required-drive, 2016.

[PRI 16] PRICEWATERHOUSECOOPERS, Tech Breakthroughs Megatrend, PwC, available at: https://www.pwc.com/gx/en/issues/technology/tech-breakthroughs-megatrend.html, 2016.

[PRO 16] PROCTOR P., WAGNER R., Special report: Cybersecurity at the speed of digital business, available at: https://www.gartner.com/doc/3426427/special-report-cybersecurity-speed-digital, 2016.

[RAY 99] RAYMOND E., *The Cathedral and the Bazaar: Musings on Linux and Open Source by an Accidental Revolutionary*, O'Reilly Media, Sebastopol, CA, 1999.

[RIC 13a] RICHET J.-L., "From young hackers to crackers", *International Journal of Technology and Human Interaction (IJTHI)*, vol. 9, no. 3, pp. 53–62, 2013.

[RIC 13b] RICHET J.-L., Laundering money online: A review of cybercriminals methods, Industry Report, White Paper, Tools and Resources for Anti-Corruption Knowledge, United Nations Office on Drugs and Crime (UNODC), 2013.

[SCH 14a] SCHLAGWEIN D., BJØRN-ANDERSEN N., "Organizational learning with crowdsourcing: The revelatory case of LEGO", *Journal of the Association for Information Systems*, vol. 15, no. 11, pp. 754–778, 2014.

[SCH 14b] SCHMARZO B., *Big Data – Tirer parti des données massives pour développer l'entreprise*, First Interactive, Paris, 2014.

[SCH 16] SCHOLZ T., *Platform Cooperativism: Challenging the Corporate Sharing Economy*, Rosa Luxembourg Stiftung/New York Office, New York, 2016.

[SEN 90] SENGE P., *The Fifth Discipline: The Art and Practice of the Learning Organization*, Doubleday, New York, 1990.

[SIM 80] SIMON H.-A., "From substantive to procedural rationality", in LATSIS S. (ed.), *Method and Appraisal in Economics*, Cambridge University Press, Cambridge, 1980.

[SLA 07] SLADE G., *Made to Break: Technology and Obsolescence in America*, Harvard University Press, Cambridge, MA, 2007.

[SRI 11] SRINIVASAN R., *Business Process Reengineering*, Tata McGraw-Hill Education Private Limited, Noida, 2011.

[STA 98] STABELL C.-B., FJELDSTAD Ø.-D., "Configuring value for competitive advantage: On chains, shops, and networks", *Strategic Management Journal*, vol. 19, no. 5, pp. 413–437, 1998.

[STA 10] STALLMAN R.-M., *Free Software, Free Society*, Free Software Foundation, Boston, 2010.

[STA 13] STALLMAN R., WILLIAMS S., MASUTTI C., *Richard Stallman et la révolution du logiciel libre. Une biographie autorisée*, Eyrolles, Paris, 2013.

[STE 87] STENGERS I., *D'une science à l'autre : des concepts nomades*, Le Seuil, Paris, 1987.

[SUC 07] SUCHMAN L.-A., *Human-Machine Reconfigurations: Plans and Situated Actions*, Cambridge University Press, Cambridge, 2007.

[TUS 85] TUSHMAN M.-L., ROMANELLI E., "Organizational evolution: A metamorphosis model of convergence and reorientation", *Research in Organizational Behavior*, no. 7, pp. 171–222, 1985.

[TUS 96] TUSHMAN M.-L., O'REILLY C.-A., "The ambidextrous organizations: Managing evolutionary and revolutionary change", *California Management Review*, vol. 38, no. 4, pp. 8–30, 1996.

[ULL 16] ULLMANN V., *Approche stratégique d'un projet ERP*, Éditions universitaires européennes, Saarbrücken, 2016.

[VAN 09] VAN GREMBERGEN W., DE HAES S., *Enterprise Governance of Information Technology: Achieving Strategic Alignment and Value*, Springer, Berlin, 2009.

[VAR 92] VARELA F.J., "Autopoiesis and a biology of intentionality", *Proceedings of the Workshop "Autopoiesis and Perception"*, pp. 4–14, Dublin, Ireland, 25–26 August 1992.

[VEL 93] VELTZ P., "D'une géographie des coûts à une géographie de l'organisation. Quelques thèses sur l'évolution des rapports entreprises/territoires", *Revue économique*, vol. 44, no. 4, pp. 671–684, 1993.

[VER 07] VERON J., *L'urbanisation du monde*, La Découverte, Paris, 2007.

[VIT 13] VITARI C., ASHTA A., BOBULESCU R. et al. *Slow management : entreprendre la transition*, Pearson Education France, Paris, 2013.

[WAK 15] WAKELIN K., STREET A.-F., "An online expressive writing group for people affected by cancer: A virtual third place", *Australian Social Work*, vol. 68, no. 2, pp. 198–211, 2015.

[WAT 10] WATSON R.-T., BOUDREAU M.-C., CHEN A.-J., "Information systems and environmentally sustainable development: Energy informatics and new directions for the is community", *MIS Quarterly*, vol. 34, no. 1, pp. 23–38, 2010.

[WEI 04] WEILL P., ROSS J.-W., *IT Governance: How Top Performers Manage IT Decision Rights for Superior Results*, Harvard Business School Press, Brighton, MA, 2004.

[WIE 48] WIENER N., *Cybernetics: Or Control and Communication in the Animal and the Machine*, MIT Press, Cambridge, MA, 1948.

[WIL 75] WILLIAMSON O.-E., *Markets and Hierarchies: Analysis and Antitrust Implications, A Study in the Economics of Internal Organization*, Free Press, New York, 1975.

[WIL 81] WILLIAMSON O.-E., "The economics of organization: The transaction cost approach", *American Journal of Sociology*, vol. 87, no. 3, pp. 548–577, 1981.

[WIL 98] WILLIAMSON O.-E., *The Economic Institutions of Capitalism*, Free Press, New York, 1998.

[WIL 02] WILLIAMSON O.-E., "The theory of the firm as governance structure: From choice to contract", *Journal of Economic Perspectives*, vol. 16, no. 3, pp. 171–195, 2002.

[WOR 15] WORLD ECONOMIC FORUM (WEF), Global Risks 2015, Report, 2015.

[ZAR 00] ZARIFIAN P., "Organisation apprenante et formes de l'expérience", *Colloque Constructivismes : usages et perspectives en éducation*, pp. 247–258, Geneva, Switzerland, 4–8 September 2000.

Index

Other titles from

in

Information Systems, Web and Pervasive Computing

2024

MAKAROV Volodymyr, MAYKO Nataliya
Traditional Functional-Discrete Methods for the Problems of Mathematical Physics: New Aspects

PINET François, BATTON-HUBERT Mireille, DESJARDIN Eric
Geographical Data Imperfection 2: Use Cases

2023

POMEROL Jean-Charles
Action in Uncertainty: Expertise, Decision and Crisis Management

REVEST Valérie, LIOTARD Isabelle
Digital Transformation and Public Policies: Current Issues

2022

ACCART Jean-Philippe
Library Transformation Strategies

BOADA Martí, LAZARO Antonio, GIRBAU David, VILLARINO Ramón
Battery-less NFC Sensors for the Internet of Things

GEORGE Éric
Digitalization of Society and Socio-political Issues 2: Digital, Information and Research

HELALI Saida
Systems and Network Infrastructure Integration

LOISEAU Hugo, VENTRE Daniel, ADEN Hartmut
Cybersecurity in Humanities and Social Sciences: A Research Methods Approach (Cybersecurity Set – Volume 1)

SEDKAOUI Soraya, KHELFAOUI Mounia
Sharing Economy and Big Data Analytics

SCHMITT Églantine
Big Data: An Art of Decision Making
(Intellectual Technologies Set – Volume 7)

2019

ALBAN Daniel, EYNAUD Philippe, MALAURENT Julien, RICHET Jean-Loup, VITARI Claudio
Information Systems Management: Governance, Urbanization and Alignment

AUGEY Dominique, with the collaboration of ALCARAZ Marina
Digital Information Ecosystems: Smart Press

BATTON-HUBERT Mireille, DESJARDIN Eric, PINET François
Geographic Data Imperfection 1: From Theory to Applications

BRIQUET-DUHAZÉ Sophie, TURCOTTE Catherine
From Reading-Writing Research to Practice

BROCHARD Luigi, KAMATH Vinod, CORBALAN Julita, HOLLAND Scott, MITTELBACH Walter, OTT Michael
Energy-Efficient Computing and Data Centers

CHAMOUX Jean-Pierre
The Digital Era 2: Political Economy Revisited

CHAMOUX Jean-Pierre
The Digital Era 1: Big Data Stakes

DOUAY Nicolas
Urban Planning in the Digital Age
(Intellectual Technologies Set – Volume 6)

FABRE Renaud, BENSOUSSAN Alain
The Digital Factory for Knowledge: Production and Validation of Scientific
Results

GAUDIN Thierry, LACROIX Dominique, MAUREL Marie-Christine,
POMEROL Jean-Charles
Life Sciences, Information Sciences

GAYARD Laurent
Darknet: Geopolitics and Uses
(Computing and Connected Society Set – Volume 2)

IAFRATE Fernando
Artificial Intelligence and Big Data: The Birth of a New Intelligence
(Advances in Information Systems Set – Volume 8)

LE DEUFF Olivier
Digital Humanities: History and Development
(Intellectual Technologies Set – Volume 4)

MANDRAN Nadine
Traceable Human Experiment Design Research: Theoretical Model and
Practical Guide
(Advances in Information Systems Set – Volume 9)

PIVERT Olivier
NoSQL Data Models: Trends and Challenges

ROCHET Claude
Smart Cities: Reality or Fiction

SALEH Imad, AMMI, Mehdi, SZONIECKY Samuel
Challenges of the Internet of Things: Technology, Use, Ethics
(Digital Tools and Uses Set – Volume 7)

SAUVAGNARGUES Sophie
Decision-making in Crisis Situations: Research and Innovation for Optimal Training

SEDKAOUI Soraya
Data Analytics and Big Data

SZONIECKY Samuel
Ecosystems Knowledge: Modeling and Analysis Method for Information and Communication
(Digital Tools and Uses Set – Volume 6)

2017

BOUHAÏ Nasreddine, SALEH Imad
Internet of Things: Evolutions and Innovations
(Digital Tools and Uses Set – Volume 4)

DUONG Véronique
Baidu SEO: Challenges and Intricacies of Marketing in China

LESAS Anne-Marie, MIRANDA Serge
The Art and Science of NFC Programming
(Intellectual Technologies Set – Volume 3)

LIEM André
Prospective Ergonomics
(Human-Machine Interaction Set – Volume 4)

MARSAULT Xavier
Eco-generative Design for Early Stages of Architecture
(Architecture and Computer Science Set – Volume 1)

REYES-GARCIA Everardo
The Image-Interface: Graphical Supports for Visual Information
(Digital Tools and Uses Set – Volume 3)

REYES-GARCIA Everardo, BOUHAÏ Nasreddine
Designing Interactive Hypermedia Systems
(Digital Tools and Uses Set – Volume 2)

SAÏD Karim, BAHRI KORBI Fadia
Asymmetric Alliances and Information Systems:Issues and Prospects
(Advances in Information Systems Set – Volume 7)

SZONIECKY Samuel, BOUHAÏ Nasreddine
Collective Intelligence and Digital Archives: Towards Knowledge
Ecosystems
(Digital Tools and Uses Set – Volume 1)

2016

BEN CHOUIKHA Mona
Organizational Design for Knowledge Management

BERTOLO David
Interactions on Digital Tablets in the Context of 3D Geometry Learning
(Human-Machine Interaction Set – Volume 2)

BOUVARD Patricia, SUZANNE Hervé
Collective Intelligence Development in Business

EL FALLAH SEGHROUCHNI Amal, ISHIKAWA Fuyuki, HÉRAULT Laurent,
TOKUDA Hideyuki
Enablers for Smart Cities

FABRE Renaud, in collaboration with MESSERSCHMIDT-MARIET Quentin,
HOLVOET Margot
New Challenges for Knowledge

GAUDIELLO Ilaria, ZIBETTI Elisabetta
Learning Robotics, with Robotics, by Robotics
(Human-Machine Interaction Set – Volume 3)

HENROTIN Joseph
The Art of War in the Network Age
(Intellectual Technologies Set – Volume 1)

KITAJIMA Munéo
Memory and Action Selection in Human–Machine Interaction
(Human–Machine Interaction Set – Volume 1)

2015

LEBRATY Jean-Fabrice, LOBRE-LEBRATY Katia
Crowdsourcing: One Step Beyond

SALLABERRY Christian
Geographical Information Retrieval in Textual Corpora

2012

BUCHER Bénédicte, LE BER Florence
Innovative Software Development in GIS

GAUSSIER Eric, YVON François
Textual Information Access

STOCKINGER Peter
Audiovisual Archives: Digital Text and Discourse Analysis

VENTRE Daniel
Cyber Conflict

2011

BANOS Arnaud, THÉVENIN Thomas
Geographical Information and Urban Transport Systems

DAUPHINÉ André
Fractal Geography

LEMBERGER Pirmin, MOREL Mederic
Managing Complexity of Information Systems

STOCKINGER Peter
Introduction to Audiovisual Archives

STOCKINGER Peter
Digital Audiovisual Archives

VENTRE Daniel
Cyberwar and Information Warfare

2010

BONNET Pierre
Enterprise Data Governance

BRUNET Roger
Sustainable Geography

CARREGA Pierre
Geographical Information and Climatology

CAUVIN Colette, ESCOBAR Francisco, SERRADJ Aziz
Thematic Cartography – 3-volume series
Thematic Cartography and Transformations – Volume 1
Cartography and the Impact of the Quantitative Revolution – Volume 2
New Approaches in Thematic Cartography – Volume 3

LANGLOIS Patrice
Simulation of Complex Systems in GIS

MATHIS Philippe
Graphs and Networks – 2nd edition

THERIAULT Marius, DES ROSIERS François
Modeling Urban Dynamics

2009

BONNET Pierre, DETAVERNIER Jean-Michel, VAUQUIER Dominique
Sustainable IT Architecture: the Progressive Way of Overhauling
Information Systems with SOA

PAPY Fabrice
Information Science

RIVARD François, ABOU HARB Georges, MERET Philippe
The Transverse Information System

ROCHE Stéphane, CARON Claude
Organizational Facets of GIS

2008

BRUGNOT Gérard
Spatial Management of Risks

FINKE Gerd
Operations Research and Networks

GUERMOND Yves
Modeling Process in Geography

KANEVSKI Michael
Advanced Mapping of Environmental Data

MANOUVRIER Bernard, LAURENT Ménard
Application Integration: EAI, B2B, BPM and SOA

PAPY Fabrice
Digital Libraries

2007

DOBESCH Hartwig, DUMOLARD Pierre, DYRAS Izabela
Spatial Interpolation for Climate Data

SANDERS Lena
Models in Spatial Analysis

2006

CLIQUET Gérard
Geomarketing

CORNIOU Jean-Pierre
Looking Back and Going Forward in IT

DEVILLERS Rodolphe, JEANSOULIN Robert
Fundamentals of Spatial Data Quality

Printed and bound by CPI Group (UK) Ltd, Croydon, CR0 4YY

27/10/2024

14580249-0001